P9-CMP-737

# COMPUTER METHODS IN THE ANALYSIS OF LARGE-SCALE SOCIAL SYSTEMS

A Publication of the Joint Center for Urban Studies of the Massachusetts Institute of Technology and Harvard University

CONCORDIA UNIVERSITY LIBRARY
GEORGES P. VANIER LIBRARY, LOYOLA CAMPUS

# COMPUTER METHODS IN THE ANALYSIS OF LARGE-SCALE SOCIAL SYSTEMS

James M. Beshers, Editor

**Second Edition**

THE M.I.T. PRESS
Massachusetts Institute of Technology
Cambridge, Massachusetts, and London, England

Copyright © 1965, 1968 by
The Massachusetts Institute of Technology and the President
and Fellows of Harvard College.

All rights reserved. No part of this book may be
reproduced or utilized in any form or by any means,
electronic or mechanical, including photocopying,
recording, or by any information storage and retrieval
system, without permission in writing from the publisher.

Second printing, June 1972

ISBN 0 262 02 041 6
Library of Congress catalog card number: 68 - 19932

# CONTENTS

# INTRODUCTION

This conference brought together people who were engaged in research involving the use of similar techniques and similar data yet came from many different disciplines. Its initial stimulus was the preparation and release of the 1-1,000 sample tape by the U. S. Bureau of the Census, an event which, though greatly increasing the volume of data that can be brought to the study of large social systems, at the same time confronted researchers with an embarrassment of riches. Few research organizations were experienced in processing such large quantities of data or in constructing appropriate computer models to guide them in data analysis and interpretation. We conceived the conference, therefore, as a means by which men experienced in computer applications might compare notes and share new knowledge with others just beginning such research.

Most of the conference participants, although experienced in the analysis of empirical social science data, were keenly aware of the shortcomings not only of their data but also of the traditional methods of processing and analyzing them. They sought from the computer ways in which to improve the quality of their research. In this conference they shared the experience of their search with others, some of whom are computer specialists.

The variety of disciplines represented might lead one to expect communication barriers among participants. Certainly much popular writing suggests an infinite increase of specialization in science, leading to an infinite decrease of communication among scientists. We predicated this conference, however, on the view that research workers from widely varying disciplines, when faced with similar problems in handling data, can communicate quite readily, despite striking differences in terminology. That different disciplines give rise to different problems can become the basis for common interest and mutual reflection rather than for antagonism or distrust. It is the suggestive quality of comparisons among disciplines that leads to creative reformulations of research within them.

In planning, the conference was divided into three parts: (1) a discussion of computer techniques for handling social data; (2) a discussion of models and problems of estimation associated with them; (3) a discussion of the possibilities of increasing the kinds of data available to research workers and of potentially fruitful next steps in the assembly of data. In fact, however, three themes recurred throughout

1

the conference: (1) control over the computer processes by the social scientists; (2) the implications of time in the interpretation of social science data; (3) the implications of the level of aggregation in the interpretation of social science data. The organization of the proceedings carried out the intentions of the plans but did not bring out these themes effectively.

Therefore, we now turn to explicit discussion of the themes. The first theme was so crucial and was expressed in so many ways from so many perspectives that we can regard it as the unifying theme that emerged from the conference. The absence of control in present computer procedures has frustrated many of the participants. They would like to express an idea in the language of social science and have the computer carry out the appropriate operations; this is a communication problem that occurs at the most rudimentary level of data analysis, at the most sophisticated level of model construction, and in the design of the data base itself.

The first four talks treat this issue with respect to techniques of computer use-programming, programming languages, and computer systems, including hardware components. Hornseth describes a program for tabulation that, by enabling the social scientist to specify his requirements with a few simple parameters, eliminates his need to comprehend the program itself. In contrast, Sakoda seeks to serve the social scientist who desires to do his own programming. After a review of the shortcoming of the programming languages now available, Sakoda proposes his own language, DYSTAL, as an appropriate tool for the social scientist.

Kennedy discusses the problems of the data base and file organization in a notably elegant manner. He shows that, in a system processing real data as a normal operation, the specification of kinship relationships in a birth-and-marriage record-linkage system may be adroitly carried out with the indirect addressing techniques of list-processing computer languages. He shows, furthermore, that the data base so organized will facilitate subsequent analysis and simulation. Thus we see that we can, indeed must, employ the same concepts and techniques in organizing the data base that we employ in analysis and in simulation; from a conceptual point of view we do not face three separate problems but one problem. This profound point echoes throughout the remainder of the conference. Incidentally, Kennedy's achievement is attained after he stops sorting records and allows them to retain their physical location permanently. This procedure directly contrasts with the unit record procedures used by many American social scientists, in which physical sorting of cards and physical merging of tapes constitute the major tools in analysis and in simulation. List-processing methods are a major innovation in the design of a data base.

Weizenbaum, the author of the computer language used by Kennedy (SLIP), describes revolutionary arrangements of men, machines, and computer languages that will increase user control far beyond anything envisioned at the typical computer center today. Many such arrangements currently exist at Project MAC at M.I.T. We see that social scientists must reorganize their concepts and heighten their aspirations in order to make effective use of these new techniques.

The next four talks are directed to model building. In the past, social scientists have achieved greatest control over their problems when they were able to specify an explicit mathematical model. How shall we exploit the opportunities that computers offer in model construction and application? The discussion of demographic applications brings out two of them. First, Keyfitz shows that the classical mathematical methods in this field (stationary Markov chains mostly developed by Lotka) have been programmed and applied in such powerful ways that few research issues remain to be explored from this perspective. Reflecting this theme, Brackett explores next steps; he is especially concerned that traditional analysis of the past become part of the computer program that processes the data rather than remain an off-line operation that is purely human. In the discussion by Demeny and others, a further search for next steps takes place. In summary, people wanted something halfway between classic mathematical methods on the one hand and greatly increased user control in computer simulation on the other hand.

The papers by Herniter and by Beshers discuss the extension of mathematical methods toward simulation. To what extent can the mathematical methods be loosened up, yet still retain their classic advantages of control? The question is two-pronged: where a classic representation is appropriate one hopes to embed it in the model and retain the elegance of analytic solution, but where a classic representation is not appropriate one may still profit from the use of explicit mathematical notation. In the application of the semi-Markov process, Herniter is able to obtain analytic solutions that could not be obtained with a Markov chain; he has much greater choice in the assumed distribution of events in time than was possible in the earlier approach. Beshers questions the ability of the Markov chain to represent many of the kinds of social theory that one might want to include in a model of a large-scale social system. He also suggests that a notation specifying sets and graphs might lead to more satisfactory alternative models.

The two papers on estimation return to data problems. Zellner considers these problems from the perspective of mathematical statistics. He stresses the influence of the choice of statistical model, and therefore the choice of the underlying theoretical model, upon estimation. Further, he notes that data are rarely in the form assumed by models, and that large errors in estimation may stem from such discrepancies between assumptions and data. In contrast, Evan considers a particular body of data, the survey data in the Roper Center at Williams College, which meets some of the assumptions of cohort analysis models but brings with it a host of difficulties of data manipulation typical of archives. Thus we are reminded that the control of the social scientist is very strongly constrained by the quality and structure of his data base.

Fleisher and Greenberger, in their papers on simulation, approach the issue of control from quite different perspectives. Fleisher calls for caution on two fronts: the first is the temptation of the social scientist to proceed to classical mathematical methods prematurely, rather than engage in an extensive exploratory and suggestive analysis of the implications of weakly defined models; the second is the temptation of the social scientist to model all the details of a system literally, rather than begin with a small set of variables and relations and then add to this set only when he has fully grasped its implications. In contrast, Greenberger views the control of simulation as a problem in the relation between the social scientists and the computer; he stresses the inflexibility of present computer language capacities and of off-line computer facilities in simulation. He regards the control by the social scientist as the essential feature in simulation of social systems; he himself has developed new concepts and a new set of procedures, OPS-2, in order to circumvent these difficulties.

A third perspective on simulation emerges from the talk by Pool. Here the issues arise from a set of substantive questions addressed to a given set of data (the survey data in the Roper Center). We see the exploratory interaction between substantive questions and characteristics of the data base within the context of building a simulation model.

The problem of the social scientist's control over his research is raised in the context of federal data policy by Taeuber, Orcutt, Kaysen, and Dunn. They explore a variety of possibilities that might satisfy both the public interest and the needs of research persons. Thus they view the problems of the structure and quality of the data base from an institutional perspective and within this context they re-examine the various technical issues that have emerged from the previous papers.

That these technical issues carry new and ominous political overtones is emphasized in the talk by Selfridge, who calls our attention to a number of issues of enormous magnitude and significance that we can only dimly perceive today. Laymen as well as computer people must face unpleasant possibilities even greater than the ordinary invasion of privacy. Both Selfridge and Weizenbaum assert that the computer man must accept the responsibility and take up the challenge at once.

Now let us turn to the second theme that emerged during the conference, the implications of time in the interpretation of social science data. We note the first hint of this theme in the paper by Kennedy. He considers it in the structure of the data base as well as in simulation. It is in the discussion of model building, however, that time is a dominant theme. Demographic models have frequently been used for projections, that is, extrapolations of trends into the future. Keyfitz notes that the classic stationary Markov chain models of Lotka may be expressed either in discrete or in continuous time. In his computer program he obtains results from solving Lotka's integral equation as well as by obtaining the characteristic roots and vectors of a matrix, thus obtaining a check. He indicates his awareness of the shortcomings of the stationary assumption, especially as it might enter into marriage probabilities. Brackett regards nonstationary population projection as requiring a choice by the social science analyst. In his computer program for projecting the population of nations, he includes subroutines that provide the social scientist with a wide and flexible range of alternative hypotheses as to the time path of death rates, birth rates, and migration rates in any nation at any point in its history.

The treatment of time is the heart of the semi-Markov process that Herniter presents. The stationary Markov assumption of the occurrence of successive events is retained, but the time interval between events is allowed to become a random variable. Difficult technical problems arise in the mathematical description of the distributions of events in time, yet the gains in ability to represent social processes are very substantial. Beshers is similarly concerned with a major bugbear of large-scale social systems — the generation as a time unit. He also questions the stationary assumption.

Again in estimation we find time a central concern. The sophistication and care with which Zellner reviews these issues contribute impressively to our understanding. The cohort technique used by Evan is one of the major options for the interpretation of social science data over time. His analysis helps us to see many of the complicated issues involved.

If, however, the implications of time were central to the issues above, how could we properly emphasize their significance in computer simulation? Simulation, dynamic systems, and dynamic modeling all refer to the same conceptual efforts; feedback is only one of many terms underlining the subtle aspects of time that must receive close attention and deep reflection if model construction is to take advantage of computer capabilities. It is here that the representation of the nonstationary stochastic process must be met and dealt with. Fleisher, Greenberger, Licklider, and Pool bring a great variety of thoughts and perspectives to this difficult problem. Both Greenberger and Licklider address themselves to the concepts of computer use that are implied, often in terms novel to most social scientists.

Needless to say, the technical issues emerging from all of these perspectives on time were crucial to the discussion of federal data policy. Orcutt, in particular, concentrates on the time implications. Indeed, his statement of the problem of economic policy from a professional economist's viewpoint brings out the fact that policy-makers want more than an extrapolation of current trends; they want to know how the system will respond to such changes as new legislation, for example. This policy interest, however, leads us back into the complex feedback relationships that are the heart of simulation models.

Next let us consider the level of aggregation as a recurrent theme. We observe first that Kennedy, by directly linking individuals in his record system, is able to estimate parameters not available to the researcher using aggregated data, say by county or state. Indeed he can choose among many methods of aggregating or disaggregating his data. Weizenbaum considers the implications of scale and aggregation for the computer systems that are likely to be available. Issues of aggregation emerge next with Herniter, who defines the states of his semi-Markov process at the level of the individual and achieves great gains in the predictability of his model thereby. Beshers treats these problems as a more general issue in the construction of social science models; there are subtle notational aspects, but more important is the need to represent social theory at both aggregated and disaggregated levels. Thus one must express the psychological or individual decision aspect of social theories directly in the model of the social system — without such components one cannot develop useful theories of social change, and consequently one cannot adequately represent the feedbacks that might result from policy alternatives — but one also must express those system parameters that serve as constraints to individual decision-making in the model.

The level of aggregation is again an important concern of Zellner's statistical discussion; his remarks are pertinent to a broad audience of social scientists. Evan also must struggle with aggregation in his efforts to unravel causal factors by the cohort method implicit in survey data.

Pool's talk raises the issue directly in a substantive context. How can we include aggregated and disaggregated data in our models of social systems? Further, how can we include theoretical concepts that stem from the tradition of psychology on one hand and the traditions of sociology, political science, and economics on the other, when the former refers to particular individuals whereas the latter usually refer to aggregations of individuals? Pool uses the attitude concept in an effort to bridge this gap and provides many insights into the general problem through his handling of the problem of voting simulation.

The issue of aggregation emerges in many forms in the papers by Taeuber and Orcutt on federal policy and is reiterated in the subsequent discussions by Kaysen and Dunn. In particular, problems of disclosure in census procedures lead Taeuber and Orcutt to consider many alternative forms of release of data. Taeuber discusses at length those forms made possible by the development of machine-readable tape. Orcutt lays stress on the use of matched groups of households in successive surveys for obtaining quasi-experimental data.

Several significant events of the conference are not reported in this volume. At our opening luncheon, Dr. Roger Revelle, newly appointed as the first Richard Saltonstall Professor of Population Policy at the Harvard School of Public Health, presented his initial conception of his task. At our second luncheon, users of the Census Bureau's 1-1,000 sample compared their experiences. Following a talk by Ithiel de Sola Pool, several participants prevailed on Martin Greenberger to give an impromptu demonstration of the Project MAC time-sharing system.

Many other themes and issues thread through the proceedings. We hope that with the help of the clues suggested here, the reader will want to search out these themes for himself and thus gain the sense of viewing old problems from new perspectives, an experience shared by the conference participants.

## POSTSCRIPT

During the three years since the conference was held, much has happened in the computer world, yet the substantive issues have remained much the same. Social scientists and other applications people are going through the painful process of developing procedures that give them greater control over the computer. A user-oriented computer system is a promise held out by many, but as yet successes are relatively few.

When the subject of a revised edition arose, the authors were queried as to their desires for updating their contributions. Most chose to stand pat, some preferred postscripts, while a few made major changes. Three papers are almost wholly new: Greenberger has extensively modified his paper. Keyfitz has contributed a new paper that I am including as well as his original paper, as it is indicative of his recent work, yet is part of his over-all recent work that is suggested in outline in the earlier paper. I have added a paper of my own that is in a very real sense an outcome of the conference. Some of us at M.I.T. continued a loose collaboration, but in particular Ithiel Pool and I developed a National Science Foundation proposal and project on computer-based social data handling; we also continued a collaboration with Weizenbaum. A progress report on this research is therefore relevant. I believe this work will lead to very different user approaches based on very different concepts from those familiar in previous computer applications. If I am right, then a new era of truly effective applications work will emerge.

In the papers that follow the affiliations of the speakers are those which they held at the time of the conference — October 1964.

SOCIAL SCIENCE COMMUNICATION WITH COMPUTERS

# SEMIAUTOMATIC TABULATIONS OF POPULATION DATA FILES SUCH AS THE 1960 CENSUS 1-1,000 SAMPLE

Richard A. Hornseth

U. S. Bureau of the Census

In the process of checking out new computers and new programming languages and techniques acquired at the Bureau of the Census over the past few years, we have been experimenting with a tabulation generator designed to tabulate population data files such as the 1960 Census 1-1, 000 sample. The main intent has been to reduce the burden placed upon the computer programmer by having the generator translate the specifications of the analyst into a form acceptable to the computer. This amounts, however, to placing the analyst in more direct contact with the computer, if only by reducing his dependence upon a programmer.

There is nothing new in this approach, either inside or outside the Bureau. As early as 1957 we had a similar, though more limited, tabulation generator for the Univac I computers. The literature is full of descriptions of techniques whereby the analyst, by supplying a few parameters in his own language, can generate a computer program. This particular generator is of interest here because it was designed to handle data files important to population analysts. A description of how it works and of our experience with it should provide some notion of what improvements in accessibility of these files analysts may expect in the coming years.

Generators stand or fall on their ability to strike a practical balance between the maximization of the variety of output result and the minimization of the variety of input parameters. A restriction on variety of input parameters often leads to impoverished output, and a lavish variety of output often requires such an array of input parameters that the burden on the analyst or programmer is not lightened but increased. Fortunately the Bureau has a very large computer, the 1107, with 65, 000 words of core memory; a good programming language, FORTRAN IV; and some experience with a quite powerful tool for organizing computer programs, Decision Logic Tables. With these advantages, we have not had to skimp on output results, and we could afford a fairly free form of input parameter with provisions for introducing great variety.

We have used the generator for the past six months on approximately 25 widely varying jobs. In the course of this experience, we have departed somewhat from the original intention of providing the analyst with an almost direct access to the computer for his own research and have tried to provide the programmer with a framework that he can easily vary to accomplish a wide variety of production jobs. This trend reflects the production character of most of our work at the Bureau. In any event, the result is about the same. We have been able to drive programming costs down for a certain range of applications to a point at which analysts can expect comparatively economical and quick tabulations of small files.

The basic structure of the generator may be described as follows: the generator initially receives as input two sets of parameters, one describing all the variables required by the tabulations, the other listing the variables that make up each table or tabulation. From the former, the program arranges look-up tables against which each input data record is checked to ascertain the ordinal category values of the variables for proper location of each tally by row or column. From the table parameters the program derives the constants, multipliers, and the like for determining the proper base core addresses for each tabulation of the data record. The tabulations are stored consecutively in a one-dimensioned array to conserve core storage. Constants are also derived for controlling the output layout. The establishment of the look-up tables and the derivation of operating constants are performed only once at the start of a run and constitute the "self-generating" aspect of the program.

Attachment A shows the punch-card layout for the specification of variables. The variables are listed in any convenient order. An abbreviated name is placed in the first field for convenience in checking only. In the second field the order number of the variable is given for use in the specification of the output tables. Field 3 shows the number of tabulation categories for the variables. Field 4 indicates the ordinal location of the variable field on the input data record, counting from left to right. In Field 5 up to 14 code values are listed to be associated with each category of the variable. Provision is made for handling one- to three-column variable fields. The FORTRAN input format statement, not shown here, indicates the field size of each variable. Variable fields greater than 3 columns require special coding.[1] To accommodate ranges of code values, T is used to indicate "through." S indicates the end of a set of code values. B indicates a blank code value. R indicates the "all other" category. The absence of an R will result in the deletion of a record from a tabulation involving the variable if the input record code matches no code in any category specified for the variable.

The code values are read in under the A, or alpha, format, as are the corresponding input data record variable fields. This permits the handling of any alphanumeric code structure, except for the alphabetics T, S, B, and R, used as scanning signals.

The signal S arises from a character set problem. Ordinarily a blank would suffice to indicate the end of a code value set. But often in the 1-1,000 sample file a blank is a legitimate code value. B arises from a language complication on the 1107. The input data file is in BCD-XS3, whereas the computer language is in Field Data. Rather than convert the input file to Field Data, in a separate program we convert the code value specifications from Field Data to XS3 before they are loaded into the look-up tables. In this process we supply the S stopper code to save the labor of writing it out, and thus we depend on a blank as the original stopper. To distinguish stopper blanks from code value blanks we used B for the latter. One additional feature of our variable specifications layout is the use of a number greater than 900 for the data input field number for the variable. The 901 in the example is a signal that the category value for the variable REAGE is to be determined by special coding. As an illustration, we assume in Attachment B that REAGE represents a reclassification of the categories for the variable, AGE. The 901 is a signal in the look-up table scanning process to suspend the scan for variable REAGE, and the programmer inserts coding indicated by Attachment B just after the scan operation to derive the proper category value for REAGE from the scanned determination for AGE. This procedure permits the easy handling of a great variety of special variables.

In Attachment C the layout for the specification of what variables enter each tabulation is shown. Field 1 provides the ordinal table number; Field 2, the basic number of columns to appear in the table, excluding totals; Field 3 and beyond list the variables, up to 18, that appear in the tabulation by their number shown in Field 2 in Attachment A, going from major to minor. The function of specifying the number of columns in Field 2 is to permit any number of variable levels to appear across the columnar dimension of the table. The number of columns must, of course, represent the product of the number of categories for each of the variables involved. A practical limitation, however, is the printer width which, on the 1107, permits up to 20 six-digit columns, including a totals column and a line serial number column. Attachment D shows how the final table layouts are related to these table specifications.

The tabulation generator consists of four sections. The logic of each is organized in Decision Table format shown in Attachment E. The first section, LOADPC, loads the variable and table specifications and computes the necessary constants required for control and operation. The next section, SCAN, searches all the variables of an input data record to determine the ordinal category value for each. These values are stored in the array H(k), where k is the ordinal variable number. The following section, TALP, takes the values of H(k) along with the necessary constants derived in LOADPC and tallies the record in the appropriate tables. The final section, RITE, outputs the tallies when required, usually at the end of the operation.

Attachment F shows a typical tabulation output. The first column is a line serial number we once inserted when we thought the serial number would be useful for preparing summaries of the output tabulations which would go out on tape as well as on the printer. It has been little used and probably will be dropped in later versions. For the same reason we put the line format statement and the row and column counts in the table header line. These we have found useful for summarization programs. The second column and the first row after the table header provide row and column totals, respectively.

The table output is one of the less satisfactory features of the generator. We have done little with it because most of our applications have involved considerable output variations requiring special coding. In Attachment G we show an output created with special coding inserted with relatively little effort in the RITE section.

Attachment H is a print of the program in FORTRAN IV. A parameter card permits the setting of the sizes of all arrays at will. Comments indicate the functions of these parameters. Input and output unit numbers are also set in the parameter statement. The common statements used are a carryover of an earlier attempt to make external subroutines of the various program sections. Running time went up so drastically, however, that this was abandoned, and the common statements were retained only for declaring the dimensions of the arrays.

The coding is interspersed with liberal comments to facilitate the preparation of an operational program with a minimum of effort by anyone with some knowledge of FORTRAN.

In conclusion, I wish to speculate a bit on the function of a generator such as I have described. If an analyst has in mind a specific series of applications, it is possible to lock in more coding to handle specific files and to provide specific options reducing the programmer involvement in the operation. The feasibility of this approach depends upon the relation of the cost of securing such a specific generator to the utility derived from it. With larger computers, advanced programming languages and techniques, and accumulated experience, the cost of preparing such generators should drop considerably.

About two man-months were required to prepare the generator we described. Thus generators of a similar level of complexity could now be prepared economically if an analyst could generalize sufficiently the computing or tabulating requirements of his research activities. Some activity in this direction has already occurred. There are now available some primitively generalized programs for handling fairly easily the preparation of life tables, interpolations, and projections. It appears to me that we are on the verge of enormous advances in this area and that it is now simply up to the analyst to specify what he wants.

### Reference

1.    We now have a version of the generator which permits the handling of six-character code fields.

### Postscript

During the four years since this tally generator was developed, it has been in constant use at the Bureau of the Census among several groups of programmers as an effective device for cutting programming costs on jobs where large numbers of tabulations for relatively small files are required. Constant use has brought about many changes to the tally generator as new programming techniques or devices became obvious or available and as the requirements of programmers and sponsors became clearer and more sophisticated. With respect to techniques and devices, the main change has been the replacement of the formatted FORTRAN read routine with machine-coded subroutines for reading and formatting tape input. This change has decreased computer running time by a factor of sometimes as much as ten. Also, this has made the tally generator compatible with all census tape files.

With respect to changes induced by users' needs, there are two of importance: the first is that the format of the input parameters has been modified to permit easier preparation. Fields are more nearly free-form in character, and overspecification is eliminated. The second is that parameters now supply legends for table titles, captions, and stubs and also provide for the derivation and insertion of subtotals.

Since the basic logic and function of the tally generator is unchanged, the latest version will not be further described here. A complete description, however, is available on request.

It is of interest here that the most surprising development in the use of the tally generator is the extent to which it has become a framework tool for a programming staff. Some programmers have become very expert in modifying the generator quite extensively to suit the needs of a particular job. Some very elegant output has been the result. Some of us, however, feel that on occasion it would have been better for the programmer to have programmed the job directly in FORTRAN rather than to have tinkered with the generator. The preference for the generator appears to indicate a need, at least among juniors, for formalized ways of organizing programming jobs that have not been too explicit in the area of data processing.

In the past few years there has been an enormous development in generators, where by generator we mean a set of computer programs designed for processing a variety of data files in a variety of ways specified by parameters that can be thought of as a "higher-level" language in the sense of conforming more nearly with the modes of thought and organization brought to bear by an analyst upon data of interest to him. [1] Unfortunately, some of the proliferation of generators is made possible by so confining attention to specialized files and restricted operations upon them that the parameter system appears to offer a "lower-level" rather than a "higher-level" language to the poor soul who attempts to use the system for what the salesman said it could do. This concern was expressed recently by Saul Gorn. [2]

Thus the hope I expressed in 1964 that "...we are on the verge of enormous advances in this area..." has not only been realized but has generated a concern that some of us may submerge in those "advances." No analyst today need want for a computer tool to ease his labor. His problem is to avoid being stuck with the wrong one.

### References

1.    Proceedings of the 1967 Spring Joint Computer Conference, American Federation of Information Processing Societies, 1967. A glance at the Proceedings reveals the presence of at least a half-dozen papers on file handling and information-retrieval systems driven by "higher-level" languages of some sort.

2.    "Handling the Growth by Definition of Mechanical Languages," ibid., p. 213.

Attachment A

Card Layout for Specification of Variables

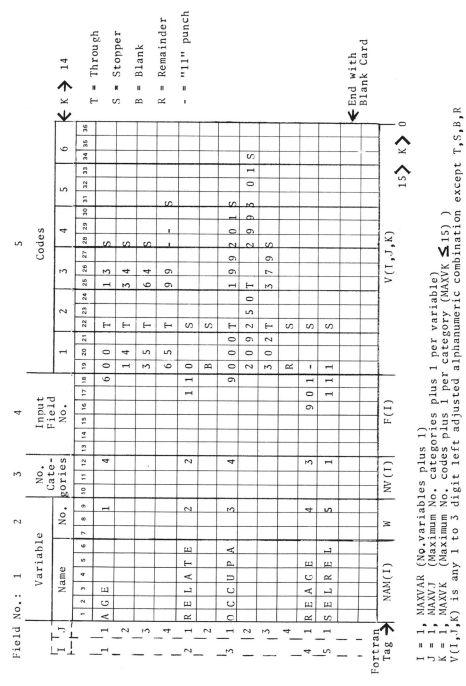

T = Through
S = Stopper
B = Blank
R = Remainder
- = "11" punch

End with Blank Card

I = 1, MAXVAR (No. variables plus 1)
J = 1, MAXVJ (Maximum No. categories plus 1 per variable)
K = 1, MAXVK (Maximum No. codes plus 1 per category (MAXVK ≤ 15) )
V(I,J,K) is any 1 to 3 digit left adjusted alphanumeric combination except T,S,B,R

Decision Logic Table

ILLUSTRATIVE SPECIFICATION FOR VARIABLE NO. 4
(FIELD NO. 901 - SEE ATTACHMENT A) ASSUMING "REAGE" IS A REARRANGEMENT
OF "AGE" SO THAT THE 1ST CLASS IS 00 THROUGH 34

| | | | | | | | | | | | |
|---|---|---|---|---|---|---|---|---|---|---|---|
| H(1) > 2 | Y | N | | | | | | | | | |
| | | | | | | | | | | | |
| | | | | | | | | | | | |
| H(4) = 1 | | X | | | | | | | | | |
| H(4) = H(1)=1 | X | | | | | | | | | | |
| | | | | | | | | | | | |
| EXIT | X | X | | | | | | | | | |

Attachment C

Card Layout for Specification of Variables

Variables in Order Major to Minor

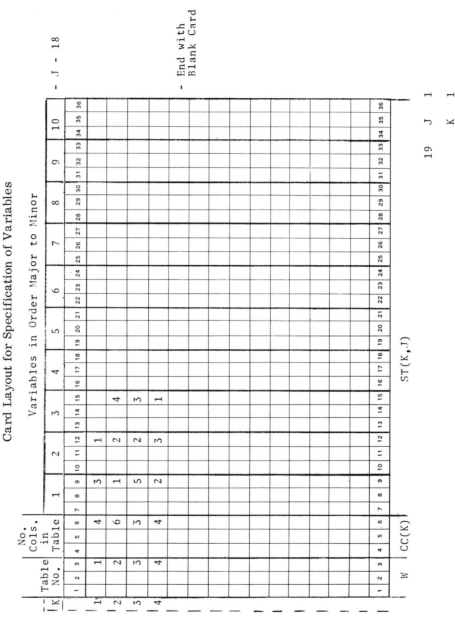

Attachment D

Table Layouts Corresponding to Variable and Table
Specifications Given in Attachments A and C
(Captions and Stubs Shown Below in Parentheses
are not Provided in the Actual Output)

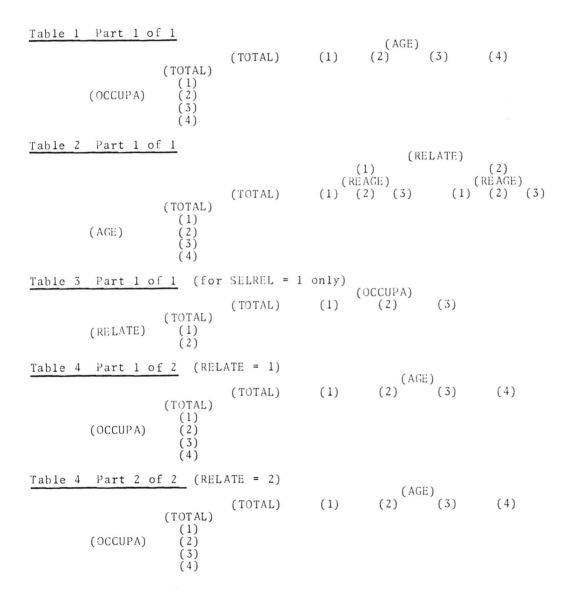

Table 1   Part 1 of 1

|  |  | (TOTAL) | (1) | (AGE)(2) | (3) | (4) |
|--|--|--|--|--|--|--|
|  | (TOTAL) |  |  |  |  |  |
|  | (1) |  |  |  |  |  |
| (OCCUPA) | (2) |  |  |  |  |  |
|  | (3) |  |  |  |  |  |
|  | (4) |  |  |  |  |  |

Table 2   Part 1 of 1

|  |  |  |  | (RELATE)(1)(REAGE) |  |  | (2)(REAGE) |  |  |
|--|--|--|--|--|--|--|--|--|--|
|  |  | (TOTAL) | (1) | (2) | (3) | (1) | (2) | (3) |  |
|  | (TOTAL) |  |  |  |  |  |  |  |  |
|  | (1) |  |  |  |  |  |  |  |  |
| (AGE) | (2) |  |  |  |  |  |  |  |  |
|  | (3) |  |  |  |  |  |  |  |  |
|  | (4) |  |  |  |  |  |  |  |  |

Table 3   Part 1 of 1   (for SELREL = 1 only)

|  |  | (TOTAL) | (1) | (OCCUPA)(2) | (3) |
|--|--|--|--|--|--|
|  | (TOTAL) |  |  |  |  |
| (RELATE) | (1) |  |  |  |  |
|  | (2) |  |  |  |  |

Table 4   Part 1 of 2   (RELATE = 1)

|  |  | (TOTAL) | (1) | (AGE)(2) | (3) | (4) |
|--|--|--|--|--|--|--|
|  | (TOTAL) |  |  |  |  |  |
|  | (1) |  |  |  |  |  |
| (OCCUPA) | (2) |  |  |  |  |  |
|  | (3) |  |  |  |  |  |
|  | (4) |  |  |  |  |  |

Table 4   Part 2 of 2   (RELATE = 2)

|  |  | (TOTAL) | (1) | (AGE)(2) | (3) | (4) |
|--|--|--|--|--|--|--|
|  | (TOTAL) |  |  |  |  |  |
|  | (1) |  |  |  |  |  |
| (OCCUPA) | (2) |  |  |  |  |  |
|  | (3) |  |  |  |  |  |
|  | (4) |  |  |  |  |  |

Attachment E

# Decision Logic Table

20

**LOADPC : LOAD VARIABLE SPECIFICATIONS**
101 FORMAT (A6, 2I3, I6, 15A3)      NI = NO. VARIABLES
102 FORMAT (1H4, A6, 2I3, I6, 15A3)
103 FORMAT (18X, 15A3)
104 FORMAT (1H4, 18X, 15A3)

| | 113 | 116 | 116 | 116 | |
|---|---|---|---|---|---|
| START | Y | N | N | N | N |
| 112 W < 1 | Y | Y | N | N | N |
| 114 F (I) > 900 | | | Y | N | N |
| 115 J = NV(I) | | Y | | Y | N |
| 116 I = I+1 | | X | X | | |
| 110 TAL(P) = 0   P = 1, MAXTAL | X | | | | |
| I = 1 | X | | | | |
| 111 J = 1 | X | X | X | | |
| READ(NTAPE,101)NAM(I),W,NV(I), | X | X | X | | |
| F(I),(V(I,J,K),K=1,MAXVK) | X | X | X | | |
| WRITE(NPRINT,102) [ABOVE LIST] | X | X | X | | |
| 117 J = J+1 | | | | X | |
| READ(NTAPE,103)(V(I,J,K),K=1,MAXVK | | | | X | |
| WRITE(NPRINT,104) [ABOVE LIST] | | | | X | |
| 113 NI = I-1 | | | | | X |
| RETURN TO 112 | X | X | X | X | |
| GO TO B (120) | | | | | X |

**LOADPC (CONTINUED): LOAD TABLE SPECIFICATIONS**
105 FORMAT (21I3)
106 FORMAT (1H4, 21I3)          NK = NO. TABLES

| | | 123 | 124 |
|---|---|---|---|
| START | Y | N | N |
| 122 W < 1 | | Y | N |
| 124 K = K+1 | | | X |
| 120 K = 1 | X | | |
| 121 READ(NTAPE,105)W, CC(K), | X | | X |
| (ST(K,J),J=1,MAXSTJ) | | | |
| WRITE(NPRINT,106) [ABOVE LIST] | X | | X |
| 123 NK = K-1 | | X | |
| REWIND NTAPE | | X | |
| RETURN TO 122 | X | X | X |
| GO TO C (130) | | X | |

# Decision Logic Table

## LOADPC (CONTINUED): DERIVE NJ(K) FROM ST (K,J)
NJ(K) = NO. VARIABLES IN TABLE K

| | 133 | 134 | 135 | |
|---|---|---|---|---|
| START | Y | N | N | N |
| 131 K = NK+1 | Y | Y | N | N |
| 132 ST(K,J) < 0 | | Y | N | |
| 134 NJ(K) = J-1 | | X | | |
| K = K+1 | | X | | |
| 130 K = 1 | X | | | |
| 136 J = 1 | X | X | | |
| 135 J = J+1 | | | X | |
| RETURN TO 131 | X | X | | |
| 133 GO TO D (140) | | | X | X |

## LOADPC (CONTINUED): DERIVE NZ(K) AND NC(K,J) FROM ST(K,J) AND NV(I)
NC(K,J) = CUM. PROD. OF VARIABLE CATEGORIES TO THE J+1 VARIABLE
NZ(K) = TOTAL PRODUCT = TABLE SIZE

| | 143 | 145 | | |
|---|---|---|---|---|
| START | Y | N | N | N |
| 141 K = NK+1 | Y | Y | N | N |
| 142 J = 1 | | Y | Y | N |
| 145 I = ST(K,J) | | X | X | |
| NZ(K) = NC(K,J)*NV(I) | | X | X | |
| K = K+1 | | X | X | |
| 140 K = 1 | X | | | |
| 146 J = NJ(K) | X | X | X | |
| NC(K,J) = 1 | X | X | X | |
| 144 I = ST(K,J) | X | X | X | X |
| NC(K,J-1) = NC(K,J)*NV(I) | X | X | X | X |
| J = J-1 | X | X | X | X |
| RETURN TO 141 | X | X | X | X |
| GO TO E (150) | | | X | X |

Note: Implication of NC(K,J) is that there must be at least 2 variables to a table.

## Decision Logic Table

**LOADPC (CONTINUED): DERIVE NW(K) FROM NZ(K)**
NW(K) = RELATIVE STARTING POINT IN TAL(P) MATRIX FOR TABLE K
107 FORMAT

| | 153 | | |
|---|---|---|---|
| START | Y | N | N |
| 151 K = NK | Y | N | |
| 150 K = 1 | X | | |
| NW(K) = 0 | X | | |
| 152 NW(K+1) = NZ(K)+NW(K)* | X | X | X |
| K = K+1 | X | X | |
| 153 WRITE(NPRINT,107)NW(K)*,NZ(K) | | X | |
| GO TO F (160) | | X | |
| RETURN TO 151 | X | | X |

**LOADPC (CONTINUED): DERIVE SB(K) AND NS(K)**
SB(K) = NO. ROWS PER PART OF TABLE K
NS(K) = NO. PARTS TO TABLE K

| | 163 | | |
|---|---|---|---|
| START | Y | N | N |
| 161 K > NK | Y | N | |
| 162 GO TO G (170) | | | X |
| 164 K = K+1 | | | X |
| 160 K = 1 | X | | |
| RETURN TO 161 | X | X | |
| 162 GO TO G (170) | | X | |
| 163 GO TO EXIT OF LOADPC AT 199 | | X | |

Note: Implication of NW(K) is that there must be at least 2 tables

# Decision Logic Table

**LOADPC (CONTINUED)**
**109 FORMAT**

| | | 177 | 175 | | |
|---|---|---|---|---|---|
| START | Y | N | N | N | N |
| 171 J  1 ≤ 1 | Y | Y | N | N | N |
| 172 W = CC(K) | | Y | Y | N | |
| 177 WRITE(NPRINT,109)K | | X | | | X |
| 174 J = J-1 | | | | | X |
| 170 W = 1 | X | | | | |
| J = NJ(K) | X | | | | |
| 176 I = ST(K,J) | X | X | X | | X |
| W = W*NV(I) | X | X | X | | X |
| 175 J = J-1 | | | X | | |
| I = ST(K,J) | | | X | X | |
| W = W*NV(I) | | X | X | X | |
| 173 SB(K) = NV(I) | | X | X | X | |
| NS(K) = NZ(K)/W | | X | X | X | |
| GO TO F (164) | | X | X | X | |
| RETURN TO 171 | X | | | | X |

**SCAN:** FOR A GIVEN INPUT DATA RECORD DERIVE FOR EACH VARIABLE I THE CATEGORY RANK VALUE AND STORE IN H(I) (IF H(I) = 0, NO CATEGORY RANK COULD BE FOUND)

| | | 205 | 207 | 209 | 212 | 212 | 212 | 212 |
|---|---|---|---|---|---|---|---|---|
| START | Y | N | N | N | N | N | N | N |
| 203 I > NI | Y | Y | N | N | N | N | N | N |
| 204 J > NV(I) | | | Y | Y | N | N | N | N |
| 206 P > 900 | | | | Y | | | N | N |
| 208 V(K,J,K) = SS | | | | | Y | Y | Y | N |
| V(I,J,K) = TT | | | | | | | Y | Y |
| 213 V(I,J,K-1) = RR | | | | | Y | N | | |
| V(I,J,K-1) = X(P) | | | | | Y | Y | N | N |
| V(I,J,K+1) ≥ X(P) ≥ V(I,J,K-1) | | | | | | Y | N | |
| 200 I = 1 | X | | | | | | | |
| J = J+1 | | | | | | | | |
| K = K+2 | | | | | | X | | |
| K = K+1 | | | | X | | | | |
| 207 H(I) = 0 | | X | | | | | | |
| 212 H(I) = J | | | | | X | X | X | X |
| 209 I = I+1 | X | X | X | X | X | X | X | X |
| 201 J = 1 | X | X | X | X | X | X | X | X |
| P = F(I) | X | X | X | X | X | X | X | X |
| 202 K = 2 | X | X | X | X | X | X | X | X |
| RETURN TO 203 | X | X | X | X | X | X | X | X |
| GO TO EXIT SCAN (299) | X | | | | | | | |

# Decision Logic Table

## TALP: TABULATE INPUT DATA RECORD ACCORDING TO VALUES OF H(I) GIVEN IN SCAN

| START | 304 | 306 | 308 | | |
|---|---|---|---|---|---|
| 302 K > NK | Y | N | N | N | N |
| 303 H(I) = 0 | | Y | N | N | |
| 305 J ≥ NJ(K) | | | Y | N | |
| Z = Z +((H(I)-1)*NC(K,J)) | | | X | X | |
| P = Z + NW(K) | | | X | | |
| TAL(P) = TAL(P)+NTAL | | | X | | |
| 300 K = 1 | X | | | | |
| J = J+1 | | | | X | |
| 306 K = K+1 | | X | X | | |
| 301 Z = 1 | X | X | X | | |
| J = 1 | X | X | X | | |
| 309 I = ST(K,J) | X | X | X | X | |
| RETURN TO 302 | X | X | X | | |
| 304 GO TO TALP EXIT (399) | | X | | | |

## RITE: WRITE TALLY OUTPUT

| START | 412 | 414 | 416 | 418 | | |
|---|---|---|---|---|---|---|
| 410 K > NK | Y | N | N | N | N | N |
| 411 W > NS(K) | | Y | N | N | N | |
| 413 I > SB(K)+1 | | | Y | N | | |
| 415 J > CC(K)+1 | | | | Y | N | |
| 400 N = 1 | X | | | | | |
| WRITE(NPRINT,401)N | X | | | | | |
| WRITE(NPT,401)N | X | | | | | |
| 417 TB(I,J) = TAL(P) | | | | X | | |
| P = P+1 | | | | X | | |
| J = J+1 | | | | X | | |
| 418 I = I+1 | | | | | X | |
| 416 GO TO B (450) | | | X | | | |
| 437 W = W+1 | | | X | | | |
| 414 K = K+1 | | X | | | | |
| P = 1 | X | | | | | |
| K = 1 | X | | | | | |
| 420 N = 1 | X | X | | | | |
| 421 I = 2 | X | X | X | | | |
| 419 J = 2 | X | X | X | X | | |
| RETURN TO 410 | X | X | X | X | X | X |
| 412 WRITE(NPT)TAL REWIND NPT | X | | | | | |
| EXIT RITE (499) | X | | | | | |

Attachment E

# Decision Logic Table

RITE (CONTINUED)
402 FORMAT (1H0,I6,7HATABLE4,I4,7HAPART4,I4,4H1A0F4,I4,5X,
6HFORMAT,12A6,4X,5HROWS4,I3,10H,COLUMNS,A,I3)

| | Y | N | N |
| --- | --- | --- | --- |
| | | Y | N |
| START | | | |
| 435 I > KAL | X | | |
| 430 KAK = CC(K)+1 | X | | |
| 431 TB(1,J) = 0   J = 1, KAK | X | | |
| KAL = SB(K)+1 | X | | |
| 432 TB(I,1) = 0   I = 1,KAL | X | | |
| 433 TB(1,J)=TB(1,J)+TB(I,J) I=2,KAL | X | | |
| 434 TB(I,1)=TB(I,1)+TB(I,J) J=2,KAK | X | | |
| L = CC(K)-1 | X | | |
| GO TO C | X | | |
| 440 N = N+1 | X | | |
| KZK = KAK+1 | X | | |
| WRITE (NPRINT,402)N,K,W, | X | | |
| NS(K),NFOR(1),NFOR(2),KAL,KZK | X | | |
| WRITE(NPT,402)  [ABOVE LIST] | X | | |
| I = 1 | X | | |
| 436 N = N+1 | | | X |
| KZK = KAK+1 | X | | X |
| WRITE(NPRINT,NFOR)N,(TB(I,J), J = 1,KAK) | X | | X |
| WRITE(NPT,NFOR)  [ABOVE LIST] | X | | X |
| I = I+1 | X | | X |
| RETURN 435 | X | | X |
| GO TO A(437) | | | X |

RITE (CONTINUED)   ADJUST FOR 1 COLUMN TABLE

| | 439 | |
| --- | --- | --- |
| | Y | N |
| | Y | N |
| I > 0 | | |
| 438 NFOR(1) = FM | X | |
| NFOR(2) = FN | | X |
| 439 NFOR(1) = FORM (L,1) | X | |
| GO TO B (440) | X | X |

25

Attachment F

P01 TABLE 4 PART 16 OF 24 FORMAT(1H , 16I7) ROWS 13, COLUMNS, 18

P15 TABLE 4 PART 17 OF 24 FORMAT(1H , 16I7) ROWS 13, COLUMNS, 18

P29 TABLE 4 PART 18 OF 24 FORMAT(1H , 16I7) ROWS 13, COLUMNS, 18

Attachment G

## Special Tabulation of Persons in Arkansas by Age for the University of Arkansas
### (Based on the 1960 Census 25 Per Cent Sample)

REGION 99  UNEMPLOYED  NONWHITE MALE  OCCUPATION LABORER  WORKED 26 WEEKS OR LESS

| | | | | AGE | | | |
|---|---|---|---|---|---|---|---|
| | TOTAL | 14-17 | 18-22 | 23-29 | 30-44 | 45-64 | 65 AND OVER |
| **UNDER 7 YEARS OF SCHOOL BY INCOME IN 1959** | | | | | | | |
| TOTAL.......... | 418 | 9 | 37 | 44 | 96 | 167 | 65 |
| $0 TO 999 OR LOSS.... | 331 | 9 | 37 | 30 | 60 | 137 | 58 |
| $1,000 TO 1,999..... | 64 | 0 | 0 | 10 | 31 | 19 | 4 |
| $2,000 TO 2,999..... | 20 | 0 | 0 | 4 | 5 | 11 | 0 |
| $3,000 TO 5,999..... | 0 | 0 | 0 | 0 | 0 | 0 | 0 |
| $6,000 AND OVER..... | 3 | 0 | 0 | 0 | 0 | 0 | 3 |
| MEDIAN INCOME........ | 631 | 0 | 0 | 0 | 0 | 605 | 0 |
| **7 TO 8 YEARS OF SCHOOL BY INCOME IN 1959** | | | | | | | |
| TOTAL.......... | 127 | 9 | 26 | 8 | 40 | 33 | 11 |
| $0 TO 999 OR LOSS.... | 85 | 4 | 26 | 8 | 18 | 25 | 4 |
| $1,000 TO 1,999..... | 26 | 0 | 0 | 0 | 15 | 4 | 7 |
| $2,000 TO 2,999..... | 4 | 5 | 0 | 0 | 4 | 0 | 0 |
| $3,000 TO 5,999..... | 12 | 0 | 0 | 0 | 3 | 4 | 0 |
| $6,000 AND OVER..... | 0 | 0 | 0 | 0 | 0 | 0 | 0 |
| MEDIAN INCOME........ | 741 | 0 | 0 | 0 | 0 | 0 | 0 |
| **9 TO 11 YEARS OF SCHOOL BY INCOME IN 1959** | | | | | | | |
| TOTAL.......... | 142 | 32 | 60 | 18 | 20 | 8 | 4 |
| $0 TO 999 OR LOSS.... | 129 | 32 | 60 | 13 | 20 | 0 | 4 |
| $1,000 TO 1,999..... | 9 | 0 | 0 | 5 | 0 | 4 | 0 |
| $2,000 TO 2,999..... | 4 | 0 | 0 | 0 | 0 | 4 | 0 |
| $3,000 TO 5,999..... | 0 | 0 | 0 | 0 | 0 | 0 | 0 |
| $6,000 AND OVER..... | 0 | 0 | 0 | 0 | 0 | 0 | 0 |
| MEDIAN INCOME........ | 550 | 0 | 0 | 0 | 0 | 0 | 0 |
| **12 YEARS OF SCHOOL BY INCOME IN 1959** | | | | | | | |
| TOTAL.......... | 84 | 0 | 35 | 19 | 8 | 18 | 4 |
| $0 TO 999 OR LOSS.... | 69 | 0 | 35 | 16 | 0 | 18 | 0 |
| $1,000 TO 1,999..... | 10 | 0 | 0 | 3 | 3 | 0 | 4 |
| $2,000 TO 2,999..... | 0 | 0 | 0 | 0 | 0 | 0 | 0 |
| $3,000 TO 5,999..... | 5 | 0 | 0 | 0 | 5 | 0 | 0 |
| $6,000 AND OVER..... | 0 | 0 | 0 | 0 | 0 | 0 | 0 |
| MEDIAN INCOME........ | 0 | 0 | 0 | 0 | 0 | 0 | 0 |
| **OVER 12 YEARS OF SCHOOL BY INCOME IN 1959** | | | | | | | |
| TOTAL.......... | 9 | 0 | 0 | 0 | 0 | 0 | 0 |
| $0 TO 999 OR LOSS.... | 5 | 0 | 0 | 0 | 5 | 0 | 0 |
| $1,000 TO 1,999..... | 0 | 0 | 0 | 0 | 4 | 0 | 0 |
| $2,000 TO 2,999..... | 4 | 0 | 0 | 0 | 0 | 0 | 0 |
| $3,000 TO 5,999..... | 0 | 0 | 0 | 0 | 0 | 0 | 0 |
| $6,000 AND OVER..... | 0 | 0 | 0 | 0 | 0 | 0 | 0 |
| MEDIAN INCOME........ | 0 | 0 | 0 | 0 | 0 | 0 | 0 |

# Attachment H

```fortran
C     FORTAL
C     GENERAL TALLY FRAME , VERSION 1, MAY 20, 1964
      PARAMETER MAXTAL=1469S,MAXVAR=26,MAXTAB=19,MAXVK=9,MAXVJ=74,
      1MAXSTJ=6,NFLD=15,NPRINT=3,NPT=1,NPT=13,NAT=10,NTAPE=9
C     MAXTAL = MAXIMUM NO. TALLIES +1
C
C     MAXVAR = MAXIMUM NO. VARIABLES +1
C     MAXTAB = MAXIMUM NO. TABLES +1
C
C     MAXVK = MAXIMUM NO. COL'S PER CATEGORY OF A VARIABLE +1    NOTE=
C                              MUST BE LESS THAN 16
C
C     MAXVJ = MAXIMUM NO. CATEGORIES PER VARIABLE +1             NOTE=
C     MAXSTJ = MAXIMUM NO. VARIABLES PER TABLE +1
C                              MUST BE LESS THAN 20
C     NFLD   = NO. FIELDS IN INPUT WORK RECORD
C     NPRINT = PRINTER UNIT NO.
C     NPT    = OUTPUT TAPE UNIT NO.
C     NAT    = INPUT TAPE UNIT NO.
C     NTAPE  = VARIABLE AND TABLE SPECIFICATION FILE UNIT NO.
C
      INTEGER F,V,X,H,ST,TAL,CC,SR,VS,FD,ZZ
      INTEGER W,P,SS,IT,PR,Z,IA,FORM,F",FN
      DIMENSION NAM(MAXVAR),NZ(MAXTAB)
      DIMENSION TB(MAXVJ,21), FORM1B(2), NFOR(2)
      COMMON/LODSC/F(MAXVAR),NV(MAXVAR),V(MAXVAR,MAXVJ,MAXVK)
      COMMON/LORTAL/TAL(MAXTAL)
      COMMON /LODTAL/ NC(MAXTAB,MAXSTJ,NJ(MAXTAB),ST(MAXTAB,MAXSTJ),
      1NW(MAXTAB)
      COMMON/NJ,NK,NJ,NK
      COMMON /LODRIT/ CC(MAXTAB),NS(MAXTAB),SB(MAXTAB)
      COMMON /SCARFD/ X(NFLD)
      COMMON /SCATA/ H(MAXVAR)
      DATA NZZ,2H /
C     NZZ FOR TWO-DIGIT SENTINEL CHECK
C     INPUT DATA FORMAT STATEMENT FOLLOWS
    1 FORMAT (5IA2,2A1,A2,4A1,2A2,A1,A3,3A2))
C     INSERT HERE CODING REQUIRED FOR INITIALIZATION SUCH AS INPUT
C     CONTROL COMMUNICATION WITH OPERATOR, INPUT TAPE SWAP SETS, ETC.
C     GO TO 100 TO LOAD VARIABLE AND TABLE SPECIFICATION INPUT
C     EXIT THERE IS TO 199
      GO TO 100
C     INSERT AT 199 CODING FOR READING INPUT DATA INCLUDING INITIALIZA-I
C     ON OF FILE, TAPE SWAPPING CONTROL, FILE CLOSING, WRITING OUTPUT,
C     AND CLOSING JOB.
C     EXAMPLE OF SUCH CODING FOLLOWS ASSUMING NO TAPE INIT OR SWAP
  199 READ (NAT,1) X
      IF (X(1) .EQ. NZZ) GO TO 400
      GO TO 200
  299 IF (H(1) .GT. 2)GO TO 900
      H(4)=1
  901 NTAL=1
      GO TO 300
  900 H(4)=H(1)-1
```

```fortran
                                    GO TO 901
  399                               GO TO 199
  499 REWIND NAT
                                    STOP
C     GO TO 400 TO WRITE TALLIES OUT ON PRINTER AND TAPE NPT
C                              EXIT THERE IS TO 400
C     GO TO 200 TO SCAN INPUT RECORD FOR CATEGORY VALUE FOR EACH
C                              VARIABLE,  EXIT THERE IS TO 299
C     AT 299 INSERT CODING TO HANDLE THE EXCEPTION VARIABLES DENOTED BY
C     FIELD NUMBERS GREATER THAN 900 IN THE VARIABLE SPECIFICATIONS.
C     CODING EXAMPLE HERE CONFORMS TO THAT ILLUSTRATED IN ATTACHMENT C.
C     NOTE ALSO THAT NTAL, THE INIT OF TALLY IS SET HERE, IF NTAL IS A
C     CONSTANT IT SHOULD BE SET BEFORE GOING TO 100 AND NOT HERE.
C     EXIT IS TO 300 WHERE THE TALLY IS MADE.
C     LOADPC
C     GO TO 100 TO LOAD RECORD CONSTANTS -EXIT IS TO 199
C     NOTE  TAL(MAXTAL) IS CLEARED TO 0 IN LOADPC
  101 FORMAT (A6,2I3,16,5A3)
  102 FORMAT (1H ,A6,2I3,16,15A3)
  103 FORMAT (18X,15A3)
  104 FORMAT (1H ,18X,15A3)
  105 FORMAT (21I3)
  106 FORMAT (1H ,21I3)
  107 FORMAT (4H NW=,16,4H NZ=,16)
  109 FORMAT (28H WRONG NO. COLUMNS IN TABLE ,I3)
C     SECTION A
  100 DO 110 P=1,MAXTAL
  110 TAL(P)=0
  111 J=1
      I=1
      READ (NTAPE,101) NAM(I),W,NV(I),F(I),(V(I,J,K),K=1,MAXVK)
      WRITE (NPRINT,102) NAM(I),W,NV(I),F(I),(V(I,J,K),K=1,MAXVK)
  112 IF(W-1)113,114,114
  114 IF(T(I)-900)115,115,116
  115 IF(J=NV(I))117,116,117
  117 J=J+1
                              READ(NTAPE,103)(V(I,J,K),K=1,MAXVK)
                              WRITE (NPRINT,104)(V(I,J,K),K=1,MAXVK)
                              GO TO 112
  116 I=I+1
  113 NI=I-1
                              GO TO 120
C     SECTION B
  120 K=1
  121 READ(NTAPE,105)W,CC(K),(ST(K,J),J=1,MAXSTJ)
                              WRITE(NPRINT,106)W,CC(K),(ST(K,J),J=1,MAXSTJ)
  122 IF(W-1)123,124,124
  124 K=K+1
                              GO TO 121
```

```
123 NK=K-1
    REWIND NTAPE
    GO TO 130
C   SECTION C
130 K=1
136 J=1
131 IF(K-NK-1)132,133,132
132 IF(ST(K,J))134,134,135
135 J=J+1
    GO TO 131
134 NJK(K)=J-1
    K=K+1
    GO TO 136
133 GO TO 140
C   SECTION D
140 K=1
146 J=NJK(K)
    NC(K,J)=1
144 I=ST(K,J)
    NC(K,J-1)=NC(K,J)*NV(I)
    J=J-1
141 IF(K=NK-1)142,143,142
142 IF(J-1)144,145,144
145 I=ST(K,J)
    NZ(K)=NC(K,J)*NV(I)
    K=K+1
    GO TO 146
143 GO TO 150
C   SECTION F
150 K=1
    NW(K)=0
152 NW(K+1)=NZ(K)+NW(K)
    K=K+1
151 IF(K-NK)152,153,152
153 WRITE (NPRINT,107)NW(K),,Z(K)
    GO TO 160
C   SECTION F
160 K=1
161 IF(K-NK)162,162,163
162 GO TO 170
164 K=K+1
    GO TO 161
C   SECTION G
170 W=1
176 I=ST(K,J)
    W=W*NV(I)
171 IF(J-1)177,177,172
177 WRITE (NPRINT,109)W
    GO TO 173
172 IF(W-CC(K))174,175,174
174 J=J-1
    GO TO 176
175 J=J-1
    I=ST(K,J)
173 SB(K)=NV(I)
    NS(K)=Z(K)/W
    GO TO 164
C   SCAN
C   GO TO 200 TO SCAN -EXIT IS TO 290
    DATA SS/1HS/,TT/1HT/,RR/1HR/,ZZ/1HZ/
200 I=1
201 J=1
    P=F(I)
202 K=2
203 IF (I-NI) 204,204,205
204 IF (J-NV(I)) 206,206,207
206 IF (P-200) 208,208,209
208 IF((V(I,J,K),EQ, SS) GO TO 213
    IF((V(I,J,K),EQ, TT) GO TO 211
    GO TO 214
213 IF ((V(I,J,K-1),EQ,RR) GO TO 212
    GO TO 210
214 IF((V(I,J,K-1),EQ, Y(P)) GO TO 212
    K=K+1
    GO TO 203
207 U(I)=0
209 I=I+1
    GO TO 201
210 IF(V(I,J,K-1),EQ, X(P)) GO TO 212
    J=J+1
    GO TO 202
211 IF ((V(I,J,K+1),GE,X(P)),AND,(X(P),GE,V(I,J,K-1))) GO TO212
    K=K+2
212 H(I)=J
    GO TO 209
205 GO TO 290
C   TALP
C   GO TO 300 TO TALLY -EXIT IS TO 399  NOTE= NTAL IS COUNT VALUE IN
C   TALLY AND MUST BE SET BEFORE ENTRY
300 K=1
301 Z=1
    J=1
309 I=ST(K,J)
302 IF (K-NK) 303,303,304
303 IF (H(I)) 305,306,305
305 IF(J-NJK(K))307,308,308
```

```
307 Z=Z+((J(I)-1)*NC(K,J))
    J=J+1
    GO TO 308
306 K=K+1
308 Z=Z+((J(I)-1)*NC(K,J))
    P=Z+NW(K)
    TAL(P)=TAL(P)+TAL
304 GO TO 306
    GO TO 390
C   RITE
C   GO TO 400 TO WRITE -EXIT IS TO 499
    DATA (FORM(L,I),L=1,18) /18*6H(1H ,/,
1FORM( 1,2) /5H 4T8)/, FORM( 3,2) /5H 6T8)/,
2FORM( 4,2) /5H 7T8)/, FORM( 5,2) /5H 8T8)/,
3FORM( 7,2) /5H10T8)/, FORM( 8,2) /5H11T8)/,
4FORM(10,2) /5H13T9)/, FORM(11,2) /5H14T8)/,
5FORM(13,2) /5H16T7)/, FORM(14,2) /5H17T7)/,
6FORM(16,2) /5H19T6)/, FORM(17,2) /5H20T6)/,
    DATA FM/6H(1H ,/,FN/6H 3I9) /
401 FORMAT (1H1,T6)
402 FORMAT (1H0,T6,7H TABLE ,I4,7H  PART ,I4,4H OF ,I14,5X,6HFORMAT,
1,A6,4X,5HROWS ,I3,10H COLUMNS, ,T3)
C   SECTION RA
400 N=1
    WRITE(NPRINT,401)N
    WRITE(NPT,401)N
    P=1
    K=1
420 N=1
421 I=2
419 J=2
410 IF (K-K) 411,411,412
411 IF (N-NS(K)) 413,413,414
413 IF (I-SB(K)-1) 415,415,416
415 IF (J-C(K)-1) 417,417,418
417 TB(I,J)=TAL(P)
    P=P+1
    J=J+1
    GO TO 410
418 I=I+1
    GO TO 419
414 K=K+1
    GO TO 420
412 WRITE (NPT) TAL
    REWIND NPT
    GO TO 490
416 GO TO 430
C   SECTION SUMOUT
430 KAK=CC(K)+1

    DO 431 J=1,KAK
431 TB(1,J)=0
    KAL=SB(K)+1
    DO 432 I=1,KAL
432 TB(I,1)=0
    DO 433 J=2,KAK
    DO 433 I=2,KAL
    TB(1,J)=TB(1,J)+TB(I,J)
433 CONTINUE
    DO 434 I=1,KAL
    DO 434 J=2,KAK
    TB(I,1)=TB(I,1)+TB(I,J)
434 CONTINUE
    L=CC(K)-1
    IF (L)438,438,439
438 NFOK(1)=FM
    NFOK(2)=FN
    GO TO 440
439 NFOK(1)=FORM(L,1)
    NFOK(2)=FORM(L,2)
440 KZK=KAK+1
    WRITE (NPRINT,402)N,K,KWNS(K),NFOK(1),NFOR(2),KAL,KZK
    WRITE (NPT,402) N,K,W,S(K),NFOR(1),NFOR(2),KAL,KZK
    I=1
436 N=N+1
    WRITE (NPT,NFOR)N,(TB(I,I),J=1,KAK)
    WRITE (NPRINT,NFOR) N,(TB(I,I),J=1,KAK)
    I=I+1
435 IF(I-KAL)436,436,437
437 N=N+1
    GO TO 421
    END
```

# A GENERAL COMPUTER LANGUAGE FOR THE SOCIAL SCIENCES

James M. Sakoda
Brown University

## Inadequacy of FORTRAN

One of the chief bottlenecks in the social scientist's use of the electronic computer, which is supposed to process data at fantastic speeds of up to a million operations a second, is the shortage of suitable programs. One reason for this is that whereas the programming requirements of the social scientist are likely to be complex, his ability to program is generally limited to the use of FORTRAN, which is basically an algebraic compiler, suited to writing formulas and solving mathematical equations. FORTRAN does not lend itself well to many of the kinds of programs the social scientist desires. It is a chore, for example, to write a data-processing program in FORTRAN involving coding of data and making cross tabulations for dozens of tables of different sizes. FORTRAN does not provide for dynamic creation of matrices that have not been anticipated in advance. Analyses by social scientists frequently include unequal numbers, missing cases, and sorting or ranking — all of which require more than routine programming skills. Content analysis of natural language data poses thorny problems, which are difficult to solve without the aid of special string operation routines. Study of kinship systems and simulation processes requires the handling of complex data structures not provided for by an algebraic compiler limited to the handling of lists and matrices.

## Special Languages

One answer to the needs of the social scientist has been the use of special computer languages, such as IPL and LISP, for complex data manipulation; COMIT for language work; and SIMSCRIPT and SIMPAC for simulation. Use of these special languages, however, involves a number of inherent difficulties: (1) They do not provide a broad range of capabilities. Even the use of list-processing language for simulation does not eliminate the need for arithmetic and matrix operations. (2) Special languages are not so easily implemented as FORTRAN, which has become a universal computer language. To maintain a language, a costly compiler or translator must be written for each machine and revised when the language is changed. This problem can be solved by writing special languages in FORTRAN, thus automatically providing all of the capabilities of FORTRAN plus its ease of use and maintenance. Joseph Weizenbaum has done this in writing SLIP, which can be described as a list-processing language in FORTRAN.

## DYSTAL

DYSTAL is a general language for complex program writing. Since it is written in FORTRAN, it is relatively easy to learn and to implement on most machines. Based on a concept of dynamic storage allocation, DYSTAL includes a variety of operations in addition to the input-output and algebraic capabilities of FORTRAN itself. The routines cover list processing, character manipulation and string operations, Boolean functions, statistical routines, matrix operations, and ranking and sorting routines. DYSTAL is therefore a general language with powerful operations that can facilitate program writing for the social scientist.

I confess that the chief impetus for the development of DYSTAL came from my inability to master IPL-V. Many of the ideas I used were, however, picked up from IPL-V and SLIP. In the following paragraphs I shall briefly describe DYSTAL, first in terms of its data handling and second in terms of the manner in which it carries out operations.

### Dynamic Storage Allocation

The key to languages for complex program writing is dynamic storage allocation. This is the ability to create lists and matrices as they are needed, even when the number needed is not precisely known at the time the program is written. It also involves the ability to specify the dimension sizes of lists and matrices at the time the program is used, so that the same program can handle data of different dimensions without reserving large storage locations in advance. IPL and SLIP use a novel method of achieving dynamic storage allocation. A list is created by taking a word and linking it to the next word. The words need not be in consecutive locations in memory, since each word carries the address of the next word. This arrangement makes it possible dynamically to create lists, to insert and delete items, and to erase lists when they are no longer needed. A price is paid for this unique arrangement, however, since it is not possible to locate an item on a list by calculating an address. It is necessary to hop from one word to the next until the desired item is reached. Much of the speed of calculation in modern computers is achieved by address modification using index registers; this novel method of linking words precludes their use.

DYSTAL achieves dynamic storage allocation while keeping contents of lists and matrices in consecutive memory locations. This achievement is DYSTAL's chief contribution to the programming art. Instead of setting up all of the required lists and matrices ahead of time, it establishes only a single large dynamic storage area called LOT or FLOT in the common area, where it is accessible from all subroutines. Lists of the desired size are created whenever needed by means of the instruction

    CALL LSTALL (MOD, N, LISTA).

The signal MOD indicates the mode of the variable, i.e., fixed point, floating point, or alphameric. N is the length of the list, and LISTA is the name assigned to the list. A space counter keeps track of the location in the dynamic storage area from which the next list is to be created. This location is the value stored in the name of the list. DYSTAL keeps track of lists for which names have not been provided by preserving their names as items on another list.

## Erasure of Lists

DYSTAL permits partial erasure of lists. The last list created can be erased without disturbing the remaining lists, by means of the instruction

CALL LERASE (LISTA).

DYSTAL allows the creation of temporary lists beginning at the end of the dynamic storage area, where they are less likely to be confused with more permanent lists located at the beginning of the dynamic storage area.

## Advantages of Dynamic Storage Allocation

The availability of dynamic storage allocation greatly increases the flexibility of program writing. All subroutines can be written as dimension-free routines, capable of processing lists and matrices of any size. They can be compiled on tape and called on without further modification. Data structure of any complexity can be read in by a single input instruction, CALL LSREAD. The data may consist of many separate lists, of lists named on other lists, or of lists connected to other lists. When DYSTAL programs are processed, space not used by one variable can be used by another, which maximizes the use of memory locations. If one routine is by-passed during a particular run, the storage locations it might have used need not even be set up. Routines can use temporary lists and then erase them to allow the same space to be used subsequently.

## Head of a List

In ordinary programming it is necessary for the programmer to have information about a list or a matrix stored separately from the list itself. In DYSTAL each list and matrix carries a five-word head, which contains valuable processing information. The head contains the external identification, a node cell which provides linkage to other lists, a mode indicator, the length of the list, and a counter that keeps track of the number of items currently on the list. Input-output is greatly facilitated by the availability of information on the head. For example, the instruction

CALL KDUMP

causes the program to print out the entire contents of the list in the dynamic storage area in the proper mode. This is a valuable instruction in debugging a program. In matrix multiplication it is not necessary to specify the size of the matrices, since these are available in the head of a list.  The instruction for multiplying MATA and MATB and placing it in MATC is

CALL MATMP (MATA, MATB, MATC).

### Complex Data Structure

Complex data structures can be created in two ways.  One is to place names of lists on another list.  This process, when continued, yields a tree structure.  Lists can also be attached to another list by placing their names in the node cell of the head of another list.  Such a list can be used to store auxiliary information.  These procedures can also be combined to form complex data structures.

### DYSTAL Syntax

DYSTAL's operations have been written to take full advantage of FORTRAN.  For repetitive operations, which are the key to programming efficiency, the FORTRAN DO loop is used.  There appeared to be little need for developing recursive routines that call on themselves.  Input-output operations make use of FORTRAN input-output instructions, which access a list or a matrix directly.  FORTRAN arithmetic statements can be used directly.  All of these have been facilitated by keeping lists and matrices in consecutive locations in memory.  SLIP's organization of memory does not permit this close integration with FORTRAN operations.

A question may be raised concerning the justification for calling DYSTAL a language when it is written in FORTRAN, which is a language in its own right.  DYSTAL observes restrictions of the FORTRAN language, but develops a syntax of its own.  Part of this is due to the method of organizing the data by having a dynamic storage area and giving each list a name.  DYSTAL operations are written as FORTRAN functions, using FORTRAN operations as primitive routines.  Each function contains one or more arguments, usually including the name of a list, and returns a value.  For example, ITEM (I, LISTA) will return the Ith item on LISTA.  One advantage of using functions is that arguments of functions are free from almost all restriction:  they can be either fixed-point or floating-point numbers or alphameric words; they can be variable names, arithmetic expressions, Hollerith characters, or other functions.  A second advantage is that functions can be nested to any depth desired.  For example, the expression "If IWD is on either LISTA or LISTB go to 100, otherwise to 200" can be written

IF (ISOR (LOCATE (IWD, LISTA, 1), LOCATE (IWD,
1 LISTB, 1) ) ) 200, 200, 100.

To place the transpose of MATA in MATT, take its inverse and place it in MATI, we can write

CALL MATINV (MTRAN (MATA, MATT), MATI).

A program written in DYSTAL consists largely of DYSTAL functions and nested DYSTAL functions.

## Growth Potential

One of the advantages of DYSTAL as a language is that new operations can easily be added or old ones modified simply by adding or modifying FORTRAN subprograms. Thus DYSTAL is capable of continued growth. For any program only those functions required need occupy space in the computer.

## Available Routines

So far, some 90 functions have been written to cover not only the basic procedures but also special routines in a variety of areas. In list processing it is possible to insert and delete items, locate items on a list, and create or read in complex data structures. A DYSTAL list can be treated as a push-down, pop-up list. Existing tree structures can be traced down to the end branches and back up again, each time returning the name of a list. String operations include unpacking characters of a word, packing characters into words, searching for patterns in a string of characters, and replacing patterns with other combinations.

In data processing, a list can be changed to a set of ranks or sorted by size. Lists can be treated as a two-dimensional matrix, and a set of matrix operations is available. Routines are available for common statistical operations on a list, such as taking a sum, sum of squares, sum of cross-products, variance, and mean and standard deviation. Boolean operations have also been written to permit combining of Boolean functions, using AND, OR, or NOT. Obviously, many other routines can be written; it is expected that users of DYSTAL will make contributions of their own.

## Applications

Once DYSTAL is learned it can be used for any program, short or long, simple or complex. The reason for learning and implementing DYSTAL, however, is likely to rest on the inability of programmers to write complex programs easily in FORTRAN. It should be particularly useful in data-processing routines, which require access to many tables of different sizes. It will be very convenient for writing statistical and matrix operations, which use precoded subroutines. It should be very helpful in writing simulation routines, which require complex data structures. It can be used to write programs involving game-playing and simulation of cognitive processes, for which machine language or special languages have been used in the past. DYSTAL can also be used for linguistic analysis. Its dynamic storage allocation is particularly useful in writing systems of programs, in which programs are combined in different ways by an executive program.

## Ease of Learning

The existence of a programming language does not automatically produce programs. It is, however, possible to train graduate students in one's own field to write complex programs in DYSTAL, thus avoiding the middleman — the professional programmer. Those who have learned to write programs in FORTRAN should, with a little additional effort, be able to write in DYSTAL. I have prepared a manual that includes exercises and answers.

**An Example of a DYSTAL Program**

The following routine demonstrates some of the basic principles of writing a program in DYSTAL. It takes items on LISTA and removes the duplicating items to create a second list, LISTB. For example, given

LISTA - DOG, CAT, CAT, COW, HORSE, COW,

we seek

LISTB - DOG, CAT, COW, HORSE.

First, dimension, equivalence, and common statements are used to provide the dynamic storage area. Next, INLOT is called to create the first list, which sets up the dynamic storage area for use. These steps are necessary at the beginning of every program.

Two constants are first read in — N, the capacity of the list, and MOD, the mode of items on the lists. For example, if MOD = 4, the items will be alphabetic words of not more than 5 characters. First, LISTA is created and labeled with the Hollerith characters. Then LREAD is called to read in N words from the card reader. These words will be read in with a standard format corresponding to the mode of the list. Then LISTB is created and labeled.

To perform the operation a DO loop is written, with I going from 1 to N. First, the Ith item is retrieved and stored in variable IWD. Next, function LOCATE is used to find IWD on LISTB, beginning with the first position of the list. If the search is successful, LOCATE will return the position on the list at which a match is found. If it is unsuccessful, after searching the whole list LOCATE returns a 0. Hence, if the returned value of LOCATE is 0, a branch is made to statement 10, where IWD is loaded into the next available location on LISTB. Otherwise, transfer is to 20, which continues the DO loop. When all of the items on LISTA have been utilized, KDUMP is called. This instruction causes the program to print out the contents of all lists in the dynamic storage area — the list created by INLOT, LISTA, and LISTB.

```
         DIMENSION FLOT (2000), LOT (2000)
         COMMON FLOT, LOT
         EQUIVALENCE (FLOT, LOT)
         CALL INLOT (10, 2000)
         READ 5, N, MOD
     5   FORMAT (5 (4X, I 10) )
         CALL LREAD (1, N, LABEL (LSTALL (MOD, N, LISTA), 1 5HLISTA) )
         CALL LABEL (LSTALL (MOD, N, LISTB), 5HLISTB)
         DO 20 I = 1, N
         IWD = ITEM (I, LISTA)
         IF (LOCATE (IWD, LISTB, 1) ) 20, 10, 20
    10   CALL LOAD (IWD, LISTB)
    20   CONTINUE
         CALL KDUMP
         END
```

# DISCUSSION

**Philip J. Stone**
**Harvard University**

Mr. Hornseth's description of new and more advanced programs for putting tabular generation at the fingertips of the analyst accords with the latest levels of technical sophistication in handling large amounts of population data. Such sophistication today begins with data preparation; flexible cleaning and editing programs arrange data storage and check on the logical consistency of the information being stored. Advanced retrieval and presentation techniques allow for information to be attractively displayed according to cross-comparison breakdowns and formats specified by the analyst. Other programs have been developed for extracting and describing major relationships; Banks' and Textor's recent book on cross-polity studies[1] and Textor's forthcoming monograph analyzing Murdock's cross-cultural sample[2] effectively illustrate this approach. As reference archives expand and as intranational and international sharing of data becomes the norm, it is heartening to see technological sophistication maintain adequate pace.

Professor Sakoda's paper describes a rather complex new language called DYSTAL, which adds approximately 90 new functions to existing FORTRAN systems. It includes many different kinds of operations potentially useful to the social scientist: list processing, Boolean operations, ranking and sorting procedures, and string packing. Rather than attempt to discuss the complete manual, I shall focus on two of DYSTAL's most unusual features: its FORTRAN compatibility and its method of dynamic storage allocation.

In my opinion, one of the more unfortunate sequences in computer history has been the separate development of fixed-dimension matrix-oriented languages (e. g. , FORTRAN, MAD, ALGOL) and of list-processing languages (e. g. , IPL-V, LISP, COMIT). Since the languages were separate, we had to choose to program using either a fixed-dimension matrix or variable list processing. No middle ground was available. Once having made a choice, we tended to be defensive in our allegiance.

Since several recent advances have made it feasible to use both kinds of procedures within the same program, the either-or polemics are out of date. On the one hand, such languages as Weizenbaum's SLIP and Sakoda's DYSTAL have directly added list-processing routines to existing fixed-dimension FORTRAN or MAD technology.

On the other hand, such an approach as that used at Carnegie Tech refers all variables to a common set of tables, and the programmer can repeatedly change computer languages while handling the same variables within the same program. In either approach, the sharing of techniques is accomplished.

As Professor Sakoda points out, dynamic storage allocation is central to complex program writing; one of the most unusual features of DYSTAL is the method by which this is done. Most languages, such as IPL-V, COMIT, or SLIP, convert the computer core memory into one long string by the use of pointers. When different string lists are required by the program, needed lengths are clipped off from this available string. As certain lists are no longer required, the pointers at the ends are redirected to clip the lists back on to the end of the available string. Soon the available string is no longer a neat sequence, but a mess of retied patches. Nevertheless, it is logically a good piece of string from which to make further lists.

Handling such strings is a relatively slow and complicated process, as Sakoda shows; the computer must continually find the current path of the strings by consulting pointers. Most variable list languages provide pointers only in one direction, although Weizenbaum's SLIP provides pointers in both directions, allowing for bidirectional search. In addition to the relatively slow speed of searching through lists, the computer must spend additional time gathering up and retying discarded lists. Indeed, such "garbage collection" can consume a considerable fraction of total processing time.

Instead of setting up pointers, DYSTAL attempts to utilize the natural order within core memory and to take advantage of index registers for searching this order. Lists are simply set up sequentially and end to end in core memory as they are created. The advantages, of course, are greatly increased speed and the ability to put more data into the core memory. The disadvantage is clear: we can only erase the last list added to each end of the current total sequence.

Many list language specialists will argue that DYSTAL is not a list-processing language. Certainly the bulk of list language complexity has been by-passed. If list creation and discarding takes place in an unordered fashion, DYSTAL will soon run out of available space, with lists that should be discarded captured, as it were, between lists still in use.

Yet, a surprisingly large number of variable list programs are quite regular in the nesting procedure of list expansion and contraction. If much use is anticipated, we must use more efficient procedures. Our own tree-building discrimination programs by P. J. Stone and E. B. Hunt, for example, demonstrated this property; we found it easy to take advantage of higher running speeds by relatively simple reprogramming in MAD and FAP. Today DYSTAL would probably be our logical choice.

However, though DYSTAL may be the _logical_ choice, it shares with SLIP a defect that, at least for me, keeps it from being a _psychological_ choice. Both SLIP and DYSTAL are based on the host language, FORTRAN, and must conform to its conventions. In my opinion, FORTRAN has long been a hopeless case of Mickey Mouse details and limitations too unyielding to be tucked in the mind of an active scholar.

**References**

1.    Banks, Arthur S. , and Robert B. Textor, <u>A Cross-Polity Survey,</u> The **M.I.T.** Press, Cambridge, Mass. , 1963.

2.    Robert B. Textor, <u>Cross-Cultural Summary,</u> Taplinger Publishing Co. , Inc. , New York City, 1967.

## FREE DISCUSSION

The first suggestion made following the discussant's remarks was that program manuals be merged, since the DYSTAL manual, although relatively new, already has 90 additions. This makes the language hard to consume and store.

Concern was voiced that in the papers no distinction had been made between the language and its implementation through a compiler or interpreter. Dynamic storage allocation is very important, but the language itself should be capable of talking about things without reference to their location. Either the compiler or the interpreter that implements the language, or the executive routine in the computer, should handle the storage allocation. If this is not done, and the allocation is built into the implementation of each language separately, chaos will soon follow.

It was pointed out that at Carnegie Tech this problem was resolved by building dynamic allocation into the over-all monitoring system with common reference tables, enabling the user to switch languages as he goes along. At M.I.T.'s Project MAC, dynamic storage allocation is built in as part of the language. This is also true of such other modern languages as MAD, ALGOL, and BALGOL. At Project MAC, using the SLIP system, each programmer is assigned a certain small amount of available space, and when this is used up, the machine automatically secures more space as long as some is available.

Some disadvantages of DYSTAL were noted: (1) The requirement that the length of the list be specified when the list is created is burdensome to the programmer; (2) Insertion and deletion are very "expensive," since they involve considerable data movement. The advantages noted lay in suggesting ideas that should be considered on their own merits by compiler writers, and in extending the capabilities of the present "de facto universal language," FORTRAN, to other than conventional data-handling or statistical problems, which have already been adequately handled by other means. Someone suggested that putting DYSTAL on MAD, FORTRAN IV, or BALGOL would be a better solution than the current one, which makes reading somewhat complicated.

For organizations (e. g., the Bureau of the Census) responsible for producing many different types of data tabulations important to analysts, the analyst's last-minute changes have customarily been expensive in both dollars and time. Consequently, a really great advantage of the newer languages is the "almost real-time" change of programs they make possible. In this regard it is important to remember that the purpose of programs is not merely "to exist, but to process data."

Concerning the 1-1,000 Census tape and Dr. Hornseth's tabulations program, the following procedure was suggested as a more efficient way of processing the tape: read the tape; extract the information wanted; and condense the data (e.g., coding) in a suitable way. This greatly simplifies subsequent tabulation runs and leads to 3- to 5-minute runs rather than the 3-hour ones that Dr. Hornseth described. These condensed runs have actually been done by use of BALGOL. The rather slow processing speed resulting in 3-hour runs may be caused by program inefficiency resulting from rushing the programming in order to get into production quickly and by relatively slow FORTRAN tape I/O.

A concluding comment concerning this census program described by Hornseth was that it does not calculate measures of relationships among variables; it merely produces cross tabulations. This was not considered a limitation, however, since it would probably be more efficient to have a separate program to do further statistical analysis on just those variables whose relationships turn out to be of interest, after the tabulations are made.

At this point, agreement was reached that those at the conference who use the 1-1,000 tape and the resulting tabulations should meet to discuss the tabulation program and the types of tabulations they would like to see produced. Dr. Beshers promised to arrange for such a get-together, despite the already crowded conference schedule.

Finally, the discussant voiced a desire to compare the speeds of DYSTAL with various other languages. For example, DYSTAL based on BALGOL (which is a high-speed matrix language, whereas FORTRAN is a low-speed one) would be a useful test and would probably result in a large gain in speed. The discussion concluded with the plea that any changes made to enable the program to run faster should not interfere with the ability to make last-minute program changes easily and rapidly.

II.      COMPUTER TECHNIQUES FOR LARGE—SCALE SOCIAL SYSTEMS

# LIST—PROCESSING METHODS FOR ORGANIZING FILES OF LINKED RECORDS

J. M. Kennedy, H. B. Newcombe, E. A. Okazaki, and M. E. Smith
Computation Centre & Research Biology Branch
Atomic Energy of Canada Limited
**Presented by J. M. Kennedy**

Many events in the life of an individual — his birth, his marriage, his illnesses, his death — are routinely recorded on punched cards or magnetic tape for accounting or other administrative purposes.  These records can provide a fertile field for many studies of human populations.  To be useful for purposes other than elementary statistical tabulations, however, the files must be arranged so that events pertaining to one person are collected together and events pertaining to one family or household are associated with one another.  When we refer to a file of "linked records, " we mean a file with this sort of structure imposed on it.

The efficient construction and maintenance of such a file by a digital computer presents a number of technical problems that are not obvious if the work is done by human clerks.  On the other hand, quite apart from the intrinsic speed and reliability of a computer, there are certain operations that are hard for a clerk but easy for a machine.  This paper reports on some experiments we have made in computer-oriented methods of file maintenance.

## The Linked-Record File

Our present study is concerned with about 50, 000 vital-statistics records from the province of British Columbia.  These represent about 10 percent of a larger collection of records covering a 15-year period; the smaller set has been chosen to include "interesting" families rather than families simply selected at random.  The records include marriages, births (including stillbirths), records of handicapped children, and children's deaths.  The object of the linkage program is to organize these into family histories in the following idealized order:

1.   Marriage record
2.   Birth of first child
2a.  Handicap record for first child
2b.  Death of first child
3.   Birth of second child,
                etc.

. . . . . . . . . . . . . . . . .

New marriage record,
                etc.

Of course, in the real file many records may be absent; the marriage may have occurred prior to the period under study; a child may have been born outside the province, etc. Our computer program is designed to surmount these difficulties insofar as possible.

The sequence of families in the file is essentially alphabetic. The surnames of the two partners to a marriage are coded phonetically to give a single key word. All records with the same key are said to belong to the same "superfamily." For example, the superfamily coded S530 A536 contains all SMITH-ANDERSON marriages, along with spelling variations like SMYTHE-ANDERSEN or even SCHMIDT-ANDREWS. As detailed comparisons of records are made only within a superfamily, the phonetic coding reduces losses resulting from errors in spelling surnames.

The task of setting up the file has two main parts. The first of these is the responsibility of the demographer or the statistician: Given a pair of records, do they pertain to the same family or not? This decision depends on the reliability of the identifying information (including the accuracy of key punching), on the size of the file being examined, and on the degree of certainty demanded in the presence of discrepancies. This question is outside the scope of this report; our reasons for believing that acceptable criteria can be supplied are published elsewhere. [1, 2]

The second task belongs to the systems programmer: If a new record is associated with an old one, it should be inserted into the file in its proper place. Much of what follows will be concerned with the implications of this rather elementary problem.

### Comparison of Manual and Computer Methods

If a new batch of records is to be added to the main file, the major steps are

1.   Encode each new record with its phonetic code.
2.   Sort the new records into phonetic sequence.
3.   Merge the two files into a single new file, comparing each
     new record with every record having the same phonetic code
     in the original file, and inserting it when a match is found.

During the merging operation the act of comparing pairs of records to establish linkages is very tedious for a human clerk, since it involves examination of a dozen or more separate items together with reference to frequency tables that give a quantitative measure of the odds for or against linkage. This job is obviously well suited to computer operation, as the machine's speed in performing arithmetical and logical operations can be fully exploited.

Unfortunately, however, the computer is inherently ill suited to the operation of inserting a new record in a given place in a file, if insertion is given its conventional meaning.  A human operator can produce a gap where he needs it by pushing with his thumb.  But with a computer file, either on magnetic tape or in the internal memory, insertion can be done only by copying all subsequent records into new locations to create the necessary gap.

This single point turns out to dominate the speed and efficiency of many file-maintenance operations in a computer.  A few years ago the task of sorting records into sequence was turned over to a card-sorter operator after a few minutes of instruction.  Nowadays sorting is a problem worthy of conferences and research papers by computer analysts.

One of the aims of introducing so-called "list structures" is to overcome the rigidity of storage allocation in a computer memory.  Several languages for manipulating lists have been devised, and each has its adherents. [3, 4, 5] Our applications are not yet exploiting the full power of list-processing techniques, but what we are using is very similar to the SLIP system of Joseph Weizenbaum. [5]

## Elementary List Structure

Many of the properties of lists are well illustrated by the layout of material in a typical ladies' magazine.  If you open at a page at random, you probably cannot tell what story the material belongs to.  The top of the page may say, "Continued from page 37" and the bottom, "Continued on page 106." This information on every page is enough to let you read forward to the end or scan backward to the beginning.

This is a simple list — a set of entities (pages, in this example) together with indicators that specify the logical sequence of the members of the set.  The editor of such a magazine can add material from many authors a page at a time in any order by using the first available space and adjusting the indicators.

Most people find this type of organization objectionable because of the nuisance of shuffling pages back and forth.  Inside a computer, however, this nuisance is absent.  The program for the machine must give a rule for getting from one record to another, anyhow, and a rule like "The location of the next record is given in the first word of this record" is scarcely more difficult than "The location of the next record is 25 words past the first word of this record."

The magazine analogy can be used to illustrate two types of freedom that are available when dealing with lists.  First, if the principle of hopping about among the pages is established, the interleaving of various stories can be more flexible than is common in magazines by relaxing the customary rule that a reader turns backward only to start a new story.  The other choice has to do with the connection of different stories to one another.  Either the end of one story can lead to the start of the next, or else it can lead to its own start ("This story begins on page 12."). In the one case, you may begin anywhere and scan the whole magazine before returning to the same place.  In the other, you must refer to the table of contents after each story to find where the next begins.  In list-processing jargon, the table of contents is the "main list," and its elements point to various "sublists" (the stories themselves).

This brief introduction to list structures is sufficient to deal with our applications to record linkage.

## Applications

Our test file consists of about 50, 000 records, each occupying 25 computer words. This can all be retained easily on a single reel of magnetic tape. The main file is sorted into superfamily groups in phonetic sequence. Each new batch of records for insertion is also sorted into phonetic sequence on a separate tape.

The tape-driving part of the linkage program makes a new merged tape, with the old and the new segments of each superfamily written side by side on the output tape (see Figure 1).

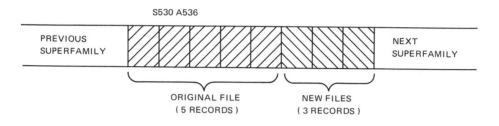

Figure 1

The relative physical order of the records in one superfamily remains unchanged.

While the complete superfamily is in the machine's internal memory, the list-processing action of the linkage program causes the logical order of the records to be altered as the new material is interpolated into existing families or made the basis of new families. This is achieved entirely by manipulating the single link word in each 25-word record; there is no gross copying of full records. The flow chart for this part of the job is roughly as illustrated in Figure 2.

Our program has several options that increase its speed and flexibility: (1) Not all old records need be considered for detailed comparison — only the first record in each family, or some other subset, can be selected; (2) The question "Are new and old related?" may be answered "Perhaps," and some additional branches of the program cope with various possibilities that may ensue.

Superficially, list manipulation looks like a programmer's trick to eliminate some unwanted operations. Actually, there is evidence that this type of file organization is a natural one for many jobs. Two by-products of our program are worth observing:

1.  The method of updating guarantees that each record linked into the file is immediately available as an old record for subsequent comparisons. We have had examples of twin births in the incoming records with the parents' marriage absent from the file. The earlier birth starts a new family, and a few milliseconds later the second is linked to it.

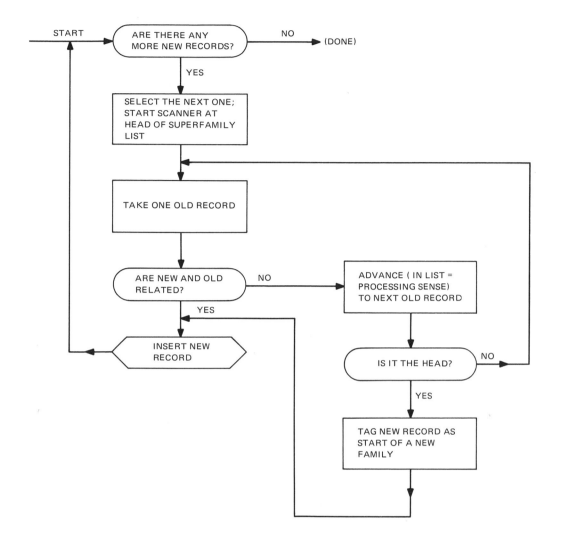

Figure 2

2. Each record automatically gets a permanent acquisition number that corresponds to its physical position within the superfamily. This number is a compact identifier for recording cross references within the superfamily list. If the records were physically rearranged during the updating process, this identifier would be meaningless.

Our largest practical test has been the linking of 35, 000 births to an original master file of 10, 000 marriages (and to one another). The merge-link operation took about 15 minutes on our CDC G-20 computer, a machine comparable in internal speed to the IBM 7040. This is a speed of about 23, 000 linkages per minute.

## Future Applications

So far we have used list-processing techniques in a rather elementary way. It is clear that as the files expand, they will acquire a structure more complex than the family groupings encountered at present. For example, the marriage of two persons whose births are in the file leads to a cross-referencing among three separate superfamilies. We intend to enlarge the programs to cope with these situations.

One short computer experiment that we have recently performed is the tracing of complete pedigrees in a small sample population covering nine generations. The population was started from 100 unrelated marriages; children were "created" by allowing one to four births per family, with a mean of two; marriages among the children were "arranged" by further use of random numbers.

The physical order of the file was chronological: events were added in order of occurrence and hence had a permanent acquisition number. The logical order of the file was alphabetic: births were attached after the marriage record for the parents, while new marriages, which might create new surname combinations, were inserted in their alphabetic positions. Cross-referencing of marriages both on the marriage record and the birth records of the participants allowed direct tracing of pedigrees either forward or backward from any record.

We have tested the methods by answering such questions as "Find all marriages of first cousins," or "How many different ancestors does a certain person have six generations back?" We believe that a list of this sort used as a master list, with detailed information about individuals as its sublists, can be of considerable use to the demographer or geneticist in studying populations of suitable size. The limits on size are set by the capacity of the random-access memory of the computer; as time goes on, this capacity shows encouraging signs of increase.

## References

1.   Newcombe, H. B., and J. M. Kennedy, "Record Linkage," ACM Communications, 5, 563 (1962).

2.   Newcombe, H. B., J. M. Kennedy, S. J. Axford, and A. P. James, "Automatic Linkage of Vital Records," Science, 130, 954 (1959).

3.   Newell, Allen, Ed. IPL-V Manual, Prentice-Hall, Englewood Cliffs, N. J., 1961.

4.   McCarthy, J., et al., LISP-1.5 Programmer's Manual, The M.I.T. Press, Cambridge, Mass., 1962.

5.   Weizenbaum, J., "Symmetric List Processor," ACM Communications, 6, 524 (1963).

# EXTRAPOLATIONS*

Joseph Weizenbaum
Massachusetts Institute of Technology

A few years ago Dr. Richard Hamming of the Bell Telephone Laboratories observed
that when any of the dimensions of a system are changed by an order of magnitude
or more, then that system has changed not only quantitatively but also qualitatively.
It can not then be used in the same way as was its predecessor, nor can its new
uses be determined by simple extrapolations or extensions of scale on its former
condition.  Dr. Hamming made this observation with respect to computer systems.
The variables he mentioned at the time were the sizes of the then emerging computer systems, as well as their prices.  The former were increasing about as
rapidly as the latter were decreasing (i. e., as measured in terms of the number of
computations performed per dollar).  A justification of Hamming's argument in its
original context is somewhat complex, by virtue of the fact that computer systems
themselves are complex.  The point is perhaps easier to appreciate when applied to,
say, aircraft.  An airplane that can carry at most 10 passengers is used very differently from one which can accommodate 100.  Similarly, a military airplane capable of sustained speeds of, at most, 100 mph is a different weapon than one which
can cruise at 1,000 mph.  A space craft is not merely an airplane that can climb to
very high altitudes.

I believe "Hamming's Law" can be applied inversely, so to speak, as well.  That is,
one can ask about the possible extrapolation of the use of a tool applied to a task that
is expanded by an order of magnitude or more.  "Hamming's Law" then states that a
mere expansion of the tool, a beefing up, will not prove adequate to the new task.
A qualitatively different, i. e., a freshly thought-through, tool will have to be developed to deal with the larger task.

---

*The work reported herein was supported by Project MAC, an M.I.T. research
program sponsored by the Advanced Research Projects Agency, Department
of Defense, under Office of Naval Research Contract NONR-4102(01).  Reproduction in whole or in part is permitted for any purpose of the U. S. Government.

The social scientist is currently in a situation in which these thoughts are of very great relevance. His successes in model building based on sophisticated uses of analyses of data emerging from carefully constructed surveys have led him constantly to increase the sizes of his data bases. Up to a point, the growth of the power and speed of computers kept pace with his requirements. But now that the early successes have whetted his appetite, now that he wishes to harvest the fruit of lessons already learned, now that he needs to apply his analytic insight to ever larger data bases, computer technology is falling behind. The principal bind is that the social scientist needs to manipulate sets of data the sizes of which are measured in units of millions of words. I say "manipulate" because his requirement is not merely to access such data sets in the sense of retrieving information from them, but to update, enrich, and reorganize the stored data. Furthermore, he is not thinking in terms of an individual investigator having a private file at his disposal, but of a number of scientists possibly geographically remote from one another, of whom each would have equal access to and authority over the data.

The tool kit provided by current computer technology contains many of the devices and techniques demanded by such applications. Very large data stores exist in the form of disk files capable of storing as many as 36 million computer words, magnetic tapes can store arbitrarily large numbers of computer words, but at the price of access times dictated by serial access disciplines. The development of computer time-sharing systems such as that of Project MAC at M.I.T. opens the door to the co-operative use of a single computer system by a number of investigators. The growth of sophistication of list-processing systems appears to be relevant to the data reorganization component of the social scientist's over-all task. Yet none of these very promising advances, taken either separately or together, solves the whole problem. It is my contention that no mere extrapolation will do, either.

Yet we have no choice but to base our predictions of future trends on what we now have. What was said above should serve as a warning that the solution of the social scientist's data access problem will not prove easy, that it will of necessity come, if at all, as a consequence of invention both in the realm of computer hardware and of technique. The hope must be that the need will serve as a stimulant to the innovators. I propose therefore to review some of the more important developments currently under way, which, in my view, contain the seeds of practicable future large-scale social science computer systems.

### Multiple-Access Computer Systems

There exist at this writing a number of computer systems in which individuals may operate the computer simultaneously from remotely placed consoles. The simultaneity is very real from the user's point of view, but may be achieved by "time sharing" of the actual computer hardware, i. e., by giving each user a small increment of time during which he has the machine all to himself, and by so spacing these time intervals that the periods during which the machine is at the service of others is well within acceptable psychological thresholds. The most highly developed of such "time-shared" computer facilities is in the system existing at M.I.T. under the name "Project MAC."

It is easy to mistake the time-sharing aspect of the MAC system as its most important feature. What is more important, from the special point of view of the individual user, is that he is operating a computer on-line. This, in turn, means that he is placed in a position such that he can converse with the computer on a give-and-take basis. An immediate consequence of this mode of computer operation is a sharp reduction in the amount of paper produced by human-computer interaction from what is considered normal in orthodox settings. The significance of this to the archivist is of course obvious; he needs no longer to print pages and pages of data in order to find the few data in which he is actually interested. A consequence of being on-line that is more subtle but even more crucial to the act of problem-solving is that conversational interaction between man and computer provides an opportunity to explore solution strategies. Under ordinary circumstances the computer is largely used as a device to generate the consequences of a solution arrived at by other means and presented to it (the computer) in the form of a program.

The system designer is impressed by the communication gear and the vast amount of software that controls it and may well mistake these as embodying the heart of the innovation. What he should see as fundamental, however, is that a time sharing system is memory centered. I bring this up in the present context because it is also of crucial significance to the design of a large-scale social science data system. The MAC system may be viewed as a large computer complex built around a hierarchical memory structure and having as its prime objective the servicing of that memory. The structure is hierarchical in that it consists of a number of storage devices of increasing speed but decreasing capacity. The line of descent may be thought of as beginning with punched cards (which will be with us for some time if only because so much historical information is already so stored), thence to magnetic tapes, to disks, to drums, and finally to the high-speed core memory of the computer itself. The computer serves this storage pyramid in that its job is to transform information retrieved therefrom and, under certain conditions, to again store the transformed data. Very often the transformations to be performed are dictated by prestored programs. Someone must have decided in advance what transformations are to be operative on what data. But in the on-line operation of the system, the investigator is part of the control loop. Certainly he will invoke previously stored programs — even many written by other people — but he will reserve for himself the prerogative to make critical decisions in those cases where he is either unwilling or unable to make prejudgments over the possible turn of events.

The interdependent properties of a multiple-access computer system, namely, that (1) it permits a number of users to operate simultaneously; (2) these users may be geographically separated from one another and from the computer; (3) the system is memory centered, shed light on the use of such systems in social science research. We can, in this light, see a very large data bank containing vast amounts of social science data, e. g. , survey data, census results, which are instantly accessible to a large number of social scientists perhaps widely scattered over the nation, each of whom may interrogate this bank by explorative techniques, and all of whom may refresh the files with newly gathered information. Programs developed by any user of the system may, of course, be made available to other users, just as is presently done in MAC. The reduction of redundant effort would be immense.

This vision may well raise fears over the privacy of certain data sets. There is an issue here which cannot be dismissed lightly. However, its discussion is beyond the scope of this paper.  Suffice it to say for the present that strong protective boundaries among individual users' files already exist within the MAC system, that, in other words, the problem is not being ignored.

### Hardware

The traditional path of expansion in computer-related hardware has been in the direction of making computers faster and giving them greater capacity.  These are not independent aims, for it has long been known that, in the computer world, one can generally buy time in the coin of space and vice versa.  The over-all objectives have not changed.  But the unmistakable success of time-shared computer systems has had an effect on the daily work of the hardware and system designer; we see an increasing amount of effort devoted to the design of hardware intended to realize the potential pointed to by MAC and related systems.  In particular, the computer industry is preoccupied with systems in which certain equipment, e. g. , processing units, are duplicated.  Future systems so equipped will permit simultaneous use in a somewhat more exact sense than is possible today.  They will also be more reliable than today's systems.  The user, however, will see them as being simply faster and more responsive.  Speed will certainly be of interest to the social scientist.  However, from the point of view of the problem being discussed here, speed is by no means the whole story.  The center of attention must be the memory system, which is to serve as the physical embodiment of the data bank.

Most computer manufacturers are hard at work designing bigger rapid-access first-level memories.  There appears to be little question that within a few years a million-word core memory, or one functionally equivalent to it, will become commercially available.  But even it does not make much of a dent on the problem of dealing with a data set consisting, say, of the 1-1, 000 tape of the Census Bureau.  The very large disks and drums also under development will have to do for quite a while.  Other mechanisms in prospect are bulk memory devices, which are physically quite small but are provided in large numbers together with mechanical means of selection such that any one of them may be placed on-line within a very few seconds.  Unfortunately, however, no device presently on the horizon will provide a data store of sufficient size and with a sufficiently short random-access time to make possible the treatment of the really large data sets we are here considering by means of present programming techniques, i. e. , techniques applicable to programs that, together with their data, can be wholly stored in one core load.  This is equivalent to saying that for some time to come, memory systems called upon to deal with social science data banks will have a hierarchical structure and perforce will bring with them all the timing problems that can be overcome, if at all, only by clever programming.  Much, if not all, of such programming may well be hidden from the ultimate user.  But its price will have to be paid in any case.

So-called "associative memories" have been talked about for almost a decade.  The central characteristic of such devices is that data are retrieved from them not on the basis of a specification of the location of the data (an address) , but on the basis of the data , or some part thereof. The program then does not say, "Give me the contents of cell number so-and-so, " but rather, "Locate the datum which begins with the set such-and-such. "  The result of such a retrieval operation might be the entire record's having the desired characteristic, the address of the cell containing the first word of such a record, or it might be the flagging of all records in the

memory which may be so described.  Any one of such records might then be retrieved or operated upon by subsequent operations.  There appears no sign that
would indicate that such memories are soon to be delivered (i. e. , in sizes which
are really interesting) or,  on the other hand,  that the attempt to build them economically has been abandoned.  It seems quite clear,  though,  that should memories like
these ever become significant components of large-scale computer systems,  they
would be of immense interest to the user concerned with linking subsets of data to
one another in arbitrary ways.

## Language Bases

The introduction of the time-shared computer system has brought with it a new
emphasis on languages designed for on-line communication with a computer.
Computers have been operated on-line from the very beginning.   It was only when
computer systems became very large and the cost of the delays imposed by a man
operating them from a console (i. e. ,  the cost of the "idle" time so introduced) became prohibitive,  that off-line operation became the normal mode.  The recent
work on such languages must here be summed up by merely saying that their aim is
to facilitate the exploratory use of the computer alluded to above.  To the extent that
they succeed in that,  they will also be of great use to the social scientist.

A language or,  in the parlance of the computer trade,  "software" problem that is
more specifically addressed to the needs of the manipulator of large archives is
related to the internal organization of such data collections.  Clearly,  it will never
be feasible to sort such collections on any conceivable key.  Even if they were
sorted to serve one objective,  their order would be wholly unsuitable to some other
objective — the whole concept of a data bank serving a number of investigators with
disparate research goals would crumble.  What is required is a storage scheme
such that each datum can carry with it pointers to other data that are related to the
first in any one of a number of ways interesting to social scientists.  List-processing languages currently in use have the ability to deal with data structured in just
that way.  These are languages that give up the successor relationship implicitly
designed into current computers (the cell with the next higher or lower address is
the successor or predecessor to the referent) ,  in favor of storing with each datum
a pointer or pointers to their successors.

In current usage,  LP languages are almost entirely core storage oriented,  i. e. ,
they deal almost exclusively with data structures residing in the first-level store
of the host computer.  However,  the data-linking techniques that were first developed as part of list processors have already found application in the task of managing the administration of the disk files of,  for example,  the MAC system.  There
the problem is that the number of tracks of disk storage available over-all is sufficient to serve all MAC users only if the tracks abandoned by one user are immediately made available to any other.  The disk is,  in other words,  organized more
like a hotel than an apartment house.  A guest in a hotel wishes to occupy a room.
He doesn't care which room it is,  or whether or not he previously occupied it.
When he leaves,  it becomes available to another guest.  If a user requires more
than one disk track,  the system management must see to it that each track contains
pointers to the next track in sequence.  We see here the generalization of concepts
arising from list-processing languages to the management of large bulk stores.

Further such generalizations must be sought as partial solutions to similar problems created by social science data banks. The lessons learned in the development and use of current list processors will undoubtedly prove valuable.

There has also been significant work on languages designed to elicit specified data from large — by today's standards — assemblages of text. Dr. Philip Stone's General Inquirer is an example.[1] The extension of the abilities of such systems to enable them to service very large data bases will not, as I pointed out, be a mere effort in scaling upward. But we will have to look to their current operation for clues as to how to build for the future.

### Conclusions

I started this paper by calling attention to "Hamming's Law." Perhaps its logic is discouraging. But I believe the advances in computer systems design, in hardware and in languages, which we have seen in the last several years, counteract any evaluation based on that law alone. We may well think of the look we might have taken into the future had it not been for the appearance of the multiple-access computer system. The whole concept of a co-operative social science data bank would have seemed absurd. If nothing else, it would of necessity have had to fall of its economic weight. Science in general has progressed most markedly whenever it operated in an atmosphere in which one of its branches was able to build on the achievements of the others. This is certainly the situation in which the social scientist finds himself today with respect to his fellow worker in the computer sciences.

### Reference

1.    Stone, Philip J., Dexter C. Dunphy, Marshall S. Smith, Daniel M. Ogilvie et al., The General Inquirer: A Computer Approach to Content Analysis, The M.I.T. Press, Cambridge, Mass., 1966.

# DISCUSSION*

Walter F. Bodmer

Stanford University

As a geneticist I would like to discuss the particular use that may be made of data from large-scale surveys such as the census. In this respect, I hope to provide, from my own rather narrow point of view, some of the substantive complement to Weizenbaum's discussion of the projected spectacular advances in computer hardware. At the same time, I shall try to re-emphasize the basic need for family-oriented data such as are provided by Newcombe's and Kennedy's record-linking studies. [1, 2]

The need to use computers in the analysis of large bodies of data like the census is self-evident. However, at the present time the primary and limiting factor in their use is the nature of the information collected rather than the ability to analyze it. Undoubtedly, the amount of information that can be analyzed on a large scale may explode beyond our wildest dreams with the promised advances in computer technology. Nevertheless, we must always ask ourselves: What information do we need within practicable limits, and why do we need it? What data should be collected, and how best can they be collected in a reliable way?

One of the major aims of the population geneticist is the construction of models that predict the changes from one generation to the next in the genetic structure of a population. Over a long period this provides the theoretical basis for evolution. Over a short period we are studying the microevolutionary changes, which are our immediate concern. To construct such models, three basic types of information are needed with respect to the characteristics of the population whose changes are being studied, namely:

---

*This work was supported by Grants GM 10452-02 and HD 00045-01 from the National Institutes of Health. I am very grateful to Professor Joshua Lederberg for many stimulating discussions which helped formulate the ideas presented here.

1.  Relative biological fitness (or combined effects of fertility and mortality);
2.  Mating patterns;
3.  Genetic determination (or genetic component in the case of a complex character, or mode of inheritance for a well-defined genetic characteristic).

Population genetics, so far, has mainly dealt with relatively simple models, although even these are sometimes analytically intractable and require computer analysis. Thus, it has been assumed that the characters have a simple genetic determination (e. g., blood groups), that mating is at random or occurs in some well-defined pattern, that the age structure of the population (discrete generations), may be ignored, and that the biological fitness is simply measured by the relative numbers of surviving offspring of different types. However, human populations have an age structure that cannot be ignored; many, if not most, of the characteristics we are interested in are complex and clearly have no simple genetic determination. The different contributions to biological fitness involve a complex interaction between mortality, fertility, and the various mating patterns. Nevertheless, a complete age-structured specification of fertility, mortality, and the mating patterns together with perhaps no more than a parent-offspring correlation for the characteristics we are interested in, provide the basis for constructing a comprehensive generalization of conventional population genetics. Our goal is to describe in detail the changes from one generation to the next in the complex structure of human populations. From census data, our characteristics would be educational achievement, socioeconomic characters, race, nativity, etc., and it is with respect to these that we require the three basic types of information mentioned above.

There is, at the moment, a lack of adequate information on the genetic determination of such characteristics. To obtain it requires the collection of data over at least two generations. As indicated above, even a simple parent-offspring correlation with respect to census classifications could provide valuable information, setting some limits to the extent of their possible genetic determination. For example, heads of households could be asked for information concerning the educational level achieved by their brothers and sisters or even simply their birth dates. The latter would at least provide some information concerning the genetic components of fertility.

The major opportunity at present in the analysis of census data lies in the study of differential fertility. This must now be the most significant component of the major differences in biological fitness, at least in the United States, following the tremendous decreases in mortality, particularly stillbirths and infant mortality, during this century. Fisher proved what he called the fundamental theorem of natural selection, namely, that "the rate of increase in fitness of any organism at any time is equal to its genetic variance in fitness at that time."[3] If there is no genetic variation in fitness, there can be no differential selection and hence no change in the gene frequencies in the population from one generation to the next. Crow provided a simple and powerful interpretation of Fisher's theorem.[4] He showed, for the case of discrete generations, that the index

$$I = \frac{variance~(x)}{(mean~x)^2}$$

where x is the observed number of offspring, is a measure of the maximum opportunity for natural selection.  Thus, if parents and offspring are counted at the same stage (that is, zygotes or mature adults), and there is complete genetic determination of fertility (each offspring has exactly the average of his parents' fertility), then the fitness of the population will increase at the rate I.  The actual rate of increase will depend on the heritability of fertility, or the proportion of the variance in fertility which can be attributed to genetic factors.  Thus, a simple initial approach to an understanding of the opportunities for differential selection would be to calculate I for a whole range of relevant cross tabulations.  The index I does not, of course, take account of the age structure of the population but could be made to do so if x was the instantaneous intrinsic rate of increase (Fisher's 1930 Malthusian parameter), rather than the number of offspring.  The census tabulations can, however, provide a much more complete specification of the major determinants of fertility than can be incorporated into one such parameter, namely, the age at marriage, the number of children ever born, and the distribution of the time interval between successive births (or child spacing).  Perrin and Sheps have recently constructed a general theory to describe child-spacing distributions based on probabilities of conception, probabilities of stillbirths and abortions, and distributions of the length of pregnancies and of the length of the sterile period following the termination of a pregnancy. [5]  This theory can be generalized to include a simple specification of contraceptive practice.  These theoretical distributions can be fitted to the observed child-spacing distributions for a series of cross tabulations with respect to relevant socioeconomic and other characteristics.  The interaction between these factors and the fertility patterns can then be studied in terms of the estimated values of the parameters used to define the theoretical distributions.  These models can be combined with a specification of the age at marriage of husband and wife to investigate the effects of the age of marriage on the total fertility.  Such an approach would, I believe, begin to answer the tremendous need for appropriate analysis of large and complicated tabular outputs such as are produced by the Census.

Mating patterns with respect to available classifications are more easily established.  These include, for example:

1.   The extent of assortive mating, that is, correlations between the characteristics of husband and wife;
2.   The distributions of the age at marriage and the distributions of the difference in age between husband and wife at marriage;
3.   The distribution of the geographical separation at birth of husband and wife;
4.   The extent of consanguinity as determined by the record-linking techniques used by Kennedy and Newcombe.

It is clear that only large-scale surveys, such as the census, can provide enough detailed data for the types of analysis discussed above.  Even the largest data files soon yield empty cells in complex cross tabulations.  Given large enough data files, the combination of these various factors can yield comprehensive models for the analysis of changes in the genetic structure of the population.  It is only the genetic components of the population structure that may be changed from one generation to the next by the mating process.  Some geneticists might argue that the relatively crude characterizations, which are all that is at present possible on such a large scale, do not allow enough detailed understanding of the nature of fertility differentials for the construction of such comprehensive models. The main need, they believe, is for smaller-scale and much more detailed surveys. I think there is a need for both types of surveys.

Special possibilities exist in such large bodies of data for the study of some more specific questions of biological and genetic interest.

(1) It has been pointed out by Lederberg (in personal communication) that since birth rank can have essentially no genetic component, correlations with respect to birth rank may be used to assess specifically the influence of nongenetic factors on, for example, educational status, occupation, and fertility.

(2) Some people have argued (for review, see Reference 6), that a male birth may partially immunize a female against subsequent male births so that the probability of a female birth following a male birth may be somewhat higher than that of a male birth following a male birth. Under this hypothesis, there should be some correlation between the interval of time between successive births and the sexes of the births. In fact, a significant observed correlation between the sexes of successive children in some bodies of data tends in the opposite direction to that expected under this hypothesis. Nevertheless, whatever the explanation of such correlations, much insight will be gained from a study of child spacing in relation to the sexes of successive births.

(3) Seasonal variation in the distribution of births differs significantly for different groups of people. The basis for this is currently being investigated by Dr. Lederberg, using census tabulations.

At Stanford we plan to investigate some of these problems through a novel co-operative venture with the Bureau of the Census, which will allow the use of larger files for research purposes than has hitherto been possible.

For the future, clearly a major need exists for the collection of more data pertaining to the family as a unit. One of the most severe drawbacks of census data is that it is collected by the household rather than the family. As we noted, information on genetic determinations can only be obtained from data collected over at least two generations. This could perhaps be provided by specially oriented smaller-scale sample surveys, such as the current population survey, or through the co-operation of the National Health Survey. In the long run, however, this might best be achieved by applying the record-linking techniques of Newcombe and his co-workers to the construction of complete family records from birth certificates accumulated over a period of two or more generations. This would be especially appropriate if more information could be collected on the birth certificates. Even dates of birth as opposed to age in years and also date of marriage would be invaluable additions. In general, considerable integration at the level of data collection could be achieved by collecting more data to accompany birth and death certificates, followed by appropriate record-linking studies. As an example, one may cite programs for testing the blood of all newborn infants to detect phenylketonuira and other similar inborn errors of metabolism. These have been initiated in Massachusetts and New York and are being planned for California. They may provide data of considerable genetic interest on an extremely large scale, provided the information is correlated with that of the family through the use of birth certificates.

A need in data collection on this scale is to combine information on mortality, stillbirths, and abortions, and hopefully also morbidity, with vital statistics. This combination would make it possible to undertake, on a large scale, studies of the familial incidence of abortions, stillbirths, and various types of illnesses, together with their correlations with fertility differences. Some of these data will, of course, come from more detailed small-scale surveys of specific diseases. As an example, at Stanford we are now undertaking such a study with respect to mental retardation in co-operation with the Pacific State Mental Hospital at Pomona, California.

Record-linking techniques should become important not so much for the linking of records on the same family collected from different sources as for the compilation of records on the same family collected at different times.

## References

1.  Newcombe, H. B., "Population Genetics, " Population records in Methodology in Human Genetics, W. J. Burdette, Ed., Holden-Day, Inc., San Francisco, 1962, pp. 92 — 113.

2.  Morton, N. F., in The Use of Vital and Health Statistics for Genetic and Radiation Studies, United Nations, New York, 1962, pp. 167 — 170.

3.  Fisher, R. A., The Genetical Theory of Natural Selection, Oxford University Press, 1930.

4.  Crow, J., "Some Possibilities for Measuring Selection Intensities in Man, " Human Biology, 30, 1 — 13 (1958).

5.  Perrin, E. B., and M. C. Sheps, "Human Reproduction: A Stochastic Process, " Biometrics, 20, 28 — 45 (1964).

6.  Edwards, A. W. F., "Genetics and the Human Sex Ratio, " Advanced Genetics, 11, 239 — 272 (1962).

## FREE DISCUSSION

The discussion began with a statement that what is needed most, so far as computing capability is concerned, is improved software, rather than better hardware. Furthermore, the need is not simply for extension of algebraic-type compilers or language-processing facilities, but for software that is oriented more to non-statistical algorithms, which can be profitably used in all the social sciences. In response to this statement the following points were made: (1) Software, in general, is in good shape. (2) There is a lag between the most advanced systems and their general applications, possibly resulting from a publication lag. (3) The real frontier today is time sharing.

Time sharing has the effect of radically changing software techniques because the rapid feedback that time sharing allows between user and computer greatly reduces the turn-around time. One specific result is that the development cycle of software techniques is greatly shortened. Also of great importance is the fact that time sharing makes it economically feasible to develop and maintain large data bases, since the base can then serve many users. This will, in turn, provide experience in dealing with extremely large data files, such as census data. In addition, the size of the bases will undoubtedly change the character of software even more extensively.

We considered next the problem of large amounts of data in less developed countries. The questions raised were: (1) How should the social scientists of these countries maintain the data or punch-card files so that they can be easily worked up for answering different computing problems? (2) Should processing be done on the punch card or on the computer level? (3) How does one handle mixed data files?

It was pointed out that structuring of the data base depends largely on what one wants to do with the data it contains. In general, restructuring is very expensive; hence the questions boil down to essentially economic ones. Within the next several years, large-scale time-shared computer systems with large disk files, drums, etc., will probably turn out to be the most economical set ups for such countries as Hungary, Israel, and Turkey, which may be small in population and economic resources but not in intellectual resources. National computer centers operating on a time-shared basis, perhaps one in each of these countries, will probably be the answer to the problems inherent in today's mixed data systems. Such centers will eliminate these problems by eliminating the mixed systems.

At this point the following extrapolations were mentioned: (1) the growing feasibility of networks of time-shared computers, because of the growing feasibility of telecommunication; (2) the development of large program bases, as differentiated from large data bases. These large program bases, containing all relevant, running (debugged) programs placed in a memory, will be capable of easily retrieving individual programs selected by a search routine. In this connection it was pointed out that when last counted several months ago, the M. I. T. system contained 35 different languages — e. g. , SNOWBALL, FORTRAN, MAD, SIM-SCRIPT — all of which are immediately available to the user at the typewriter.

An offer was made to show the conferees the M. I. T. time-sharing system in operation, with such programs as tree-building by computer, psychiatric interview by computer, and game-playing with the computer (blackjack and three-dimensional tic-tac-toe).

In further discussion of his paper Dr. Kennedy pointed out: (1) There are more data about individuals than are contained in census records (e. g. , the Canadian study he talked about makes extensive use of vital statistics records). (2) Linking individuals by household units provides data useful for genetic studies (e. g. , still- plus live-birth data, grouped by family or household, provide fertility rates and child-spacing data). (3) Identification of records is accomplished by a Soundex code, which determines the main sequence of the file and sets up the superfamilies, and by a position number. (4) Dead persons are not erased from the file, since the object is to keep entire life histories (mortality data included) of all individuals entered in the file.

The Soundex name code is not meant to be a foolproof identifier, but rather a coding scheme that helps to link records that would not otherwise have been linked because of slight spelling discrepancies. Its use in the Massachusetts General Hospital computer system exemplifies this point. In this hospital's data-processing system, a nurse types in the name of a drug to be administered to a patient; the computer uses Soundex to match the drug against a list of drugs; if the nurse has misspelled the name, the type-out states, "We don't have such a drug, but did you mean . . . ?" (Names in the file with the same Soundex code are listed. ) The nurse then corrects the spelling and proceeds. This kind of feedback demonstrates the usefulness of Soundex coding.

Record matching was pointed out as a useful technique for data evaluation. It has, for example, been used to estimate census underenumeration and the under-registration of births in the United States. The reliability of record-matching techniques is, however, sufficiently in question to cast doubts on the results. Consequently, it is important to pursue development of these techniques in the hope that this will lead to higher matching accuracy and hence more useful computer-linkage procedures.

The concluding remarks were concerned with the development of computers for the control of human behavior, such as teaching machines, which correct behavior by utilizing immediate feedback.  It may well be, however, that useful social science data will emerge as a fortuitous by-product of these developments.

The discussion ended on the optimistic note that a common terminology will probably arise and enable social scientists to communicate with one another more easily than is now possible.  Central data banks and a common inquiry language will eventually be developed to make this feasible.

# III. DEMOGRAPHIC APPLICATIONS OF COMPUTER MODELS

# HOW MUCH DEMOGRAPHIC RETURN CAN A SINGLE PROGRAM EXTRACT?*

Nathan Keyfitz and Edmund M. Murphy
University of Chicago

**Presented by Nathan Keyfitz**

The following outline of an extensive program goes somewhat beyond present
practice at the Population Research and Training Center, but not so far beyond that
there can be any serious doubt about its implementation. It is an extrapolation of
procedures already put on the machine, debugged, applied to large amounts of data,
and, in part, published.

The direction of extrapolation is toward the construction of more flexible, comprehensive, and self-contained programs. Initial work tends to be very specific. One
wants to know the intrinsic rate of natural increase for a few countries for which one
already has life tables and age-specific fertility rates. Then one comes across
countries for which life tables are lacking or untrustworthy in the relevant years.
One writes a longer program to read in such fundamental data as death rates or
absolute numbers of deaths and population, and instructs the machine to compute the
life table itself and then use it to find the intrinsic rates, perhaps adding the age
distribution of the stable population, which is easily calculated from the life table
and intrinsic rates.

At the next stage one may be interested in the trajectory by which the age distribution moves from its present condition to the stable; this is readily found as a population projection. In some circumstances it is useful to carry out the projection by
using an operator on the age distribution that takes the form of a 9 x 9 or 18 x 18
matrix. The program is expanded to include the assembly of this matrix.

---

*In a field in which there is a good deal of oral exchange and independent
invention, and relatively little in writing, it is not easy to give credit.
The thoughts above have been influenced by discussions with members
of the U. S. Bureau of the Census, the Office of Population Research of
Princeton, and colleagues at the University of Chicago, none of whom is
responsible for their errors.

Having the matrix, one incorporates the calculation of its latent roots in the expectation that they will permit a classification into types of population change. The dominant root incidentally gives the intrinsic rate of natural increase, or at least another approximation of it. The matrix itself is a convenient summary of the growth processes in a population.

By this time the program has become a group of ordered subroutines, which might be represented as a string of beads, as in Figure 1.

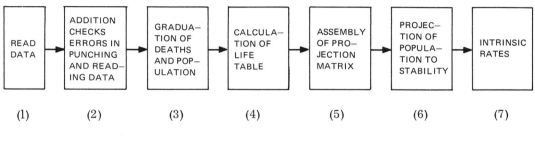

| READ DATA | ADDITION CHECKS ERRORS IN PUNCHING AND READING DATA | GRADUATION OF DEATHS AND POPULATION | CALCULATION OF LIFE TABLE | ASSEMBLY OF PROJECTION MATRIX | PROJECTION OF POPULATION TO STABILITY | INTRINSIC RATES |
| (1) | (2) | (3) | (4) | (5) | (6) | (7) |

Figure 1

The output of each subroutine is the input for the next. Results needed by later subroutines are placed in common storage. Obviously, the sequence is vital; if any two of the subroutines are interchanged, the program is nullified.

The first departure from this straight-line sequence arises because one would like to check the calculation. The checks are desirable to protect oneself from program errors or machine errors. Machine errors are highly unlikely; program errors are common.

These checks can also serve to cope with a type of error inherent in most demographic calculations — that arising from the finite approximations that must be used at every stage. Typical of these is the integration of the life table $1_x$ curve (the number of persons attaining exact age x in the stationary population) to obtain $_nL_x$ (the number of persons in the stationary population living in the range of n ages). A number of ways for carrying out this integration are available; it seems only reasonable to program more than one method if there is any chance that the differences can be of consequence. This portion of the sequence will then involve some subroutines that are parallel so far as the logic of the work is concerned, as shown in Figure 2.

Here the subroutine (4) of Figure 1 has been split into three parallel subroutines. They are parallel in logic only; the machine will carry them out one at a time, but within this portion the order is no longer important. What is essential is (4b), the comparison of the sets of results and the determination of the best. If the several results are within a tolerance specified in the program — say 0.2 per cent for $_5L_x$ — then the program will continue. If the results diverge beyond the tolerance, this will be noted conspicuously on the printout. The program can then stop at this point, or it can perform the rest of the program several times, once using each version of $_5L_x$. When the results are indifferently precise, the program continues on to subroutine (5), etc., using one set of results — either an average of the various results or one arbitrarily selected from them.

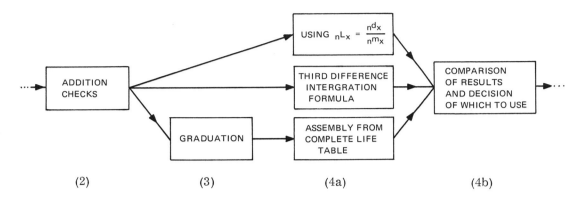

Figure 2

Similar routines have been used in parallel for the intrinsic rates of natural increase, the stable age distribution, etc. The more dissimilar these parallel routines are in the method of finite approximation, the more assurance one has. It is plain that no worker with a desk calculator can enjoy the luxury of such methods of attaining accuracy.

The program has also been extended in other respects. These include calculation of powers of latent roots, moments and cumulants of important distributions, graphs of the latent roots and of the trajectory to stability, and various standardized rates. These, however, involve nothing more than a lengthening of the string of calculations; they need not be taken up here.

A different kind of extension is needed to put more flexibility into the program. Some progress on this has been made. For example, work with Swedish and French data from the nineteenth century involves age groups quite different from the standard 0, 1 — 4, 5 — 9, etc., which are familiar to readers of modern data sources. It was plainly necessary to place between (2) and (3) of the string of subroutines in Figure 1 a new subroutine, which would make the adjustments necessary to convert the data read in, into the standard age groups in which the rest of the program was written. (To rewrite all that followed so as to use the various eccentric groupings of age that were found might have added slightly to precision, but was not considered for obvious reasons.)

A second and more important interposition early in the sequence is a subroutine to make comparisons and improvements in the original data. What is done in (2) in Figure 1 is only a check against mechanical errors in card punching (for example, the machine-calculated total of the age groups is checked against a prepunched total). It is possible to make use of redundancies in the data to improve them in a fundamental way. These corrections become more important as one extends the study beyond countries whose censuses and registrations are sensibly complete.

This subroutine compares the number of births registered and the population under 1 year of age; the number of births and the population aged 1 — 4; and the number of births and the population aged 5 — 9. In each case it adjusts the number of births by the life table calculations from (4). If the adjustment is more than a given tolerance, all the following routines are rerun with the adjusted figures. In the version that has been used up to now, the entire sequence is run with the original data, and then if the test has shown that the number of births is short by more than 5 per cent, the program reverts to (5), and the sequence runs again with the adjusted data. More sophisticated tests are to be worked out; if these show the raw data to be grossly deficient, say 10 percent, then only the adjusted data will be processed. This improved adjustment routine might make several estimates of the underlying figures, each of which will be run through the rest of the program.

The previous discussion pertains to the use of a standard set of data, which up to now has been fed in on 11 punch cards. There will, however, be instances in which something more than this minimum is to be had. Work is now being done with parity for countries whose data include this. It is easy to include in the input the simple distribution of women of each age by parity and the births by order. Code numbers punched on the title card will tell the machine how much data to expect for each country. This changes the program from a single-line sequence to a branching one, as in Figure 3.

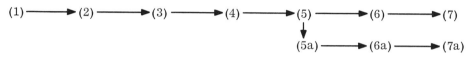

Figure 3

After going through the sequence from (1) to (7), the machine would come back to (5) and go through the parallel sequence (5a) to (7a), which takes account of parity. Included in the results are sex-age — parity — specific figures and the intrinsic rates that result from these, which turn out to be quite different from intrinsic rates that do not recognize parity.

Work now under way at the Population Research and Training Center will add another level to the existing program. Up to now the program has processed only a single set of data referring to a given population at a given date. But if, as is common, data for more than one date are available for a given population, additional data-correction techniques can be used. This improved program will read in all of the data available for a given country. The correction subroutine will then work with all of this information, using survival techniques to link and make consistent the various census and registration figures. After the figures for all of the dates have been adjusted, they will be processed one at a time by the remainder of the program.

This program might strain the storage capacity of the computer since, after the correction routine, it must store a great deal of data beyond that which it is processing. The use of scratch tapes, which can be written, rewound, and reread at will, could solve this problem, however.

This process envisions a new set of parallel routines. Each of the parallel branches will consist of the complete string of computation routines that has been discussed above, arranged as in Figure 4.

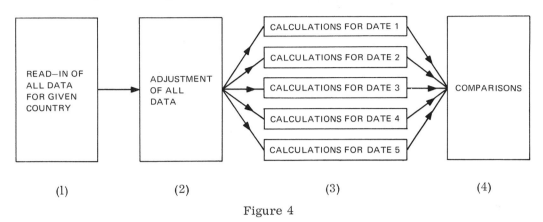

Figure 4

It may also be desirable to link the data for the different time periods at the end of the calculations. For instance, the user may wish to establish a trend in mortality over the period, or to see how some parameter describing fertility through time is evolving. The necessary results from the branches in (3) above could be stored, and a further routine (4) could process them.

All the discussion up to this point has been applicable to one sex. In general it has been customary for demographers to trace the evolution of the female population, but where the data are available, the program will evidently work for the male population equally well. The results for males and females will in general not be consistent in that the continuance of the age-specific rates for each will result in a changing sex ratio down to a limit of 0 or infinity. What happens in real populations, of course, is that relative ages at marriage, and hence at childbearing, of men and women shift, so that approximate numerical equality of the sexes is retained through time. Nothing prevents running the sequences for the two sexes at a given period and then joining the two sequences together, having the program execute a projection of male and female populations in which the results of one in any period would influence the matrix of the other. Specifically, if over a 5-year period the sex ratio was shifting towards males, the top row of the male matrix, representing ages of fathers at the births of their children, would be shifted upward, and that of females, downward. This and other devices would be designed to simulate actual population movements.

The final step would be to retain within the machine or on a scratch tape the results for a large number of populations, in respect to the same sex and date, and to have the program classify these results. This is applicable to all the ways in which populations and their changes may be categorized, but we need only refer here to one example — life tables. Among the other things that the machine would turn out for a large number of countries would be fully detailed life tables, and it would be necessary only to preserve any one column — say $l_x$ — from which any other could be constructed at the end if required. Along with this column would be retained the identification of the life table it was from (in alphabetical or numerical code) and various indices that might be used in the subsequent arranging and comparing; these would include $\overset{o}{e}_0$, $\overset{o}{e}_1$, possibly $\overset{o}{e}_{10}$, etc. It might also include such other elements as the constants of a Makeham fitting. These indices would be used to classify the life tables along one or several dimensions, and they would be printed out as arranged. The program might compare those that came next to one another in the arrangement according to the indices, and if they were closer than a certain amount, they would be aggregated. As with life tables, so with age distributions, age-specific fertility rates, etc.

The foregoing discussion has been limited to programs that have been completed or are now in progress at the Population Research and Training Center. These programs assume only the present results of demographic theory. The lines along which a uniform population analysis will develop in the future are, however, quite clear. It is relatively easy to describe the ideal program implicit in today's work. The computer techniques described below are all available today and have all been used in other contexts.

Let us then assume that the necessary demographic work has been accomplished. Model life and fertility tables are available. Parameters for basic demographic functions and for the demographic transition have been constructed. What will the program for uniform population analysis look like?

The program will have several levels of subroutines. It will make full use of the flexibility provided by the several tape drives available on large computers like the IBM 7094.

The first and most general level will be the control routine, which will have storage space reserved only for various control codes. These codes will tell the control program how to choose among the various subroutine options available to it. They will also tell the machine what to expect in each group of data — how much data, how precise, how detailed, how the data are grouped by age. The codes might also include any demographic, economic, or sociological parameters that have been left to the demographer's judgment.

Some of these codes will be read in as data with each block of population data; some of them might be generated by various lower-level subroutines and transferred up to be stored and used by the control routine.

Because the control routine reserves only the small amount of space needed to store these codes, each of the major subroutines starts with virtually a "clean" machine — in the case of the 7094, almost 32,000 cells.

The first major subroutine called will be the data input and correction sequence. This sequence will be similar to that already discussed. It will work with blocks of data; each block will contain data for one country from as many dates as possible. One addition to the correction procedures might be comparison with the demographic models assumed to be available. These models will be available to the machine on a reference tape that will read them in as needed.

If the data are found to be deficient, the machine will make several estimates of the underlying "true" figures and will write these onto scratch tape to be called as needed. The choice among the estimates could be made in several ways: Control codes could tell the machine what set of criteria to apply. The machine could read the appropriate criteria from the reference tape and make its own decision. An alternative, and probably better, method would stop the program at this point, after printing out the various estimates and any useful summary measures of them. The demographer could then make his own decision about which estimate or combination of estimates to use. The scratch tape would then be reloaded onto the machine, the appropriate codes would be punched into cards, and the rest of the program would be run.

The control routine will next call the basic analysis routine, which will be similar to that already developed. This routine will compute life tables, stable populations, intrinsic rates, etc.

The basic analysis will be carried out independently for each sex. Then the machine will do the calculations involving the interaction of the male and female populations. The necessary data for these calculations will have been stored either on scratch tape or in storage cells allocated in an intermediate routine between the control and the basic routines.

After printing the results of the interaction analysis, the machine, which again has stored the necessary information, will call the prediction routines. These routines will inspect the necessary codes, read in from reference tapes the appropriate parameters of change, and make several realistic predictions on various assumptions.

A final sequence of routines will make comparisons between countries. As described above, the necessary information will have been stored on scratch tape as each set of data passed through the computer.

This ideal program, except for the demographic progress assumed, is only an extrapolation of techniques already in use at the University of Chicago. The system of options that will be the key to the program has already been used extensively by James Palmore, of the Community and Family Study Center, in an elaborate program for analysis of cross tabulations. His program has extensive options for varying the size of the table, combining or deleting columns and rows, making various kinds of statistical tests, and calculating various types of per cent distributions. His program, thoroughly tested and operational, already includes more options than envisioned here.

## Postscript

The preceding article has something of a programmatic character; at the time it was written, some four years ago, we had hopes but little experience. Since that time Dr. Wilhelm Flieger and I have prepared for publication a set of tables regarding all the populations for which we could obtain data, and printed out for each several hundred figures. These are to appear shortly under our joint authorship with the title World Population. Specimens of the more detailed techniques of computation which have been developed are presented in the next article.

# MACHINE COMPUTATION AND THE WORKING DEMOGRAPHER

Nathan Keyfitz
University of Chicago

The computer encourages a rethinking of numerical procedures in demography as in other fields. Suggestions of the new directions will here be presented on several specific problems concerning deterministic birth and death calculations.

## Graduation

Data provided in 5-year age groups are often graduated to single years by polynomial interpolation. The fitting of a polynomial through a series of given values is a process that is linear in those values, and each interpolated number may be expressed as a weighted average. In the form of interpolation due to Sprague, for instance, in which successive interpolated values lie on a curve that is continuous and has a continuous derivative, the number of the population at age 20 last birthday, $_1K_{20}$, may be written in terms of the data given in 5-year age groups $_5K_{10}$, $_5K_{15}$, $_5K_{20}$, $_5K_{25}$, $_5K_{30}$ as follows:

$$_1K_{20} = -0.0128 \; _5K_{10} + 0.0848 \; _5K_{15} + 0.1504 \; _5K_{20}$$

$$- 0.0240 \; _5K_{25} + 0.0016 \; _5K_{30},$$

and similarly for $_1K_{21}$, etc.

But collections of such linear expressions are readily expressed in matrix form, and Table 1 shows three alternative sets of multipliers, each set designated $\underset{\sim}{A}$ and capable of ascertaining numbers in interpolated intervals of one-fifth the width of the data, or of the preceding interpolation.

TABLE 1.  Exhibit of Midpanel Sprague, Greville, and Beers
Multipliers in Form of Matrix $\underset{\sim}{A}$, Showing

$$\underset{\sim}{A}_5\underset{\sim}{V}_{20} = {}_1\underset{\sim}{V}_{30}.$$

---

Sprague

$$\begin{bmatrix} -.0128 & +.0848 & +.1504 & -.0240 & +.0016 \\ -.0016 & +.0144 & +.2224 & -.0416 & +.0064 \\ +.0064 & -.0336 & +.2544 & -.0336 & +.0064 \\ +.0064 & -.0416 & +.2224 & +.0144 & -.0016 \\ +.0016 & -.0240 & +.1504 & +.0848 & -.0128 \end{bmatrix} \times \begin{Bmatrix} {}_5K_{20} \\ {}_5K_{25} \\ {}_5K_{30} \\ {}_5K_{35} \\ {}_5K_{40} \end{Bmatrix} = \begin{Bmatrix} {}_1K_{30} \\ {}_1K_{31} \\ {}_1K_{32} \\ {}_1K_{33} \\ {}_1K_{34} \end{Bmatrix}$$

Greville

$$\begin{bmatrix} -.0117 & +.0804 & +.1570 & -.0284 & +.0027 \\ -.0019 & +.0156 & +.2206 & -.0404 & +.0061 \\ +.0048 & -.0272 & +.2448 & -.0272 & +.0048 \\ +.0061 & -.0404 & +.2206 & +.0156 & -.0019 \\ +.0027 & -.0284 & +.1570 & +.0804 & -.0117 \end{bmatrix} \times \begin{Bmatrix} {}_5K_{20} \\ {}_5K_{25} \\ {}_5K_{30} \\ {}_5K_{35} \\ {}_5K_{40} \end{Bmatrix} = \begin{Bmatrix} {}_1K_{30} \\ {}_1K_{31} \\ {}_1K_{32} \\ {}_1K_{33} \\ {}_1K_{34} \end{Bmatrix}$$

Beers

$$\begin{bmatrix} -.0117 & +.0804 & +.1570 & -.0284 & +.0027 \\ -.0020 & +.0160 & +.2200 & -.0400 & +.0060 \\ +.0050 & -.0280 & +.2460 & -.0280 & +.0050 \\ +.0060 & -.0400 & +.2200 & +.0160 & -.0020 \\ +.0027 & -.0284 & +.1570 & +.0804 & -.0117 \end{bmatrix} \times \begin{Bmatrix} {}_5K_{20} \\ {}_5K_{25} \\ {}_5K_{30} \\ {}_5K_{35} \\ {}_5K_{40} \end{Bmatrix} = \begin{Bmatrix} {}_1K_{30} \\ {}_1K_{31} \\ {}_1K_{32} \\ {}_1K_{33} \\ {}_1K_{34} \end{Bmatrix}$$

## Matrix Expressions for Polynomial Graduation

The premultiplication of the vector of five consecutive 5-year age groups, say $\{_5V_{20}\}$, by $\underset{\sim}{A}$ gives 5 consecutive single years of age, say $\{_1V_{30}\}$. On the definitions of the 5-element vectors,

$$\{_5\underset{\sim}{V}_{20}\} = \begin{Bmatrix} _5K_{20} \\ _5K_{25} \\ _5K_{30} \\ _5K_{35} \\ _5K_{40} \end{Bmatrix}; \quad \{_1\underset{\sim}{V}_{30}\} = \begin{Bmatrix} _1K_{30} \\ _1K_{31} \\ _1K_{32} \\ _1K_{33} \\ _1K_{34} \end{Bmatrix}; \quad \{_{0.2}\underset{\sim}{V}_{32}\} = \begin{Bmatrix} _{0.2}K_{32.0} \\ _{0.2}K_{32.2} \\ _{0.2}K_{32.4} \\ _{0.2}K_{32.6} \\ _{0.2}K_{32.8} \end{Bmatrix}; \ldots;$$

the successive application of $\underset{\sim}{A}$ gives $\underset{\sim}{A}\ \{_5\underset{\sim}{V}_{20}\} = \{_1\underset{\sim}{V}_{30}\}$; $\underset{\sim}{A}^2\{_5\underset{\sim}{V}_{20}\} = \{_{0.2}\underset{\sim}{V}_{32}\}$; $\underset{\sim}{A}^3\{_5\underset{\sim}{V}_{20}\} = \{_{0.04}\underset{\sim}{V}_{32.4}\}$; etc. $A^3\{\underset{\sim}{V}\}$ gives numbers at intervals of twenty-fifths of a year. Table 2 shows the operation of the three sets of multipliers on males of ages $10-14$, $15-19$, . . . , $30-34$, to provide single years of age $20-24$ and fifth of a year of age. The reader may verify some of the numbers on a desk calculator, given the following values for United States males, 1963, omitting armed forces abroad:

$$_5K_{10} = 9170$$

$$_5K_{15} = 7892$$

$$_5K_{20} = 6331$$

$$_5K_{25} = 5453$$

$$_5K_{30} = 5625.$$

This approach to the use of matrix multipliers for graduation merely rearranges a limited number of well-known techniques. Ways of obtaining the graduating matrix which will meet extensive sets of conditions are provided by Kimeldorf and Jones,[1] using a technique known as Bayesian graduation.

## Life Table Construction by Double Graduation

To make a life table the multipliers may be applied once, twice, or three times in succession. Twice is recommended, to give intervals of one-fifth of a year for $K_x$ and $D_x$, the latter being the number of deaths. It may be assumed that the life table central death rate, $_{0.2}m_x$, is the same as $_{0.2}M_x = {_{0.2}D_x}/{_{0.2}K_x}$ from the observations. Let $_nq_x$ be the probability of a person of age x dying before age x + n;

TABLE 2. Graduation to Fifths of a Year of Age, United States Male Population, 1963.    Programmed by Nancy Wang.

| Age | Sprague multipliers One year | 1/5 year | Greville multipliers One year | 1/5 year | Beers multipliers One year | 1/5 year | Beers - Sprague | Beers - Greville |
|-----|------|------|------|------|------|------|------|------|
| 20 | 1382176 |        | 1381517 |        | 1381517 |        | -659 | 0 |
|    |         | 281811 |         | 281804 |         | 281803 |      |   |
|    |         | 279138 |         | 279008 |         | 279005 |      |   |
|    |         | 276456 |         | 276253 |         | 276250 |      |   |
|    |         | 273743 |         | 273551 |         | 273552 |      |   |
|    |         | 271028 |         | 270902 |         | 270907 |      |   |
| 21 | 1316142 |        | 1316322 |        | 1316382 |        | 240 | 60 |
|    |         | 268360 |         | 268294 |         | 268307 |      |   |
|    |         | 265737 |         | 265727 |         | 265745 |      |   |
|    |         | 263166 |         | 263210 |         | 263228 |      |   |
|    |         | 260660 |         | 260748 |         | 260759 |      |   |
|    |         | 258220 |         | 258343 |         | 258343 |      |   |
| 22 | 1256902 |        | 1257861 |        | 1257741 |        | 839 | -120 |
|    |         | 255834 |         | 255994 |         | 255978 |      |   |
|    |         | 253501 |         | 253707 |         | 253679 |      |   |
|    |         | 251268 |         | 251494 |         | 251461 |      |   |
|    |         | 249155 |         | 249361 |         | 249333 |      |   |
|    |         | 247145 |         | 247306 |         | 247290 |      |   |
| 23 | 1207918 |        | 1208098 |        | 1208158 |        | 240 | 60 |
|    |         | 245190 |         | 245303 |         | 245302 |      |   |
|    |         | 243288 |         | 243362 |         | 243374 |      |   |
|    |         | 241482 |         | 241520 |         | 241537 |      |   |
|    |         | 239785 |         | 239781 |         | 239800 |      |   |
|    |         | 238173 |         | 238131 |         | 238144 |      |   |
| 24 | 1167861 |        | 1167202 |        | 1167202 |        | -659 | 0 |
|    |         | 236607 |         | 236550 |         | 236557 |      |   |
|    |         | 235094 |         | 235002 |         | 235003 |      |   |
|    |         | 233586 |         | 233452 |         | 233451 |      |   |
|    |         | 232055 |         | 231885 |         | 231882 |      |   |
|    |         | 230519 |         | 230313 |         | 230309 |      |   |

$l_x / l_0$ the probability of a child just born surviving to age x; $_n d_x = l_x - l_{x+n}$ the number dying in the life table population; $_n L_x = \int_0^n l(x+t)\, dt$ the number living between ages x and x + n in the life table or stationary population, all according to standard demographic usage. Then for n = 0.2 we may use the approximations:

$$_{0.2}q_x = \frac{0.2\, m_x}{5 + \frac{1}{2}(_{0.2}m_x)}; \qquad _{0.2}d_x = (l_x)\,(_{0.2}q_x);$$

$$l_{x+0.2} = l_x - _{0.2}d_x; \qquad _{0.2}L_x = 0.1\,(l_x + l_{x+0.2});$$

$$T_x = T_{x+0.2} + _{0.2}L_x; \qquad \overset{o}{e}_x = T_x / l_x.$$

Consolidation back to 5-year age groups means <u>adding</u> 25 values for columns $_5 d_x$ and $_5 L_x$, etc; <u>selecting</u> the required values for columns $l_x$, $T_x$, $\overset{o}{e}_x$; <u>recomputing</u> from these grouped values $_5 q_x = _5 d_x / l_x$; $_5 m_x = _5 d_x / _5 L_x$.

The variation that results from different sets of multipliers (as among Sprague, Greville, and Beers) can be ascertained without any change of program other than substituting alternative matrices. In general the differences are trifling. Taking Austria females, 1963, we have for $1000\,_5 q_x$ the quantities shown in Table 3. Sprague multipliers are somewhat further from the iterative life table than Greville and Beers. However, the graduations are all grossly wrong in the allocation of deaths as between ages 0 and 1 − 4, as one would expect of any polynomial fitting. A hyperbola does much better.

TABLE 3.   Comparison of $1000\,_5 q_x$ on Four Calculations of the Life Table for Austria Females, 1963.

| | Graduation to fifths of a year | | | Iterative life table using (14) below |
|---|---|---|---|---|
| | Sprague | Greville | Beers | |
| $1000\,_5 q_0$ | 31.61 | 31.85 | 31.79 | 31.84 |
| $1000\,_5 q_{20}$ | 3.01 | 2.99 | 2.99 | 2.99 |
| $1000\,_5 q_{40}$ | 11.05 | 11.04 | 11.04 | 11.04 |
| $1000\,_5 q_{60}$ | 65.78 | 65.80 | 65.80 | 65.96 |
| $1000\,_5 q_{80}$ | 488.36 | 487.33 | 487.49 | 485.45 |

For the same Austria females, 1963, the values of $\overset{o}{e}_0$ on double graduation to fifths of a year were

Sprague 72. 775  Greville 72. 699  Beers 72. 721

as compared with $\overset{o}{e}_0 = 72.677$ for the iterative life table of the following section. Observe again that Sprague multipliers stand somewhat away from the other graduations.

### Interpolation by Evaluation of Determinants

The direct way of looking at interpolation is as the establishing of a polynomial, say $y = A + Bx + Cx^2 + Dx^3 + \ldots$, which passes through the given points $x_1$, $y_1$; $x_2$, $y_2$; $\ldots$. If we have three given points, not necessarily at equal intervals, and wish to interpolate with a quadratic, say $Ax^2 + Bx + C$, then the condition under which the four equations linear in the constants,

$$
\begin{aligned}
Ax^2 + Bx + C - f(x) &= 0, \\
Ax_1^2 + Bx_1 + C - y_1 &= 0, \\
Ax_2^2 + Bx_2 + C - y_2 &= 0, \\
Ax_3^2 + Bx_3 + C - y_3 &= 0,
\end{aligned}
\tag{1}
$$

are consistent is

$$
\begin{vmatrix}
x^2 & x & 1 & f(x) \\
x_1^2 & x_1 & 1 & y_1 \\
x_2^2 & x_2 & 1 & y_2 \\
x_3^2 & x_3 & 1 & y_3
\end{vmatrix} = 0,
\tag{2}
$$

from which[2]

$$
f(x) = \frac{
\begin{vmatrix}
x^2 & x & 1 & 0 \\
x_1^2 & x_1 & 1 & y_1 \\
x_2^2 & x_2 & 1 & y_2 \\
x_3^2 & x_3 & 1 & y_3
\end{vmatrix}
}{
\begin{vmatrix}
x_1^2 & x_1 & 1 \\
x_2^2 & x_2 & 1 \\
x_3^2 & x_3 & 1
\end{vmatrix}
}.
\tag{3}
$$

The verification that Equations 2 and 3 pass through $x_1$, $y_1$ is to put $x = x_1$ and expand by the fourth column; nothing remains of Equation 2 but $f(x_1) = y_1$. That the other conditions are met is verified in the same way. The extension to n given values takes the form of an $n + 1$ by $n + 1$ determinant, fitting a curve of degree $n - 1$, as is similarly verified.

To be satisfied that the determinantal equation (Equation 2) is the same as Newton's divided difference formula, we first subtract the third row from the fourth and divide the new fourth by $x_3 - x_2$, the second row from the third and divide the new third by $x_2 - x_1$. The third as it then stands is subtracted from the fourth and divided by $x_3 - x_1$, writing

$$[y_1, y_2, y_3] = \frac{[y_2, y_3] - [y_1, y_2]}{x_3 - x_1}.$$

The result is

$$\begin{vmatrix} x^2 & x & 1 & f(x) \\ x_1^2 & x_1 & 1 & y_1 \\ x_1 + x_2 & 1 & 0 & [y_1, y_2] \\ 1 & 0 & 0 & [y_1, y_2, y_3] \end{vmatrix} = 0 \qquad (4)$$

which when expanded by its last column is

$$f(x) = y_1 + (x - x_1) [y_1, y_2]$$
$$+ (x - x_1)(x - x_2) [y_1, y_2, y_3]. \qquad (5)$$

**Data Given as Areas Rather than Points**

What has been set forth above is not directly applicable as such in demography because the typical data are not points but areas under a curve: the population over 45 and under 50 years of age, for example. Such data can be converted so that they represent points by cumulating them, which is to say, dealing with

$$F(x_1) = \int_0^x f(x) \, dx,$$ where $F(x_1)$ is the total of the frequency up to $x_1$. After the operation of graduation has produced $F(x)$, we can differentiate $F(x)$ to obtain $f(x) = F'(x)$. If, as is more likely, we need the total of the distribution between x and $x + 1$, $\int_x^{x+1} f(a) \, da$, we obtain it by subtraction, as

$$\int_x^{x+1} f(a) \, da = F(x + 1) - F(x)$$

Through such means the multipliers of Table 1 were derived.

### The Estimate of Interpolation Error

The classical remainder terms for Taylor series and Newton interpolation have their uses but in some circumstances a different procedure may provide more information on error and be better suited to machine computation.

When we are given n values of a function and wish to interpolate or graduate to find intermediate values, we can study the precision likely to be attained by using $n - 1$ of the points to interpolate the nth. The comparison of the interpolated with the given nth value will then constitute an estimate of error for any new point that is to be interpolated. If the interpolated nth value is written $f(x_n)$, and the given nth point $y_n$, then $f(x_n) - y_n$ is the error of $f(x_n)$.

Suppose $n = 4$. We know by solving Equation 2 for $f(x)$ that the interpolated value for the fourth point is Equation 3. Then $f(x) - y$ is the same as Equation 3, with the sole difference that the zero in the upper right-hand corner of the numerator is replaced by $y$.

When interpolated $f(x_4)$ is compared with observed $y_4$, the error is

$$f(x_4) - y_4 = \frac{\begin{vmatrix} x_4^2 & x_4 & 1 & y_4 \\ x_1^2 & x_1 & 1 & y_1 \\ x_2^2 & x_2 & 1 & y_2 \\ x_3^2 & x_3 & 1 & y_3 \end{vmatrix}}{\begin{vmatrix} x_1^2 & x_1 & 1 \\ x_2^2 & x_2 & 1 \\ x_3^2 & x_3 & 1 \end{vmatrix}} = - \frac{\begin{vmatrix} x_1^2 & x_1 & 1 & y_1 \\ x_2^2 & x_2 & 1 & y_2 \\ x_3^2 & x_3 & 1 & y_3 \\ x_4^2 & x_4 & 1 & y_4 \end{vmatrix}}{\begin{vmatrix} x_1^2 & x_1 & 1 \\ x_2^2 & x_2 & 1 \\ x_3^2 & x_3 & 1 \end{vmatrix}} = \frac{\Delta}{-\Delta_{44}} , \quad (6)$$

where $\Delta$ is the determinant in the numerator and $\Delta_{44}$ is $\Delta$ with the last column and last row deleted.

There being four points available, each of them in turn could be taken as $x_4, y_4$ in Equation 6 and four indications of the error of the process obtained. With n points n indications would be given, which in an extension of the above notation might be designated

$$f(x_i) - y_i = \frac{\Delta}{(-1)^{i+n+1} \Delta_{in}} , \quad i = 1, 2, \ldots, n. \tag{7}$$

The points may be far from equidistant; the interpolating formulas may involve derivatives as in Taylor's expansion or in osculatory interpolation; polynomial interpolating functions may be replaced by exponentials or other forms; these more general situations require at most obvious modifications of Equation 7. Insofar as n points will give a better result than n-1, the application of Equation 7 somewhat exaggerates the error to which the final interpolation will be subject.

The procedure may be exemplified with three points, say $l_{25}$, $l_{30}$, and $l_{35}$. If we interpolate single years, then the errors with straight lines through the known points are

$$\frac{\Delta}{\Delta_{11}} = \frac{\begin{vmatrix} 25 & 1 & l_{25} \\ 30 & 1 & l_{30} \\ 35 & 1 & l_{35} \end{vmatrix}}{- \begin{vmatrix} 30 & 1 \\ 35 & 1 \end{vmatrix}} , \tag{8}$$

and two other ratios which differ only by their denominators

being $- \begin{vmatrix} 25 & 1 \\ 30 & 1 \end{vmatrix}$ and $\begin{vmatrix} 25 & 1 \\ 35 & 1 \end{vmatrix}$, respectively. The denominators are seen to equal 5, 5, and -10 respectively, and for United States males, 1964 ($l_{25} = 94906$, $l_{30} = 94071$, $l_{35} = 93074$), the common numerator is 810. Hence the three estimates of error are $\frac{810}{5} = 162$, $\frac{810}{5} = 162$, and $\frac{810}{(-10)} = -81$, as may be verified without the use of determinants in this simple example.

We described earlier a modification of the method used in demography for making a life table, and this showed how the computer can be helpful. But it constitutes only a small departure from conventional graduation methods. We proceed to an iterative life table that is a sharper break from the desk calculator.

## A Method for Improving the Life Table

Having the computer renders unnecessary a method for _making_ a life table; all that is needed is a method for _improving_ one. Starting with an arbitrary life table (for instance, one in which $_5q_x = 0.1$ at all ages), successive improvement may be readily programmed; the computer is at its best when performing the same operation again and again on different numbers.

When we have the $l_x$ on a particular iteration, we wish to produce $_5M'_x$ from this iteration in such fashion that it will be comparable with the $_5M_x$ constituting the data. One way of achieving this is to convert the stationary population of the life table into a stable population, or at least one that is stable in sections. If this stable population is increasing at the rate of the observed population, then it is proper to compare its $M'_x$ with that of the observed. Our problem is thus reduced to finding $M'_x$ from an arbitrary set of $l_x$ and r.

As $_5M'_x$ is the ratio of deaths $_5D'_x$ to population $_5K'_x$ (both on the assumption of sectional stability), we need to define these in a way that will be calculable. The stable population is

$$k'(x) \, dx = e^{-rx} \ell(x) \, dx \tag{9}$$

between ages x and x + dx, and hence we need the integral

$$_5K'_x = \int_0^5 e^{-r(x+t)} \ell(x+t) \, dt. \tag{10}$$

For the deaths we need a continuous curve corresponding to $\ell(x)$, which might be represented as $\ell(x) \, \mu(x)$, such that

$$_5d_x = \int_0^5 \ell(x+t) \, \mu(x+t) \, dt.$$

In fact $\ell(x) \, \mu(x)$ is simply $-\left[\dfrac{d\ell(x)}{dx}\right]$. To represent $_5D'_x$, the deaths in a population growing at rate r, we write

$$_5D'_x = \int_0^5 e^{-r(x+t)} \ell(x+t) \, \mu(x+t) \, dt = -\int_0^5 e^{-r(x+t)} \, d\ell(x+t).$$

Fortunately this latter may be integrated by parts to provide

$$_5D'_x = e^{-rx}\ell_x - e^{-r(x+5)}\ell_{x+5} - r \int_0^5 e^{-r(x+t)} \ell(x+t) \, dt, \tag{11}$$

in which the only integral is the same $_5K'_x$ of Equation 10.

Now our age-specific rate of $_5M'_x$ as worked out from the life table for an increasing population being

$$_5M'_x = \frac{_5D'_x}{_5K'_x},$$

we substitute $_5D'_x$ from Equation 11 and $_5K'_x$ from Equation 10 to obtain the basic result

$$_5M'_x = \frac{_5D'_x}{_5K'_x} = \frac{e^{-rx}\ell_x - e^{-r(x+5)}\ell_{x+5}}{\displaystyle\int_0^5 e^{-r(x+t)}\ell(x+t)\,dt} - r. \tag{12}$$

Note that no approximations are required for Equation 12 once we have r and the $\ell_x$ of the previous iteration. An approximation will of course enter for the integral $_5K'_x$ of the denominator of the first term of the right-hand side of Equation 12.

The agreement of the life table with the data is mediated only by how we ascertain this integral, and different formulae for the integral will produce different life tables. An explicit result will be shown for a cubic through $k'_{x-5}$, $k'_x$, $k'_{x+5}$, and $k'_{x+10}$.

A familiar means of evaluating $_5L_x$ is

$$_5L_x = \int_0^5 \lambda(x+t)\, dt$$

$$= \frac{65}{24}\left(\lambda_x + \lambda_{x+5}\right) - \frac{5}{24}\left(\lambda_{x+10} + \lambda_{x-5}\right).$$ (13)

The method is perfectly valid when $e^{-rx}\lambda_x$ is written for $\lambda_x$, and it then gives $_5K'_x$. Hence Equation 12 becomes, after canceling out $e^{-rx}$,

$$_5M'_x = \frac{\lambda_x - e^{-5r}\lambda_{x+5}}{\frac{65}{24}\left(\lambda_x + e^{-5r}\lambda_{x+5}\right) - \frac{5}{24}\left(e^{-10r}\lambda_{x+10} + e^{5r}\lambda_{x-5}\right)} - r.$$ (14)

The $M'_x$ of Equation 14 — dropping the prefix 5 — may be compared with the $M_x$ from the data and a correction provided for $q_x$. The simplest form of correction is by the ratio of $M_x$ to $M'_x$:

$$q^*_x = \frac{M_x}{M'_x}\, q_x,$$

where $q^*_x$ is the improved $q_x$. The process is repeated with $q^*_x$ until a test of convergence such as

$$\left| q^*_x - q_x \right| < 10^{-6}$$

is satisfied. It suffices to apply the test for $x = 75$.

The iterative process has involved explicitly only the $\lambda_x$ and $q_x$ columns of the life table. Once convergence has been attained on these, the remaining columns may be evaluated. The only one on which any discretion is possible is $_5L_x$, for which one might use Equation 13.

The basic result (Equation 12) may be made to apply to an interval other than 5 years, say n, by entering n in each of the three places where 5 appears. We will ordinarily want to use it with n = 1 for the interval under 1 year of age; with n = 4 for the 1 — 4 at last birthday; with n = 15 for the open interval 85+ with which the table ends. Some comments may be made on integration formulas suitable to these.

For the ages under 5 a hyperbola for $\lambda_x$ through x = 0, 1, and 5 is recommended. If the hyperbola with $\lambda_0 = 1$ is

$$\lambda(x) = \frac{ax + b}{x + b},$$

then it will be found that

$$b = \frac{5(\lambda_1 - \lambda_5)}{4 + \lambda_5 - 5\lambda_1},$$

$$a = \lambda_1 (1 + b) - b.$$

Now the integral required in Equation 12,

$$\int_0^1 k(x + t) \, dt = \int_0^1 e^{-r(x+t)} \lambda(x + t) \, dt,$$

cannot be represented exactly in a simple form. An efficient way of evaluating it is the Gauss formula

$$\int_0^1 k(x + t) \, dt = \frac{64}{225} \left( k(0.5) \right)$$

$$+ 0.2393143 \, (k(0.2307653) + k(0.7692347))$$

$$+ 0.1184635 \, (k(0.0469101) + k(0.9530899)). \quad (15)$$

For the interval from x = 1 to x = 5 this would be applied four times.

Between ages 5 and 10 it may be preferable to use a one-sided integral rather than the symmetric Equation 14. This is obtained from a quadratic through $\lambda_5$, $\lambda_{10}$, and $\lambda_{15}$ as

$$\int_0^5 k(5 + t) \, dt = \int_0^5 e^{-r(5+t)} \lambda(5 + t) \, dt$$

$$= \frac{25}{12} k_5 + \frac{10}{3} k_{10} - \frac{5}{12} k_{15}.$$

A case may be made for using the Gompertz curve

$$\frac{\lambda(x + t)}{\lambda(x)} = g^{c^t - 1}$$

to fit three successive values of $\lambda_x$, or the more general Makeham to fit four values:

$$\frac{\lambda(x + t)}{\lambda(x)} = s^t g^{c^t - 1}.$$

The subsequent integration of $e^{-r(x+t)} \Lambda(x+t)$ could be carried out by means of the Gauss formula (Equation 15) applied five times for each 5-year interval.

The intrinsic rate of increase $r_x$ for sectional stability is given by

$$r_x = 0.1 \ln \left( \frac{{}_5K_{x-5}}{{}_5L_{x-5}} \Big/ \frac{{}_5K_{x+5}}{{}_5L_{x+5}} \right).$$

**Computing the Intrinsic Rate of Natural Increase**

The equation

$$B(t) = \int_\alpha^\beta B(t-x) \frac{\Lambda(x)}{\Lambda_0} m(x) \, dx \tag{16}$$

relates B (t), births at time t, to B (t - x) in a population of fixed regime of mortality, $\Lambda(x)$, and fertility, m (x), where x is both age and time. $\alpha$ is the lowest age of reproduction and $\beta$ the highest. Only one sex, say female, is under discussion. A solution to Equation 16 is found by trying $e^{rt}$, where r is to be determined. Entering B (t) = $e^{rt}$ in Equation 16 gives the characteristic equation

$$\Lambda_0 \psi(r) = \int_\alpha^\beta e^{-rx} \Lambda(x) \, m(x) \, dx = \Lambda_0. \tag{17}$$

In order to solve this equation we need to translate it into the discrete form

$$\Lambda_0 \psi(r) = e^{-2\frac{1}{2}r} \sum_\alpha^\beta e^{-rx} {}_5L_x \, {}_5F_x = \Lambda_0, \tag{18}$$

where ${}_5F_x$ is the age-specific fertility rate between ages x and x + 4 at last birthday.

The modern iterative approach to the solution of Equation 18 was first suggested by Ansley Coale.[3] Several routes of iteration suggest themselves:

a.    If r, r*, and r** are successive iterates, the rule:

if $\psi(r*)$ is greater than 1, take r** as $r* + 0.5 \left| r* - r \right|$;

if $\psi(r*)$ is less than 1, take r** as $r* - 0.5 \left| r* - r \right|$.

This requires programming only $\psi(r)$, and gives one binary digit per iteration, starting, for example, from r = 0.0 and r* = 0.025. Fifteen to twenty iterations in practice provide six-decimal-place accuracy.

b.    The Newton-Raphson method,

$$r* = r - \frac{\psi(r) - 1}{\psi'(r)}, \tag{19}$$

which may be derived from the first term of Taylor's expansion, and converges in about 5 cycles.

c.     The secant method.  If $r^*$ and $r^{**}$ are two approximations to a root of $\psi(r) = 0$, then the straight line through these points is a kind of approximation to the curve $\psi(r)$.  The straight line is

$$\frac{\psi(r) - \psi(r^{**})}{\psi(r^{**}) - \psi(r^*)} = \frac{r - r^{**}}{r^{**} - r^*},$$

and the intersection of this with the horizontal line one unit above the r-axis gives a better approximation $r^{***}$.  Hence

$$r^{***} = r^{**} + \left(\frac{1 - \psi(r^{**})}{\psi(r^{**}) - \psi(r^*)}\right)(r^{**} - r^*).$$

For the United States, 1960, we started with arbitrary $r^* = 0.02$ and $r^{**} = 0.025$.  Then the iterative sequence was

$$r^* = 0.02,$$

$$r^{**} = 0.025,$$

$$r^{***} = 0.01908,$$

$$r^{(iv)} = 0.02084,$$

$$r^{(v)} = 0.02083,$$

$r^{(v)}$ being correct to the places shown.

d.     Functional iteration.  By multiplying the characteristic equation (Equation 18) by $e^{27\frac{1}{2}r}$ and transposing, we obtain the alternative form with $\alpha = 10$ and $\beta = 50$:

$$\lambda^{*5\frac{1}{2}} = \lambda^3 \left(\frac{5^L10}{\Lambda_0}\right) {}_5F_{10} + \lambda^2 \left(\frac{5^L15}{\Lambda_0}\right) {}_5F_{15} + \lambda \left(\frac{5^L20}{\Lambda_0}\right) {}_5F_{20} + \left(\frac{5^L25}{\Lambda_0}\right) {}_5F_{25}$$

$$+ \lambda^{-1} \left(\frac{5^L30}{\Lambda_0}\right) {}_5F_{30} + \ldots + \lambda^{-4} \left(\frac{5^L45}{\Lambda_0}\right) {}_5F_{45}, \tag{20}$$

where $\lambda$ has been written for $e^{5r}$ to avoid unnecessary taking of exponentials in the course of iteration.  We start by choosing some arbitrary value for $\lambda$, evaluating the expression on the right with $\lambda$, then taking the 5 1/2th root, which is to say the 2/11th power, in order to find the improved $\lambda^*$, substituting $\lambda^*$ for $\lambda$, and repeat.  The test for convergence might be that $\lambda^*$ differs from $\lambda$ by less than 0.000001.  Once the sequence has converged to $\lambda^*$, the required r is $0.2 \ln \lambda^*$.  In practice only 2 to 4 cycles are necessary for six-decimal-place accuracy.  This method combines ease of programming with economy of computer time.  If we multiply Equation 18 by $e^{37\frac{1}{2}r}$ for United States females, 1964, and start with $r = 0.02$, some 20 cycles are necessary. Waves of slowly diminishing amplitude appear in the successive iterates. When we multiply Equation 18 by $e^{32\frac{1}{2}r}$, convergence to six decimal places requires 7 iterations; multiplying by $e^{17\frac{1}{2}r}$ requires 12 iterations. What is the optimum power of $e^r$ by which to multiply? Theory on convergence in functional iteration is provided in Scarborough and Ralston.[4, 5]

e.    A solution that dispenses with the characteristic equation. The method of Daniel Bernouilli converts a polynomial equation into a recurrence equation in order to solve the former.[6, 7] In demography we start with the recurrence equation (Equation 16). Instead of converting it into the polynomial equation (Equation 17) in $e^{-r}$, we should be able to use Bernouilli's method directly.

We seek then a direct solution for Equation 16 expressed in finite form as

$$B(t) = B(t - 12\frac{1}{2}) \frac{{}_5L_{10}}{\lambda_0} F_{10} + B(t - 17\frac{1}{2}) \frac{{}_5L_{15}}{\lambda_0} F_{15}$$

$$+ \ldots + B(t - 47\frac{1}{2}) \frac{{}_5L_{45}}{\lambda_0} F_{45} , \tag{21}$$

The B (t) for values of the argument less than 0 may be put equal to 1 to start the process. Then the first calculated B (t) from Equation 21 will be $B(0) = R_0$, the net reproduction rate. We now move along in the trajectory by adding 2.5 to the arguments of B in all terms of Equation 21, and find again that $B(2.5) = R_0$. Next we add another 2.5 and so find B (5). The process of increasing the argument of B (t) and evaluating the right-hand side of Equation 21 continues step by step until stability is reached, for example, as tested by

$$\left| \frac{B(t + 2\frac{1}{2})}{B(t)} - \frac{B(t)}{B(t - 2\frac{1}{2})} \right| < 10^{-7}.$$

The value of r may then be extracted as

$$r = \frac{2}{5} \left( \ln B(t + 2\frac{1}{2}) - \ln B(t) \right),$$

since at stability $B(t + \frac{5}{2}) = e^{5r/2} B(t)$.

The method does converge, but very slowly. Large waves of very slowly diminishing amplitude are generated in B (t), and convergence typically requires about 250 iterations, corresponding to a projection of over 1,000 years. The main reason for presenting this here is to show that the characteristic equation (Equation 17) is helpful.

f.    Simultaneous iteration for r and other constants of the stable population. This is useful when intrinsic birth and death rates are required as well as r;

it converges in 4 or 5 iterations and produces a number of quantities relating to the stable situation.

The stable age distribution will result from the operation of a given regime of mortality and fertility, specified by age for a one-sex population. It equals

$$c(x) = be^{-rx} \frac{\lambda(x)}{\lambda_0} \tag{22}$$

in continuous terms, or

$$_5K'_x = be^{-r(x+2\frac{1}{2})} {}_5L_x \tag{23}$$

for the discrete age group x to x + 4 at last birthday, where b is the intrinsic birth rate. But b is also

$$b = \frac{\sum\limits_{\alpha}^{\beta} e^{-r(x+2\frac{1}{2})} {}_5L_x {}_5F_x}{\sum\limits_{\alpha}^{\beta} e^{-r(x+2\frac{1}{2})} {}_5L_x} = \frac{\sum\limits_{\alpha}^{\beta} {}_5K'_x {}_5F_x}{\sum\limits_{\alpha}^{\beta} {}_5K'_x}, \tag{24}$$

the crude birth rate in the stable population. And the corresponding intrinsic death rate is

$$d = \frac{\sum\limits_{\alpha}^{\beta} e^{-r(x+2\frac{1}{2})} {}_5L_x {}_5M_x}{\sum\limits_{\alpha}^{\beta} e^{-r(x+2\frac{1}{2})} {}_5L_x} = \frac{\sum\limits_{\alpha}^{\beta} {}_5K'_x {}_5M_x}{\sum\limits_{\alpha}^{\beta} {}_5K'_x}. \tag{25}$$

The preceding is the basis of the iterative method of simultaneously ascertaining r, b, d, and c (x). The steps are

1.    With arbitrary r and b and the given life table ${}_5L_x$, construct $\lambda_0 c(x) = be^{-rx} \lambda(x)$ or ${}_5K'_x$ for the several ages, using Equation 23.

2.    From ${}_5K'_x$ and given ${}_5F_x$, find b from Equation 24

3.    With ${}_5K'_x$ and given ${}_5M_x$, find d from Equation 25

4.    Improve r to r* = b – d, and repeat.

Following is the sequence of quantities calculated for Nicaragua females, 1962 (programmed by S. K. Sinha):

| 1000b | 1000d | 1000r |
|-------|-------|-------|
| 50. 000 | – | 20. 000 |
| 40. 219 | 8. 737 | 31. 482 |
| 39. 834 | 7. 523 | 32. 312 |
| 39. 733 | 7. 467 | 32. 266 |
| 39. 738 | 7. 470 | 32. 268 |

Four cycles provide convergence to five places in r. This is nearly as quickly convergent as functional iteration Equation 20, the best preceding method, and provides more information.

From the viewpoint of machine computation, we may express some preferences among the above methods. The secant formula (c), requiring no derivative, is more easily programmed than the Newton-Raphson (b), and converges about as quickly. Either may be used for complex roots; the only problem is to find an initial value close enough to the desired root that the iterative process will converge to that one and not to some other.

The functional iteration (d) is easiest of all to program; it converges at least as quickly as any other method; it involves no theory other than the multiplication of Equation 18 by $e^{27\frac{1}{2}r}$. If all that one wants is the root r, this is the preferred method. If one wants b, d, r, and the stable age distribution, then the preferred method is (f), which secures them all simultaneously.

### Translation from One Finite Approximation to Another

Different finite approximations to Equation 17 present themselves, of which Equation 18 may well be preferred for accuracy. An alternative is

$$\sum_{\alpha}^{\beta} e^{-rx} ({}_5L_{x-5} \; {}_5F_{x-5} + {}_5L_x \; {}_5F_x) = \lambda \Lambda_0, \tag{26}$$

which arises in a natural way out of the matrix formulation of essentially the same population process.[8] Somewhat different numerical results will be obtained; for United States females, 1965, the intrinsic rate r, which is obtained from Equation 18, is 12. 65 per thousand, while that from Equation 26 is 12. 67. For Honduras, 1965, the difference is greater, the numbers being 34. 06 and 34. 19. Under some circumstances one already has the solution to Equation 26 and wishes to know the solution to Equation 18. The two are related to one another in a simple way; the r* from the integral equation (Equation 18) is $r* \doteq r - r^2/8$, where r is the solution to the matrix form (Equation 26), if the mean age of childbearing is about 25 years.[9]

In hand computation the differences among finite approximations to the same quantity are lost amid rounding and other errors. With the computer, consistent differences, such as the differences between the roots of Equations 18 and 26, become conspicuous. We proceed to derive formulae which permit the ready expression of one set of approximations in terms of the other, bearing in mind that the $\lambda$ of Equation 26 is the positive root of $|M - \lambda I| = 0$, where $M$ is the projection matrix in 5-year age groups; $e^{5r} = \lambda$; the eigenvectors of $M$ are readily computed as $(M / \lambda)^t$.

## Stable Populations Changed from One Finite Approximation to Another

In the stable age distribution the improved $_5K^*_x$ based on the integral equation $r^*$ may be obtained by correcting $_5K_x$, a column of $(M/\lambda_1)^t$:

$$_5K^*_x = {}_5K_x \left( \frac{e^{-r^* (x+ (5/2))}}{\lambda^{- (x+ (5/2)) / 5}} \right) = {}_5K_x e^{- (r^*-r) (x+ (5/2))}$$
$$\doteq {}_5K_x + {}_5K_x (r - r^*) (x + (5 / 2)) \tag{27}$$

if both the original and the improved distributions are on the same radix, say unity. Since $r - r^* = 25r^2/8A_r$, where $A_r$ is the mean age of childbearing in the stable population,[9] we have

$$_5K^*_x \doteq {}_5K_x (1 + \frac{25r^2}{8A_r} (x + 5/2)) \doteq {}_5K_x (1 + \frac{r^2}{8} (x + 5/2)).$$

The values of $_5K^*_x$ will be larger than those of $_5K_x$ at older ages in rapidly increasing populations.

The corresponding improved intrinsic birth rate is

$$b^* = \frac{\lambda_0}{\Sigma {}_5K^*_x}, \tag{28}$$

if the radix of $_5K^*_x$, which may be thought of as the limiting value $_0K^*_0$, is equal to $\lambda_0$. Entering Equation 27 in Equation 28,

$$b^* = \frac{\lambda_0}{\Sigma {}_5K_x + (r - r^*) (\Sigma {}_5K_x (x + (5/2)))}$$
$$= \frac{b}{1 + (r - r^*) \bar{A}_r},$$

where $\bar{A}_r$ is the average age in the stable population. Inserting in this last $r - r^* = 25r^2/8A_r$ as earlier, we find

$$b^* = \frac{b}{1 + (25r^2\bar{A}_r/8A_r)} \doteq b \left( 1 - \frac{r^2\bar{A}_r}{8} \right).$$

It may likewise be shown that the improved mean age in the stable population, $\bar{A}^*_r$, is

$$\bar{A}^*_r = \bar{A}_r + (r - r^*)\bar{\sigma}^2_r,$$

where $\bar{\sigma}^2_r$ is the variance of the stable population; the improved mean age at childbearing in the stable population, $A^*_r$, in terms of the variance of age at childbearing in the stable population, $\sigma^2_r$, is

$$A^*_r = A_r + (r - r^*)\,\sigma^2_r;$$

and the improved length of generation $T^*$ is

$$T^* = \frac{\ln R_0}{r^*} \doteqdot \frac{T}{1 - \dfrac{25r}{8A_r}} \doteqdot T\left(1 + \frac{r}{8}\right).$$

The preceding paragraphs have shown how the estimates from the matrix, unstarred, may be changed into estimates according with the integral equation, written with a star. The following results for Togo females, 1961, based on the matrix and the integral equation, will show the magnitude of the differences.

|  | Matrix | Integral equation |
|---|---|---|
| Intrinsic rate of natural increase | $r = 0.02729$ | $r^* = 0.02721$ |
| Intrinsic birth rate | $b = 0.05039$ | $b^* = 0.05030$ |
| Stable age distribution |  |  |
|     Ages 0 — 4 on radix unity | $_5K_0 = 3.8521$ | $_5K^*_0 = 3.8529$ |
|     Ages 20 — 24 on radix unity | $_5K_{20} = 1.7416$ | $_5K^*_{20} = 1.7449$ |
|     Ages 40 — 44 on radix unity | $_5K_{40} = 0.7952$ | $_5K^*_{40} = 0.7981$ |
| Mean age in stable population | $\bar{A}_r = 21.030$ | $A^*_r = 21.055$ |
| Mean age at childbearing in stable population | $A_r = 27.234$ | $A^*_r = 27.239$ |
| Length of generation | $T = 27.89$ | $T^* = 27.97$ |

To find $\bar{A}^*_r$ the value $\bar{\sigma}^2_r = 307.4$ was used, and for $A^*_r$, the value $\sigma^2_r = 50.5$. The differences between the two columns would be smaller for a population of slower rate of increase.

## Summary

The preceding limited review of demographic work has shown several points at which the use of the computer drastically modifies the technique of calculation: The double application of graduation formulae for smoothing population and deaths;

the life tables that emerge from such double graduation; interpolation by evaluation of determinants and a procedure for finding the error of interpolated values by its means; computation of a life table that agrees with the data by a process of successive improvement; a method of functional iteration for obtaining the intrinsic rate; and finally, the elucidation of differences in finite approximations to intrinsic rates, average ages, and stable population.

## References

1.   Kimeldorf, G. S., and D. A. Jones, "Bayesian Graduation," Transactions of the Society of Actuaries, 44, 66 — 112 (1967).

2.   Nörlund, N. E., Vorlesungen über Differenzenrechnung, Verlag von Julius Springer, Berlin, 1924.

3.   Coale, A. J., "A New Method for Calculating Lotka's $r$ — the Intrinsic Rate of Growth in a Stable Population," Population Studies, 11, 92 — 94 (1957).

4.   Scarborough, J. B., Numerical Mathematical Analysis, 2nd ed., Johns Hopkins Press, Baltimore, 1950, 4th ed., 1958, p. 206.

5.   Ralston, A., A First Course in Numerical Analysis, McGraw-Hill Book Co., New York, 1965, p. 320.

6.   Hildebrand, F. B., Introduction to Numerical Analysis, McGraw-Hill Book Co., New York, 1956, p. 458.

7.   Ralston, p. 364.

8.   Keyfitz, N., "Reconciliation of Population Models: Matrix, Integral Equation, and Partial Fraction," Journal of the Royal Statistical Society, 30, 61 — 83 (1967).

9.   Keyfitz, N., "Finite Approximations in Demography," Population Studies, 19, 281 — 294 (1966).

# SOME COMPUTER APPLICATIONS TO POPULATION PROJECTIONS AND DEMOGRAPHIC ANALYSIS

James W. Brackett

U.S. Bureau of the Census

Many people think of computers as oversized desk calculators capable of performing only routine work of a highly repetitive nature. They tend to think of computer programs as a series of instructions for carrying out simple operations, not unlike the directions prepared for a clerical staff. Computers, however, might more properly be thought of as devices designed to perform operations in logic. Whether these operations instruct computers to carry out routine computations, or to perform a series of complex tests leading ultimately to a particular selection from among many possible alternatives, depends upon the skill and ingenuity of the persons using them.

In their paper "Simulation of Individual and Group Behavior, " Clarkson and Simon describe computers as devices capable of employing various operations for manipulating symbols. [1] Computers can read symbols (for example, sense patterns of holes on punched cards); write symbols (for example, create magnetic patterns on coated tape); and erase symbols (change such patterns). They can store symbols (retain patterns in magnetic cores or other kinds of internal memories); copy symbols (write patterns identical with patterns presented); and compare symbols (determine whether two patterns are identical or different). Finally, and most important, they can behave differently, depending on whether a pair of patterns turns out on comparison to be identical or different. By virtue of this last capacity, they can follow strategies — make decisions that are conditional upon any kind of symbolic information.

To quote Clarkson and Simon:

The symbols, or patterns, that computers can read, write, compare, and process can be interpreted as numbers, as words, as English sentences, or even as geometric diagrams. How they are interpreted depends on the programs that process them. Historically, computers were specifically designed to process symbols as numbers — to perform arithmetical operations on them. The computer "hardware" of standard computers in use today does not incorporate this limitation. If computers are used mainly to do rapid arithmetic, that is because people want to use them in this way and not because this is the only way they can be used. [2]

To date, applications of electronic computers to demography have been limited chiefly to what Clarkson and Simon call "rapid arithmetic." They have been used to process schedules, to prepare population projections, and to do certain other essentially clerical operations on demographic data. The experience we have gained over the past 6 years, working mainly with programs to prepare population estimates and projections and more recently with a program to construct population pyramids, leaves little doubt that computers can assume a much more sophisticated role in demography. In this paper I should like to describe some of the things computer programs developed by the Foreign Demographic Analysis Division of the Bureau of the Census have been designed to do, and to present some thoughts on the further development of computer applications to demography, particularly the development of programs capable of doing more than "rapid arithmetic."

Our first computer program was designed to carry out the extensive computations required to prepare detailed population estimates and projections by age and sex. This program was the logical first step, from our standpoint, because the basic procedure to be programmed had already been worked out for our statistical clerks. By converting this operation to the computer we were able not only to relieve our clerical staff of the time-consuming task of preparing population projections but also to relieve the professional staff of the responsibility of supervising the clerical operation.

Once the basic procedures were operational, we began expanding the program to make it more versatile. We have added new projection techniques, which offer virtually every means of preparing population projections by the cohort-survival method, with the possible exception of the cohort technique for projecting fertility. The program does, however, offer the option of using a different set of age-specific fertility rates for each year in the projection period, and the Population Division of the Bureau of the Census has written a FORTRAN program for the IBM 1401, designed to convert cohort fertility rates to period rates and to put the results on punched cards in the format required by the projections program.

The program was also expanded to permit data input in a wider variety of forms. For example, the base population distribution may be by single years of age, by 5-year age groups, or by a combination of the two. When the program encounters 5-year age groups, it uses Sprague's osculatory interpretation factors to obtain values for single years of age. It counts the number of 5-year groups and uses Sprague's "midpanel" multipliers on the maximum number of groups. A further example is that of life-table functions, which may be in the form of values of $_1L_x$, $_5d_x$, $_Q_x$, or survival ratios.

Perhaps the most significant additions to the program, however, were devices to test the data and results for "reasonableness." These tests can detect such things as questionable or unacceptable survival ratios, control totals for deaths that imply unreasonable levels of mortality, and certain inconsistencies between the types of data supplied and the projection techniques selected. The tests may lead to any of three results: The data or results being tested may be deemed acceptable, in which case the program proceeds with the run. They may be found unacceptable, in which case the program writes a warning on the output tape, then terminates the run. Finally, the data may be found questionable but not totally out of bounds, in which case the program writes a warning on the output tape but continues with the run.  In the last case the person using the program must decide whether his final results are acceptable.  For example, each survival ratio is tested to determine whether that ratio exceeds the hypothetical "maximum" survival ratio for the age-sex group that has been built into the program.  If the ratio does not exceed this hypothetical maximum, it will be accepted.  If one or more (but not all) of the ratios are higher than the hypothetical maxima for the respective age groups, the program will write a warning on the output tape indicating (1) that one or more of the survival ratios exceed their maxima; (2) the year in the projection period to which the ratios apply; and (3) the age-sex groups to which the questionable survival ratios relate.  The program next performs one additional test before deciding whether to continue:  it checks each of the ratios to determine whether any of them exceeds unity.  If none do, the program will proceed with the projection.  If, however, any ratio does exceed unity, the program will state on the output tape that this is so and then will terminate the run.  Since a survival ratio greater than unity implies resurrection from the dead, even one such ratio is clearly unacceptable.

The program performs one additional test, which will result in the rejection of the entire series of survival ratios if all or a substantial proportion exceed the hypothetical maxima.  If, on comparison, the number of deaths implied by the survival  ratios the program is expected to use is less than the number implied by the hypothetical maximum ratios, the program will reject the entire set.

Thus the program will reject a set of survival ratios if the set as a whole is unreasonable (for example, if it implies too few deaths), or if any one of the ratios is completely illogical (for example, if it implies negative deaths).  It will not, however, reject the entire set out of hand simply because one or two ratios fall into the "questionable" category.

Because conditions may vary from one run to another, the program permits special instructions altering the outcome for certain tests to be included with the input.  For example, the program may be instructed to reject a set of survival ratios if any ratio in the set exceeds the hypothetical maximum.  Moreover, although the program has a built-in set of "maximum" ratios, alternative sets may be provided in the input, and the sets may be changed at any point in the projection period.

I might add one other point before leaving the discussion of the tests.  Over the years during which these tests have been evolved, we have tended to build into the program more and more of the logic required to judge the acceptability of the questionable cases, to the end that the program rejects virtually all the runs that should be rejected and completes only those runs that have a high probability of being accepted by the user.  Since runs rejected by the program are terminated after only a few minutes of computer time, while those that will ultimately be rejected by the user must go to completion, we have realized significant savings by permitting more of the decisions to be made by the computer.

The output from the program consists of (1) estimates and projections of the population, by single years of age and sex, for each calendar year in the projection period; (2) 5-year and summary age groups, by sex; (3) estimates and projections of the total population, by sex, for the beginning of each projection year and for midyear; (4) estimates and projections of the components of population change and vital rates, by sex; (5) life expectancies for each sex; and (6) maternal and paternal gross reproduction rates. In addition, the program lists the input at the beginning of the output tape, thus providing a permanent record of the data used and the techniques selected.

The program regulates the table format for most of the output, setting the column widths for tables showing population by age, on the basis of the number of digits to be shown. Thus, spacing <u>between</u> the numbers in the various columns is the same for all countries, regardless of the size of their populations. Because the program offers the option of preparing four series of projections for persons born up to a maximum of 25 years in the future, the stub on the age tables must provide for either one or four series for each age up to 24 years. In order to minimize the problem of preparing stubs, we decided that if any single year of age within a standard 5-year group had four series, the stub for all the single ages within that group would provide for four series, even though some of them had entries on only one of the four lines. This decision limited the number of possible stubs to 6 — that is, a stub with no provision for four series up to one in which provisions for four series are made for all age groups up to 24 years. All of the possible stubs have been assembled on a special stub tape, and the program selects the specific stub for any given run from this tape. Deciding which is the appropriate stub is done entirely by the program, on the basis of self-generated parameters.

The column heads for the age table and the stubs for the tables showing annual series, which consist of the calendar years to which the respective data refer, are generated by the program on the basis of an input card that delimits the projection period. Finally, the program will, in certain circumstances, supply headnotes for the various tables. These headnotes are, to a limited degree, constructed by the program on the basis of self-generated parameters or of input parameters.

At the present time the titles and source notes for the tables are supplied as part of the input. Although the source notes may contain anything one wishes, our practice has been to give the name of the unit responsible for the projection; the month and year in which the projections were prepared; and a brief description of the underlying assumptions regarding fertility, mortality, and migration. Most of the information necessary to construct such a source note is, of course, available in the input, and we have been experimenting with having the computer compose it. This particular approach appears to hold considerable promise.

One other program that illustrates the versatility of the computer is designed to construct population pyramids for printing on the high-speed printer. Some examples of the output from this program are shown in Figure 1. The print symbol selected for the pyramids shown is the letter I. The program, however, permits the user to select any character available on the high-speed printer. It also provides the options of constructing pyramids based on percentages as well as absolute numbers and for either single years or 5-year age groups. It can also construct, on a common scale, pyramids for several countries or pyramids for different dates for the same country. When this program is used to generate a number of pyramids during a single computer run, the cost per pyramid is only a few cents.

The programs just described were written in the USE language for the UNIVAC 1105. USE is a symbolic machine language compilable only on that computer. Although the choice of this particular language was made because during the late 1950's, when the development of these programs began, the Census facility did not offer any other, the FORTRAN compilers available at that time were bound by restrictions that probably would have prevented their use for so complex a program. For example, one of the earlier barriers to the use of FORTRAN for complex programs was that it did not permit transfer of address control from one program to another. Thus, very long programs that exceeded the capacity of the computer could not be segmented — that is, broken up into two or more technically separate programs designed to run serially and to carry over certain data from one segment to the next. Our projections program, for example, consists of six parts. A more advanced FORTRAN and several other shortcut languages have, however, been made available at the Census facility for the recently acquired UNIVAC 1107, and it is possible that one or more of these languages can be used for future programs, perhaps in combination with symbolic machine coding. Our limited experience with the new FORTRAN suggests that it will be most effective for arithmetical operations. The output format, however, apparently does not offer the flexibility of standard machine language table-edit subroutines. For example, the program-controlled variations in the table format described earlier appear to be, at best, difficult to obtain with FORTRAN.

Our plans for the immediate future call for the development for the UNIVAC 1107 of a program that will be able to process output from the 1105 population projections program. This new program, as it is initially conceived, will have two functions: (1) to produce summary and comparative data for two or more countries; and (2) to provide greater flexibility in the tabular presentation of the output from the projections program. It will, for example, be able to construct consolidated tables for groups of countries (for example, Eastern Europe or South America), or to compare data for two or more countries (for example, the United States and the Soviet Union). It will also be able to prepare, for individual countries as well as for groups of countries, tables and charts featuring functional age groups. For example, it might prepare a table showing the projected numbers of children of primary-school age over the next 20 years and a line or bar graph illustrating the projected changes in the size of the group. (The Bureau of the Census has recently acquired a line plotter, which should prove very useful for computer-generated graphics.) The definition of what constitutes the primary-school ages for a given country may be either built into the program or supplied as a part of the input. Ultimately, we hope the program will be able to use the population data to generate "end-product" measures. For example, it might convert the projected numbers of school children into classroom and teacher requirements, thus providing information required for school-building and teacher-training programs. It might also draw comparisons between projected requirements and planned accomplishments, thus providing the essentials for judging the adequacy of the plan.

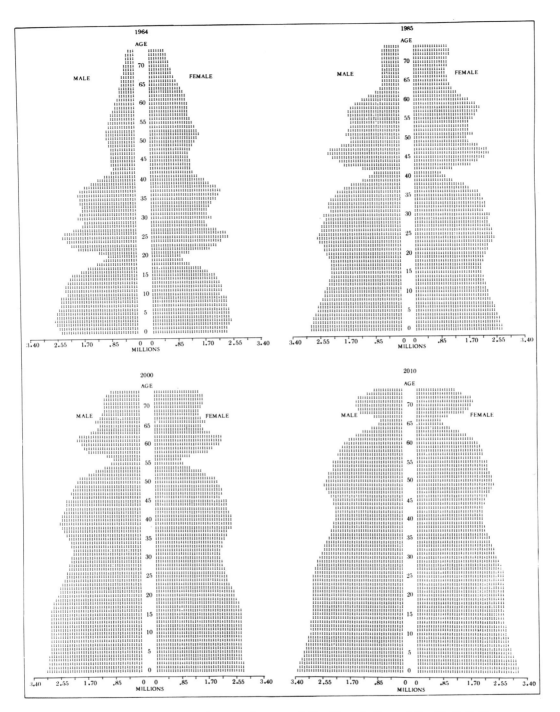

Figure 1. — Hypothetical Distribution of the Population of the U. S. S. R.,
by age and sex: 1964, 1985, 2000, and 2010.

99

We hope that this program will serve as a nucleus for the ultimate development of a truly analytical program.  As I envision it, an analytical program would be designed to examine the demographic and related data available for a particular country — or perhaps some segment of these data — for "reasonableness" and internal consistency.  Faulty segments in the data would be corrected or rejected; then the program would proceed to an estimating phase, in which missing segments were filled in and existing series projected into the future.  Next the program would analyze the data to determine, according to a given set of rules, their demographic, economic, social, or other implications.  It would then set up a series of tables and charts designed to present the findings of the analysis.  Although the output would be constructed around a basic theme, in accordance with the particular goals of the analysis, the program would vary the format and add or delete tables and charts to fit the specific conditions for each country.  It might also provide statements to point out the relevant aspects of the data presented in the tables and charts and might perhaps present additional materials that did not warrant tables.  For example, migration is a major factor for such countries as the Federal Republic of Germany and Australia, but the number of migrants entering or leaving Czechoslovakia has not been significant since the late 1940's.  Thus, the program might produce tables or charts relating to migration for Germany and Australia but none for Czechoslovakia unless the period prior to 1950 was to be covered.

Similarly, if the data for a given country point to wide fluctuations in, say, the working-age population, the program might produce tables and charts emphasizing this fact.  This does not mean that the program would ignore the working-age populations of other countries.  The difference would be in the type and number of tables and charts produced.  Since the number of persons of working age is significant for most countries, regardless of the rate of change in the group, tables showing absolute numbers of persons and perhaps annual increments would probably be produced for all countries.  For countries experiencing unusual changes in the size of the group, however, the program might produce special charts and tables designed to emphasize that change.  It might also write statements giving the highlights of the changes in the series.

The program might also incorporate procedures permitting the user to determine what course of action would be required to produce a given result.  For example, we might wish to know what demographic histories could have produced a given population distribution, or perhaps whether any reasonable history could have produced it.  Such devices would, of course, be very useful in the evaluation of census results and might be used to indicate where adjustments in these results should be made.  Countries whose official policy is to bring the rate of population growth into line with economic development might use these devices to determine the proper course of action consistent with a given development plan.  Suppose, for example, that a government wished to reduce unemployment by 50 per cent within 25 years and that the economic plan provided for a given increase in employment during that period.  The program might then be used to determine what birth rate would be consistent with this goal, and, if the expected birth rate would produce too large an increase in the future working-age population, the program might also indicate what course of action would be likely to bring the birth rate into line.  It might, for example, indicate that a certain group of women should be encouraged to limit the size of their families, estimate the number of these women who must be reached, and perhaps point out the geographic areas with the largest concentrations of such women.

The output from such a program might serve as the nucleus for a written report, the tables and charts being incorporated more or less intact, or the output itself might constitute a "report" of sorts to be used by, say, economists charged with the responsibility of evaluating or perhaps evolving a development plan for a given country. Since the computer can be programmed to tailor the output to the prospective audience, the users need not be specialists in either computers or demography. Such an output would not preclude the derivation of conventional demographic measures nor the use of advanced mathematics in the analysis. The program would serve as the "interpreter," presenting the results of its analysis in nontechnical terms. An auxiliary output consisting of the more technical aspects of the analysis might, however, be provided as a sort of appendix.

The advantages of an analytical program of this type are many. First, the data for a series of countries could be analyzed on a much more consistent basis than that attainable by conventional methods, even when the same demographer performs the analysis for all the countries in the series. Second, the quality of the analysis could be higher than that offered by conventional means because the collective experience of several demographers could be built into the program and because greater attention could be given to each phase of the analytical process than would be feasible for the individual-country approach. Third, the time and cost required to complete the analysis would be markedly reduced. Fourth, the present critically short supply of competently trained demographers could be used more efficiently. Many could turn their attentions to the more creative aspects of demography, and perhaps some effort could be devoted to improving the writing in demographic reports. The long period of time required to complete demographic reports, the scarcity of competent demographers, and the tendency for demographic reports to be dull have been among the main barriers to a fuller utilization of demography in the formulation of policy decisions in both government and business.

Although the development of computer applications to demography for other than rapid arithmetic will undoubtedly take many forms, highly complex, integrated programs, incorporating a wide range of demographic techniques and capable of transforming basic demographic data into a form meaningful to users in other disciplines, appear to me to be one of the more promising. Since a program of this sort was first proposed, about 2 years ago, many arguments have been advanced against it. The most frequent ones stem from the old concept of computers being merely big desk calculators. If, as Clarkson and Simon suggest, we think of computers as devices capable of manipulating symbols and if, in turn, we accept demography as a science based on certain hypotheses, theories, and laws, then clearly, to the extent that these can be expressed symbolically, they can be committed to computer programs. The question, then, is not whether analytical programs are feasible, but whether there is a need for them, and how the cost of development can be met. The growing acceptance of population as a proper consideration in the formulation of public policy and the needs of the policy-makers for reliable information on a relatively short-term basis leave little doubt in my mind that analytical programs are needed.

The problems associated with developing analytical programs should not be minimized, for they are indeed complex; but neither should their complexity be exaggerated, for many problems of much greater complexity have been solved. Moreover, much of what I have outlined can be accomplished without solutions to some of the more complex problems. Computer programs capable of performing demographic analysis will be developed; how soon depends upon the ingenuity and dedication of the demographer-programmers and upon the resources placed at their disposal.

### References

1.   Clarkson, Geoffrey P. E. , and Herbert A. Simon, "Simulation of Individual and Group Behavior, " Journal of the American Economic Association, 50, 920 — 932 (Dec. 1960).

2.   Clarkson and Simon, p. 925.

## DISCUSSION

Paul Demeny
Princeton University

The topic of the papers and discussions that we heard yesterday dealt with problems of new computer techniques, in particular with problems of communicating with computers. It seems to me that with the two papers presented by Professor Keyfitz and Mr. Brackett this focus has now shifted to the question of applying already existing computer technology and programming techniques to the solution of substantive problems in demography. Thus I am somewhat at a loss in trying to determine the subject to which I should be addressing myself. Listening to the latter two very interesting papers, I see that all the questions that occur to me concern issues of demographic analysis rather than problems of computation. The effort involved in programming problems of the sort outlined by Professor Keyfitz and Mr. Brackett is certainly considerable, and complications of a computational nature are numerous. Yet the underlying principles of their solution are already well established and should offer no basis for disagreement. The crucial question is not how to calculate but, instead, what are we calculating? I am afraid the discussion of the latter question would lead us to problems of demographic analysis rather remote from the subject of this conference.

I will, nevertheless, voice some thoughts along this line, taking the risk that they will merely reveal me as a somewhat old-fashioned parochial demographer. Let me point out first that while the demographic applications of computer technology described or suggested in the papers under discussion are very important, they are essentially what Mr. Brackett calls "rapid arithmetic." This is not a deprecatory statement: rapidity in one's calculation provides a great deal of convenience. But in the instances given, this rapidity does not seem to create a qualitative difference; the problems could have been attacked by somebody having access to a desk calculator only, or even by a diligent person using pencil and paper. When I read the demographic literature of the 1930's or 1940's, I do not notice any particular shortage of population projections, or calculations of intrinsic rates, or life tables, not to mention standard presentations of population data in terms of rates, distributions, and other statistics preliminary to an evaluation of such data. The demographers of those days had no access to electronic computation, yet they turned out their projections proficiently. If the success of these in coming true was less than spectacular, it was not the fault of their slow arithmetic, but rather the fault of analysis, resulting from weaknesses of the underlying theory. I think it is still true that when we are faced with the analysis of a body of census data, or a mass of vital statistics on the conventional lines (a situation to which both papers have addressed themselves), computational matters represent but a minor headache. If one has access to a computer, one would naturally have those rates, distributions, and other calculations performed by the machine as a matter of routine. It is also quite likely, however, that one will end up doing more computation than would otherwise be the case, particularly when one deals with a large number of countries. Projections, for example, might be prepared for a long time period, even if one is only interested in the next 30 years, and the truism of what a population structure will be like under specified conditions may be spelled out on the basis of many different assumptions as to the future time paths of fertility and mortality. But such calculations, whatever the mechanics used to obtain them, are merely preliminary to analysis and in themselves are of secondary interest.

Mr. Brackett's paper, besides presenting interesting examples of computer applications for various demographic computations, discusses the intriguing possibility of programming the machine to perform the actual analysis that follows the raw calculations. Undoubtedly the analysis of a body of data, the demographer's work par excellence, can be decomposed to a series of logical steps, each having an outcome that is, or should be, uniquely determined by certain features of the data that are being analyzed; hence they can be programmed on a computer. Contemplating already existing technology only, the result of such a program might be the selective printing out of English sentences, perhaps with some modifications, that were prestored in the machine, summarizing the results of the analysis. I have some qualms about this prospect, not because I question its feasibility but because I question its economics. The economic issue boils down to the simple and rather unimaginative proposition that there are too few countries or provinces (or whatever unit we choose sufficiently large that demand for its demographic make-up may be still forthcoming) to make such an effort worthwhile. This is not a reflection on the merit of the proposal but rather on the limited scope of demography, at least as far as applications of the nature discussed by the two papers are concerned.

The point becomes clearer if I illustrate analogous attempts in another field. Promising steps have been taken to write programs that would, after analyzing medical reports on sets of symptoms observed in patients, come out with the proper diagnosis. Clearly, the essence of the two problems is the same: Mr. Brackett intends to feed in data displaying symptoms of various statistical "sicknesses," hoping to produce the appropriate diagnosis. Such a diagnosis may consist simply of an estimate of the actual level of the birth rate or death rate of a country as opposed to the erroneous reported rates. Now, though I know little about medicine, it seems to me that there is obvious justification for putting a great deal of energy and effort into developing and refining a program doing medical diagnosis. Since, unfortunately, sick people are in apparently inexhaustible supply, there would be a chance to apply certain sequences of logical steps built into that program hundreds of thousands of times. In demography not only is there a relative scarcity of countries, provinces, censuses, and surveys, but my experience in analyzing population data tells me that there are also as many diagnoses as sick bodies of demographic information. To build the logical structure and evaluation of each such case into a huge computer program, then, seems a rather roundabout operation; after a few initial steps the analysis in each case would branch out into a sequence never destined to be used more than once, or perhaps a few times. Other reasons, too, make me sceptical as to the field of applicability of truly analytical programs in demography. For example, in the past 2 years I have been working with a group analyzing demographic data on Subsaharan Africa. Of course our first step was to gather all the pertinent information. The material resulting from our search was extensive enough so that the use of the computer was economical for doing rapid arithmetic and for turning out the various cross tabulations, rates, distributions, and correlations that demographers use. On the basis of inspecting these statistics we gradually developed the techniques and methods to adjust the raw information. Indeed it would have been impossible to program these methods at the outset; their very existence was largely a by-product of our analysis itself. Also, it is unlikely that the logic of our analysis, once developed and built into a computer program, would be extensively applicable to other populations or even to future African data. For instance, recently in working with Sudanese data, I found that one peculiarity of the statistical information provided by this country is that the main outlines of the age distribution are provided in qualitative terms, such as "under puberty" or "past menopause." Obviously this feature of the data determines the character of the whole analysis. One or two other countries, perhaps, provide information of a similar type, but naturally even these differ sharply in other respects. No country may collect such data in the future. We would have gained little, therefore, had we programmed the procedure applied in analyzing these data for a computer, except the pedagogical advantage of insuring a logic free from ambiguities, which we would strive to achieve anyhow. I believe that most data have their own idiosyncrasies, even though to a less spectacular extent than those just mentioned. If so, the prospects of turning over the preparation of even "skeleton" population reports to machines are limited indeed.

I find myself, however, in full agreement with Mr. Brackett's insistence that computer applications in demography should grow beyond the use of "rapid arithmetic" toward utilizing the logical capabilities of the machine. By far the most important way of doing so is constructing stochastic "micro" models of demographic behavior and applying these to simulate various kinds of population processes. A number of remarkable efforts have been made in this direction; I should especially mention the work of Dr. Sheps and her collaborators. The application of Monte Carlo techniques, which would indeed be unfeasible without the help of computers, opens up truly spectacular analytical possibilities in demography. Clearly, the utilization of "rapid logic" in simulation is very different from the kind advocated by Mr. Brackett.

Let me add finally that my brief comments on computer applications in population analysis were as much a criticism of my own work as that of the papers I have discussed. I have been a steady co-practitioner of the art of rapid arithmetic since I first wrote stable-population and projection programs some 5 years ago. It is sometimes said that there is some danger that fascination with the machine tends to make computation a master instead of a more efficient servant. But as the use of computers becomes common, this danger will recede. How calculations are made will be gradually relegated to a brief footnote, if that, and our attention as demographers will be again focused on what. By that time our abilities to be meaningful in the latter will have benefited greatly from electronic computation.

## FREE DISCUSSION

Commenting on Professor Demeny's remarks on his paper, Mr. Brackett indicated that he did not mean to imply that all existing demographic problems can be handled by building them into computer programs. Indeed, each population has its own problems, which must be handled on an individual basis. Many specific demographic techniques can, however, be built into analytical programs for computers, and these same techniques can then be employed on other populations. In fact, a library of programmed techniques can be built up in this manner, permitting subsets to be put together when needed for a particular population study. While Mr. Brackett saw a need for this, Professor Demeny questioned whether specific techniques once programmed and used would ever be reused. Mr. Brackett thought they could and would.

As the group pursued the above thoughts, it was pointed out that basic demographic problems are not essentially computational in nature. While this is fundamentally true, demographic data must still be used and so should be prepared and published quickly. Obviously, the computer is admirably suited to this. It seemed to be the consensus that there must be a balance between demographic programs that merely do calculations and hence produce needed data rapidly and economically, and programs that experiment with theory via models and simulations and thereby aid in resolving demographic problems.

Someone remarked that a better title for this session would be "Computer Applications of Demographic Models," rather than "Demographic Applications of Computer Models." Both papers deal with the use of computers as an embodiment of demographic theory (e.g., Professor Keyfitz's paper deals with the mathematical simulation of a population carried through time and based on current demographic theory). But computers can also be used to develop theory by the development of computer programs that help to formulate which variables belong in demographic equations. The computer is suited for this task because the necessary large-scale simulations and data manipulations are possible only on computers.

A crucial point raised during the open discussion dealt with the limitation of intrinsic rates and reasons why this will lead to greater use of computers in demography. While the intrinsic rate theoretically represents a generation or cohort and should apply to that group as it passes through life, demographers choose period rates from a single year. These cannot possibly represent the experience of a real cohort because of the different life histories of the various cohorts existing at a given time period. In developing realistic measures of a cohort, Mr. Murphy has taken parity into account. Although this is an advance, J. Schachter's work in national vital statistics shows that it still does not yield realistic rates. If demographers would add birth intervals to age and parity, they might then get realistic rates that can be applied to a real cohort. With this kind of matrix (age, parity, and interval) a desk calculator is inadequate, and a computer is necessary.

Professor Keyfitz felt that the discussion cited in the preceding paragraph came closer to the subject of the session than did either of the two speakers. The matrix and intrinsic rates mentioned in his paper can be adapted to the cohort approach. The question then becomes one of interpretation of the elements of the matrix as coming from different ages and time periods. The interpretation of the matrix to make it represent a cohort is a vital advance. Still more relevant, however, is interpreting the matrix to take into account parity (in the cohort sense) as well, and then using it to generate period rates. If we subsequently add the essential stochastic element, we create a computational task that cannot be conceived with a desk calculator; a computer is absolutely necessary.

Because of its appropriateness to the discussion, Dr. Sheps outlined her work to the audience. By starting with a cohort, she is trying to generate cohort rates specific by age and parity. She puts each individual woman of the cohort stochastically through a number of contingencies, year by year. First, she ascertains how long each woman is likely to live; when she is likely to marry for the first time; and when she is going to become sterile. Once a woman is married and fertile, the program ascertains, by the same kind of stochastic process, whether or not she is a family planner. Then her history through childbearing is determined from her age, parity, and the other contingencies that occur. Dr. Sheps expects to emerge with duration- and age-specific birth rates, which might then be incorporated into a population model that does not yet exist. Her ultimate hope is to combine a population approach with the present cohort one.

The concluding comments at this session dealt with the fact that Mr. Brackett's use of computers to analyze data is identical to the approach taken by H. Selvin in a seminar on the analysis of survey research data. Two results emerged from Selvin's work: (1) Some analytical operations could be successfully computer programmed, while others could not; (2) Confronted with the use of computers, the research group was forced to consciously think through how they were analyzing the data. This proved very valuable in itself.

IV.    MATHEMATICAL DESIGN OF LARGE—SCALE SOCIAL SYSTEMS

# MATHEMATICAL DESIGN OF MARKETING SYSTEMS

**J. D. Herniter**

**Arthur D. Little, Inc.**

## Introduction

Claude Shannon once said that the perfect predictor is a black box into which we feed questions and out of which come correct answers. Since we have no such black box at present, we must construct models of phenomena interesting to us if we are to answer questions concerning these phenomena. Although the models should be judged solely on their ability to predict observable effects, and not on their resemblance to the real world, we generally find it necessary to describe the phenomena as realistically as possible in order to obtain models that predict well.

Here we shall discuss models of market behavior — specifically, market models for frequently purchased, low-priced consumer items, such as soap powder or tooth paste. The approach used is to describe mathematically the behavior of the individual consumer. The market's behavior is then the composite behavior of the individual consumers. In the formulation of the model we use the mathematics of the semi-Markov process.

Although the models we shall discuss were designed to describe the behavior of the market, the mathematics and methodology used are appropriate for many other social systems as well.

## Background

The early work on mathematical market models was done 5 to 10 years ago. The data used were primarily market shares or sales reported by brand or by month. By following market-share data in time, certain types of patterns could be observed. One pattern of considerable interest was that resulting from an intensive advertising campaign. It was observed that if the advertising expenditures for a brand were substantially increased for a period of time, sales increased to a new level. When the additional advertising was withdrawn, sales fell back to their original level. This behavior is shown in Figure 1. We note that the effects of neither the increase in advertising nor its withdrawal are immediate, but instead follow an exponential curve. It was found that this behavior could be duplicated by a Markov-process model.

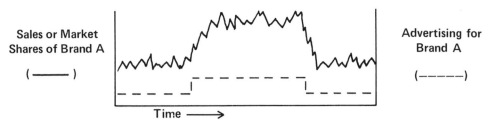

| Sales or Market Shares of Brand A | | Advertising for Brand A |
| :--- | :---: | :--- |
| ( ——— ) | | (—————) |

Figure 1.   Effect of advertising on sales

## Markov Models

The simple Markov model is a discrete time model.   Time is segmented into equal-length periods, and states of the system are defined.   The Markov process is the simplest process in which successive state occupancies are not independent events, but are governed by the transition probabilities that define the probability of entering a state, given the last state occupied.   In the simple Markov model of the market the brands are numbered $i = 1, 2, . . ., N$, and the state of the system is defined as the brand purchased during the time period.

To describe the effect of advertising on sales or market shares we define a system with two states:   Brand A and Other Brands.   A transition matrix such as that shown in Figure 2 is derived from the market-share data.

**Brand**

| From \ To | A | Other |
| :---: | :---: | :---: |
| **Brand** A | .90 | .10 |
| Other | .12 | .88 |

Figure 2.   Two-state transition matrix

This matrix is interpreted as follows:   If Brand A was purchased during one time period, the probability that Brand A is purchased during the following period is .90, and the probability that Other Brands is purchased is .10.   The transition from Other Brands to Brand A is .12 and from Other Brands to Other Brands .88.   The rows necessarily sum to 1, since by definition a customer must purchase some brand during the time period.

Brand A's market share at the end of the period is composed of (1) 90 per cent of the market share that it had at the end of the previous period, plus (2) 12 per cent of the market share of Other Brands.   For the transition matrix described, this leads to a stable market share for Brand A of .545.   When an advertising campaign is instituted, the elements of this transition matrix change, and a new matrix is obtained. An example of this modified matrix is shown in Figure 3.

**Brand**

|  | To / From | A | Other |
|---|---|---|---|
| **Brand** | A | .92 | .08 |
|  | Other | .14 | .86 |

Figure 3.  Modified transition matrix

The probability of going from Brand A to Brand A is increased to .92, and the probability of going from Other Brands to Other Brands is decreased to .86. This new transition matrix leads to a market share for Brand A of .636. The approach to this new market share is geometric. The matrix will be appropriate so long as the higher level of advertising expenditure is maintained. If after several time periods the advertising expenditures are reduced to their original level, the initial transition matrix is once again appropriate. A geometric decay to Brand A's original market share will result from the reduction of the advertising expenditures.

Since this model appears to yield the type of behavior actually observed, it has been used extensively with varying degrees of modification. Although the model is applicable only to market-share data, we discussed it in terms of customers' purchasing the product and switching from brand to brand. A natural follow-up was to test the model on data that explicitly show individual consumer purchases.

**Panel Data**

The Consumer Purchase Panel is used to satisfy the need for detailed observations of consumer activity. The Chicago Tribune, from which we obtained our data, maintains such a panel, composed of a large group of consumers who have agreed to record every purchase they make in the course of their daily lives. The purchases are described by time, quantity, brand, source, and price. These data are reported weekly in a diary. Figure 4 illustrates the typical form of the purchase history for one consumer's soap-powder purchases.

We represent the purchase pattern by a diagram whose horizontal axis is divided into calendar time. A bar is erected on this axis whenever a purchase of soap powder is made. The height of the bar represents the size of box purchased. We shall assume there are three sizes of soap powder — regular, giant, and economy; the contents of these sizes are in the ratio of 1 to 2 to 4. If both a regular and an economy size are purchased at the same time, the regular bar of length 1 will be constructed upon the economy bar of length 4. The brand, price, and store of purchase are indicated in an appropriate code beside each box purchased.

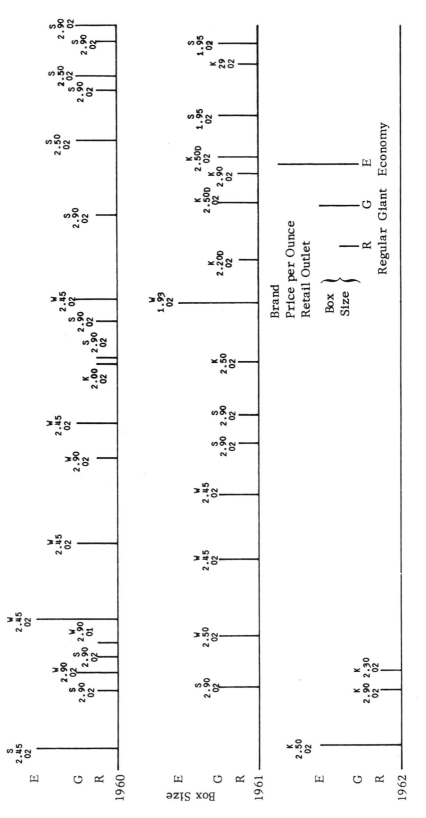

Figure 4. Consumer purchase pattern for soap powder

It is easy to read the customer's pattern from Figure 4. We see, for example, that on January 11, 1960, this customer purchased an economy-size box of Snowite (S) in a National Food Store (02), and paid the equivalent of 2.45¢ per ounce.

Several interesting observations may be made about this customer's behavior. First, the customer obviously does not purchase periodically; the time between purchases varies from 3 to 43 days. An indication of the random quality of this behavior is obtained from the histogram of the time between purchases, shown in Figure 5. The mean time between purchases is 22 days; the variance is 127 days squared.

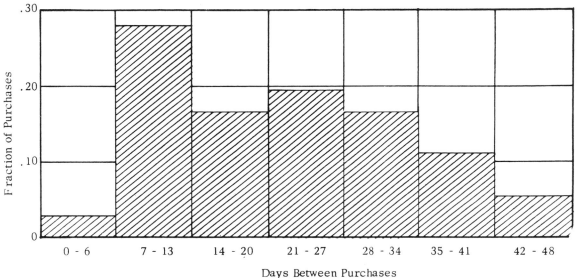

Figure 5. Histogram of days between purchases

There does not seem to be any obvious regularity of the purchase pattern for this customer in terms of the size of purchase; all three sizes are purchased in seemingly random order. In Figure 6, the histogram of the purchase size, we see that this customer purchases almost as much of the giant size as he does of the regular size; he purchases the economy size much less frequently.

We might expect a strong relationship between the size purchased and the interval between purchases. Such an interdependence of size of purchase and interpurchase time would appear in a joint histogram of these quantities, like that in Figure 7. The average number of days that followed the purchase of a given size before another purchase is indicated by an arrow. The average time to the next purchase is 15 days when the regular size is bought, 27 days when the giant size is bought, and 29 days when the economy size is bought. If soap powder is used at a uniform rate, then we would expect that the purchase of a large quantity would be followed by a rather long time until the next purchase. Such behavior is indicated when purchases of the regular size are compared with purchases of the giant size, but not when purchases of the economy size are examined.

The brand purchased by the consumer varies from purchase to purchase; it, too, appears to be a random variable. The transitions from one brand to another are

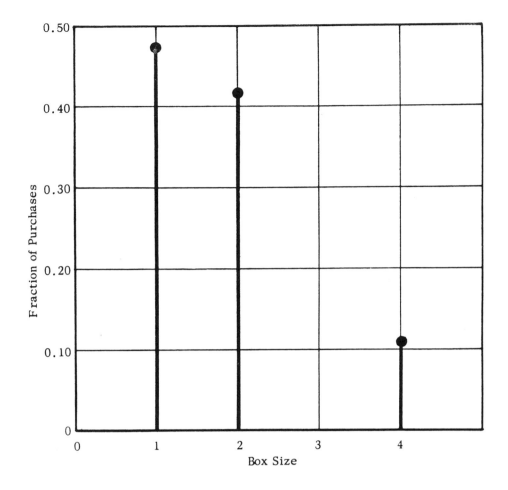

Figure 6.   Histogram of box size purchased

described by Figure 8.   Each entry in this table represents the number of times
that the purchase of the brand in the column followed the purchase of the brand in
the row.  We see that, although there is a tendency to repurchase a brand, there
is also considerable variation in the brand purchased.

To explain the panel data, researchers initially used the simple first-order Markov
model described previously.  The states were defined as the brand purchased during the previous period, and transition matrices were constructed.  The simple
statement that transition matrices were constructed is not very realistic; problems
arose almost immediately.  After the time period had been defined as either one
month or a quarter, it was found that a customer occasionally did not purchase during a month and that occasionally he made multiple purchases during a month.
The problem of no purchases was "solved" simply by adding a new state — "no-
purchase."  Customers were considered to go from a state defined by a brand to a
no-purchase state, from a no-purchase state to a brand, and from a no-purchase
state to a no-purchase state.  This solution, however, aided the researchers very
little when it came to the problem of multiple purchases during a time period.

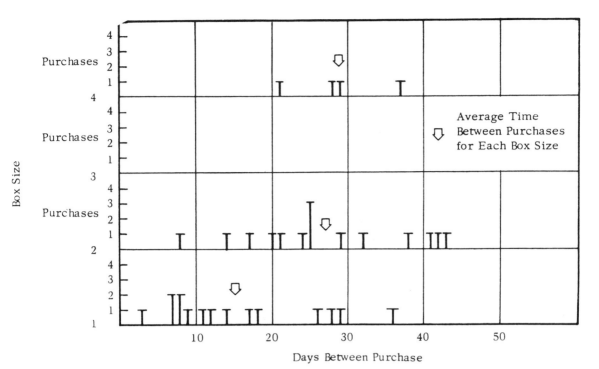

Figure 7.  Joint histogram of the box size per
purchase and days between purchase

| To<br>From | Washrite | Snowite | Kleenbrite | Total |
|---|---|---|---|---|
| Washrite | 6 | 3 | 2 | 11 |
| Snowite | 4 | 9 | 3 | 16 |
| Kleenbrite | 1 | 3 | 5 | 9 |
| Total | 11 | 15 | 10 | |

Figure 8.  Transition frequencies
January 1960 — February 1962

One proposed solution was to decrease the length of the time period, say from a
month to a week.  This would obviously decrease multiple purchases, but it would
vastly increase the number of no-purchases and would create the additional problem of very small sample sizes.  Other solutions were proposed; indeed, there
were as many methods of attacking the problem as there were investigators.

The cause of the problem and its solution are readily apparent from the consumer purchase pattern. The simple Markov model was for a discrete time system in which consumers were assumed to purchase periodically. It is obvious from Figure 4 that the consumer purchases are randomly distributed in time; there is no periodicity to the purchase pattern. The system with which we are dealing is continuous in time rather than discrete. The definition of state that presents itself is the brand last purchased, regardless of when the purchase was made. This state definition eliminates the problems of no purchases and of multiple purchases during a time period.

Because time is an integral component of the system, the mathematics of the discrete-time Markov process is inappropriate; rather, we must use the mathematics of the semi-Markov process.

## Semi-Markov Process

In the semi-Markov process we redefine the states as the brand last purchased by the customer. In addition, we must define not only the transition probabilities, $p_{ij}$, but the time between purchases, $\tau_{ij}$, as well. The $p_{ij}$'s are the same transition probabilities that govern the ordinary Markov process and must satisfy the relations

$$p_{ij} \geq 0, \sum_{j=1}^{N} p_{ij} = 1.$$

The $\tau_{ij}$'s are random variables that specify the time the system will spend in state $i$ before it makes a transition to stage $j$, given that it is going to make its next transition to state $j$. We call these $\tau_{ij}$'s the "holding times" of the process and define each $h_{ij}(.)$ to be the density function of $\tau_{ij}$. When we know $p_{ij}$ and $h_{ij}(.)$ for all pairs of states $i$, $j$, we have a complete description of the brand-to-brand purchase behavior described as a semi-Markov process.

When we model the actual set of consumer purchase histories with the semi-Markov model, the first problem we face is how to evaluate the transition probabilities $p_{ij}$ and the holding-time density function $h_{ij}(.)$. We can estimate $p_{ij}$ by observing the number of times the purchase of brand j followed the purchase of brand i in the data. If the $p_{ij}$'s are assumed to be the same for all customers, the purchase-frequency tables of all customers are superimposed on one another, and from this the transition probabilities are obtained.

We find $h_{ij}(.)$ by constructing a histogram for the time that separates the purchase of brand i and brand j every time a purchase of brand j follows a purchase of brand i. It may happen, as it did in the case of the soap powder, that times between purchases are independent of the brand last purchased. In this case the distribution of time between purchases could be described by the equation

$$h_{ij}(t) = h(t) = (2\lambda)^2 t e^{-2\lambda t}$$
$$1 \leq i, j \leq N, t \geq 0,$$

where the parameter $\lambda$ is the inverse of the average time between purchases.

Thus far we have been describing the behavior of an individual consumer.  Our goal, however, is to describe the over-all behavior of the market.  Since this is the composite behavior of many individual consumers, we must determine how the behaviors of individual consumers can be related to one another.  For the product we have paraphrased as soap powder we found that consumers could be considered to behave identically except for their purchase frequencies.  Consumer purchase frequencies were found to vary from no purchases to 70 purchases in 18 months.  A histogram of the fraction of customers who purchased n times during a 28-month period is shown in Figure 9.  From this histogram we can infer that the distribution of $\lambda$ can be represented by the equation

$$f\,(\lambda|\mu)\ = \alpha\delta(\lambda) + (1-\alpha)\mu e^{-\lambda\mu} \qquad\qquad \lambda \geq 0,$$

where

$$\delta(\lambda)\ =\ \begin{cases} 1 \text{ if } \lambda = 0 \\ 0 \text{ if } \lambda \neq 0 \end{cases}$$

and $\mu$ is a parameter of the population.

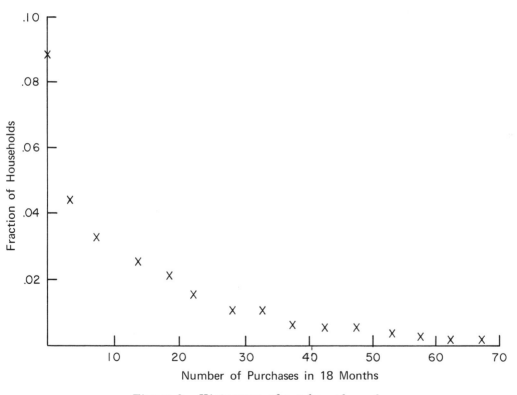

Figure 9.  Histogram of number of purchases

The coefficient of $\delta(\lambda)$, $\alpha$, represents that portion of the consumer population who are not in the market for this product.  The distribution of $\lambda$ is exponential for the $(1-\alpha)$ portion of the consumer population who are customers for this product.

The mathematical characterization of the average time between purchases for the entire population, together with the average-time-between-purchase distribution for the individual consumers, and the transition matrix allow us to describe the behavior of the market for this product.

The model we have described, though complex, is still sufficiently simple to obtain analytic results. We can determine analytically such quantities as market shares of purchases; fractions of the population purchasing each brand once, twice, three times, etc., during a time interval; first-passage times (the time between the purchase of brand i and the next purchase of brand j); and run lengths. These predicted statistics can be used to validate the model. The model gives us additional insight into the behavior of the market and allows us to determine more precisely how to analyze market data and extend the model.

If we expand the model to incorporate some additional features, we can no longer obtain analytic results. One such simple extension of the model would be incorporation of the fact that transition matrices vary from consumer to consumer and depend on the average time between purchases. At this stage it is possible, however, to use the computer to obtain numerical solutions. One technique about which I am sure you will hear more is the use of simulation to analyze and predict the behavior of large-scale social systems. It is a technique that allows us to analyze very complex but, we hope, realistic models. The simulation can, however, be no better than the model used.

# SUBSTANTIVE ISSUES IN MODELS OF LARGE-SCALE SOCIAL SYSTEMS

James M. Beshers

Massachusetts Institute of Technology

Suppose we regard a computer model of a large-scale social system, whether a "simulation" model or a "projection" model, as a statement of a social theory. How can we assure ourselves that the computer model represents a particular theory? Can we explicitly specify the translation of a theory from its conventional form to its form in the computer model? If the translation can be described with mathematics, then these questions can be answered. [1]

Let us consider methods for the explicit statement of social theory in mathematics. That there is a need for such methods would come as a surprise to physicists and perhaps to some economists. For them it is customary to regard mathematics as the appropriate form in which to state theory. But for the kinds of social theory with which I work, the issue is very much in doubt. This state of affairs arises in part because the substantive theory is stated in ordinary language or in a jargon that does not readily yield mathematical equivalents or even simple sentences that can be translated into propositions in set theory. In part, however, the situation stems from an apparent inappropriateness of the conventional mathematics of physics or economics for expressing these theories.

The purpose of this paper, then, is to suggest some ways in which a more effective mathematical statement of social theory might be brought about. These suggestions grow largely from my own experiences in making models of social mobility, human fertility, and migration.

The appropriate mathematical statement of social theory will have to be embedded in complex computer models. The nonexperimental character of social research requires the inclusion of a large number of variables in the theory, and it also requires a large amount of data. Complex computer programs will be involved in the deduction of implications from the theory and in the statistical analysis of data that are to be compared with the predictions from the theory. These programs will place constraints upon the type of mathematical formulation of social theory that is appropriate. But these constraints are not my main concern, which is the explicit statement of the social theories that the computer program seeks to represent or to test.

At present I believe that the mathematical statement must enable us to deduce the "future time path of the system, " and that this deduction must be in terms of probabilities. I am very dubious about the usefulness either of differential equations or regression for representing the substantive social theory with which I work. Differential equations can be employed in the deductions of the time path of the system, as in the case of semi-Markov processes; regression techniques can be the workhorse of statistical analysis; but neither effectively embodies the substance of these social theories.

Let me sketch out the methods that currently seem helpful. These methods are not by themselves adequate to define satisfactory models, but they do permit one to examine some of the substantive issues that arise.

In passing, let me note that prior to any mathematical work on a particular problem I spend a great deal of time, usually years, attempting to summarize and restate those theories and empirical generalizations that seem to have enough merit to be worth formalizing. It is so difficult to obtain any kind of mathematical representation that it hardly seems worth the effort for a bad theory.

When I get to the mathematics I proceed more or less in this fashion. First I try to establish definitions using the language of finite sets and relations. This is useful in getting a notation that is close to the language and form of the statement of the substantive theory. The next step is to employ many graphs, usually tree diagrams, in order to bring out more clearly the possibilities implicit in the relations that I am considering. Then I attempt to define vectors and matrices in such a way that I end up with a stochastic process.

This description of the mathematics is not very helpful, as it does not indicate the nature of the substantive problems that arise, or how one grapples with them. In order to do this I will have to introduce some highly simplified notation and illustrate with some simplified models.

Let us suppose that among the elements in our system are persons. Consider now the problem of social mobility, ignoring births and deaths. We shall attempt to represent this problem as a finite Markov chain. [2] In order to do this we shall have to define a distribution vector and a transition matrix. This task requires us to define states of the system and to define a time unit during which the transitions occur.

The simplest procedure for defining states of the system is this. First, one sets down the status symbols, such as occupation, and the categories of each status symbol, such as "manual" and "nonmanual, " that one wishes to include in one's model. Then one constructs a new set of categories that represents all of the possible combinations of categories that have already been defined. (This is the procedure used to define states in the Simulmatics voting model by Pool, Abelson, and McPhee. ) [3] We say that the set C of states of the system can be defined as the

Cartesian product of the sets of status symbols,

$$C = S_1 \times S_2 \times S_3 \ldots \ldots ,$$

where the status symbols are defined as $S_1$, $S_2$, and so on.  Let us suppose that n categories are defined in the set C.  Then we can arbitrarily designate the states as $C_1$, $C_2$, ..., $C_n$.

The distribution vector for any given time period t, say m(t), is then defined as a (1xn) vector with elements $m_1$, $m_2$, etc., that define the number of persons in $C_1$, $C_2$, and so on.  The transition matrix P will be an (nxn) matrix representing the states of the system at any two different time periods, say t and t+1.  If we define the time unit as a year, then our substantive definitions are complete. [4]

There are many convenient mathematical theorems for such a Markov chain that describe the future history of the system.  The basic equation used in deriving these results is

$$m(t + 1) \ = \ m(t) P.$$

Thus the basic equation is a matrix multiplication.

The Markov chain that we have defined is a vast improvement over many of the available verbal theories of social mobility.  It is, even in this simple form, rather useful in investigating certain empirical problems.  Yet it falls far short of expressing many of the more interesting theoretical notions about social mobility.

What substantive social theories have been ignored in the Markov chain?  Here is a partial list.  (1)  There is no explicit psychological theory in this model.  (2) There is no theory of the transmission of culture across generations.  (3) There is no way to let the probabilities change as part of a system response — no feedback mechanism.  (4)  There is no way to represent the influence of "supply" upon the system, neither the supply of persons determined demographically nor the supply of status symbols determined by a production process.  (5)  There is no way to represent the influence of discontinuous events, such as wars and depressions.

Let us see how some of these deficiencies might be remedied.  First, consider the states of the system.  In defining these we have overlooked an alternative.  Social mobility may be viewed as a process in which people move with reference to status symbols, or in which status symbols move with reference to people.  The difference between these two views can be brought out in two graphs.

One graph, which we shall call the micrograph, has persons for nodes, or points, and relations among the persons for the lines.  Of particular interest are those relations that define flows among persons, say of commodities, money, behavior patterns, or genetic characteristics (disease, information, and emotion are examples that occur in other problems).

The other graph, which we shall call the macrograph, has <u>sets</u> of persons for nodes and relations among the sets of persons for lines.  Among these relations are the flows of persons among the nodes.   The states of the Markov chain were defined for the macrograph alone.   Note that migration is also represented by such a macrograph, in which the nodes are areas.

Psychological theories are more effectively stated over a micrograph than over a macrograph.   In order to get psychological consequences into the mathematical model we should first consider the micrograph.

Interesting and very difficult problems emerge when we try to relate micrographs and macrographs in one theoretical system.   The simplest procedure is to derive the latter from the former by combining points of the micrograph.   Thus statements about specific individuals become statements about classes of individuals. But relations among individuals within the same node are no longer defined on the macrograph.   Frequently one wants to preserve information on two kinds of relationship — those within the household (as done by Orcutt et al. ), [5] and relationships within friendship or sociometric groups (as done by Coleman). [6]

In order to retain information defined on the micrographs, Orcutt's and Coleman's groups define states of the system over a set of micrographs.   They obtain definitions of the state over macrographs by summing over micrographs.   They also obtain parameters defined over macrographs by summing over the micrographs. In this way macrograph "constraints" can be computed, and these can, in principle, be introduced into the mathematical theory of behavior within the macrograph. In Orcutt et al. , these macrograph constraints are largely used as correction factors in a statistical operation.   But these constraints may also be used to define states of "markets," the supply aspect.   We shall return to this point later.

When the states of the micrograph can be ignored in the study of the system, then other ways of relating the micrograph and the macrograph can be used.   A classic method is to state a mathematical hypothesis over a micrograph and then deduce the mathematical expression that defines a distribution over a macrograph.   For example, the contagion models of epidemiology are derived by considering contacts defined over a micrograph and then employing an assumption of random contacts in order to deduce the state of the system, the proportions of persons in various health categories.

Another example of obtaining a macrograph by deduction can be found in the classical theory of economic use of utility.   In this instance an explicit psychological hypothesis is stated over a single node in the micrograph, an entrepreneur; consequences are derived for flows of money and commodities among nodes; and then further consequences are derived for states of the system defined by distributions of prices of commodities.   (Classical economists use the macrograph that I have defined above where they wish to deduce income distributions; otherwise, they tend to ignore it. )

Despite these examples, there is, to my knowledge, no very satisfactory solution at present to the problems posed by the micrograph and the macrograph.   The published computer simulation models do not contain sufficiently well-developed decision-theory models, or other psychological models of behavior.   Further, the published models leave much to be desired in the way that parameters computed over the macrograph are used to express constraints on behavior defined in reference to a micrograph.  The path to solution is to embed explicit psychological theory within the existing framework of computer simulation models.

Let us turn from substantive issues raised by the definition of states of the system to substantive issues raised by the choice of time units.  In effect we must commit ourselves to some statement about "causality" in the system.  In other words, we must commit ourselves to a description of the "memory" of the system.  For we must not only select time units that relate to our measurements, but we must also indicate the time lags that relate variables in the system.

In many models of social systems the generation must be used to represent the causality, or memory, of the system.  In Orcutt et al., the generation is needed in order to describe household formation.  But the generation is also the unit required to represent the transmission of cultural or of genetic characteristics.  We might argue on this basis that a maximum time lag of one generation would be used in the model, because the cultural and genetic influence of persons would extend only to their children.  Thus we would define a social system as a first-order Markov process over generations.  If we are dealing with a social system (perhaps China) in which the influence of grandparents upon grandchildren seems great, independent of the intervening parental linkage, then we would want to express this in our model — a second-order Markov process.

If we try to use the generation to express cultural or genetic transmission, then we will have to define the marriage relation among the persons in the system, ordinarily a nasty little problem.  Theories that explain the empirical distribution of marriages in a society are more likely to solve this problem than theories that explain that society's idealized kinship rules.

The generation also raises some nasty mathematical problems, since it is not of fixed length in years.  Suppose a particular model uses the generation and the year as time units.  How do we relate these two?

One approach is to carry out computations on the basis of the year as a time unit and to use a table of empirical distributions of age at marriage in years as an approximate generation.  A procedure of this type was used in Orcutt et al.  Another approach is that of semi-Markov processes in which the generation is a random variable with a specified distribution in years. [7]

Let us now turn our attention to substantive issues as they arise in the definition of the transition matrix P.  Since the transition matrix is defined over a set of states of the system and over a time unit, we have already implicitly been dealing with it.  The question we can now raise however, is:  Do we really want to assume that the same set of probabilities determines the history of the system for all time?

Much substantive theory is not represented by the constant, or stationary, transition matrix.  Many of the notions of equilibrium, or of adjustment, or of feedback, no matter how ambiguously expressed in language, are not equivalent to or represented by the stationary transition matrix.

How shall we represent the transition matrix as a variable in time? Let us define P(t) as the matrix at time t that defines the transition from t to t+1. A first-order nonstationary Markov process can be defined if the n-squared elements of the matrix P(t) are expressed in n-squared equations (ignoring row normalization) as functions of numbers that are calculated in the preceding time period t-1. Suppose we confine our attention to the elements of the distribution vector and the transition matrix in time period t-1. Then we can define a function G of n-squared equations corresponding to the n-squared equations in P(t) as follows:

$$P(t) = G(m(t-1), P(t-1)).$$

This function G has the property that, given definitions of G, m, and P, and any constants defined in G, then the future history of the system is determined (probabilistically).[8]

Many other functions have this property. Indeed, many of them can be defined simply by extending the range of the function G; for example, simultaneous relations can be expressed if m(t) is included in the range of G. However, the definition of G above is sufficiently complicated for present purposes. Note that many of the computer simulation models are defined by this function.

Let us first note that G allows us to represent the system as adjusting to the distribution of elements within it. Thus we can consider the supply of elements within the system as influencing the transition probabilities. One example of such a system for social mobility can be seen in Beshers and Reiter (Reference 4). The transition probabilities (mobility rates) are made to depend upon the relative power of the social classes, and relative power in turn depends upon changes in the distribution of persons throughout the class system. An example of such a system for migration of persons among areas is the "gravity model," in which each transition probability for a pair of areas is a function of the product of the numbers of persons in the two areas.

Next let us note that the form of G could be determined by psychological theory. If P(t) is defined over the macrograph for social mobility, as is our initial definition of P, then each category $C_i$ contains persons having the same status symbols. If we can define a psychological theory that has different behavior implications for persons who have different status symbols, such as the classic theory of marginal utility, then changing distributions of persons throughout the system would imply changing distributions of behavior in the system. If we regard status striving as an example of behavior, then we might represent the total volume of changes in the stratification system as a function of the distribution of persons in the system.

In our discussion of the nonstationary case we have already introduced the problem of representing the system as sensitive to supply. The notation above can be used to represent further notions of supply. For example, the contagion models, although usually written in continuous notation, share in common with those of the present discussion the fact that the transition probabilities are a function of the distribution of persons over the states of the system — not infected, contagious, recovered, immune, and so on.

The notation above also seems to have some merit as a means of representing the workings of a market. For example, consider a marriage market. The probabilities of intermarriage among various categories of persons could be represented as a function of the supply of "eligible" persons. The degree of eligibility might be represented as a utility function defined over the set of categories of persons. The utility function need not assume the same form throughout. The preferences might vary according to the relative ranks of persons, they might vary according to the similarities of persons, and they might vary according to the probability of persons ever having a contact with each other (visibility). The point is that the results of the market depend on the initial distribution, and the initial distribution is defined as the distribution vector. By defining utilities appropriately, one should be able to deduce distributions of spinsters and bachelors implied by different marriage systems. [9]

The problem of supply can be pursued further if we turn our attention to birth and death processes for the elements, in addition to the transitions already defined. From a purely formal point of view these processes can be represented in the transition matrix simply by including the unborn and the dead as categories to be added to the definition of states. But the pure formalism tends to obscure the substantive issues involved.

Birth and death not only change the internal distribution of persons in the system, but they also change the total number of persons. If substantive theory says that the total number of persons is an important variable, then our mathematical model must represent it.

Birth and death raise theoretical problems because they require explicit recognition of nonsocial variables, specifically biological variables. The probabilities of birth and death are not independent of the social variables. The simplest way to introduce birth and death probabilities is to employ a table of empirical probabilities differentiated by age and sex, and perhaps some empirical regression relationships with some of the social variables. This procedure will not, however, be sensitive to certain kinds of social change, such as the introduction of new medical technology. [10] If the purpose of the model is to project births, it would be well to make the probabilities of births depend on the distribution of birth control methods in the population.

If the elements in question are not persons, but perhaps commodities that flow among persons, then similar difficulties are likely to occur in the representation of birth and death processes, although not because of biological theory in this case.

Note that if our social system has categories defined by areas, then migration plays a similar role for each of these areas that birth and death processes play for the total system. This point is implicit in the definition of G, but it might have escaped notice.

Now let us turn to the last substantive issue that the simple Markov chain could not represent — the occurrence of discontinuous events, such as wars or depressions. If the event occurred prior to the history of the system that we wish to represent, we simply adjust our initial time period and our initial distribution vector appropriately. But if we are interested in studying the "response" of our system to such events, then we must define the adjustments in terms of the equations of the system. For the first-order nonstationary Markov process defined previously, we have three ways to express the adjustment. The adjustment can (1) influence the distribution vector, (2) influence the transition probabilities, (3) influence the function G. It is well to define these adjustments explicitly. Note that adjustment of the distribution vector alone is equivalent to an arbitrary modification of the "supply" available.

In summary, the main concern of this paper is to call attention to the need for representation of substantive social theory in computer models of large-scale social systems. If possible, it would be nice to have an explicit mathematical description of the substantive social theory embedded in the computer model. This is no simple task. Nevertheless, the illustrations of difficult cases in mathematical representation were not chosen simply to discourage work on problems of this type. Perhaps some of the suggested paths toward solution will turn out to have some merit. Much mathematical and empirical research remains before such judgment can be made.

### References

1.    For a definition of "model" and its part in the representation of substantive theory, see Beshers, James M., "Models and Theory Construction," American Sociological Review, 22, 32 — 38, 32 — 38 (Feb. 1957).

2.    See Kemeny, John G., and J. Laurie Snell, Finite Markov Chains, Van Nostrand Co., New York, 1960, pp. 191 — 200.

3.    See Pool, Ithiel de Sola, and Robert A. Abelson, "The Simulmatics Project," Public Opinion Quarterly, 25, 167 — 183 (Summer 1961).

4.    See Beshers, James M., Urban Social Structure, The Free Press of Glencoe, New York, 1962, Chapter 7 and Appendix; and Beshers, James M., and Stanley Reiter, "Social Status and Social Change," Behavioral Science, 8, 1 — 13 (Jan. 1963).

5.    Orcutt, Guy, Alice M. Rivlin, Martin Greenberger, and John Korbel, Microanalysis of Socio-economic Systems, Harper & Row, New York, 1961.

6.    Comment based on participation in seminar on computer simulation led by James S. Coleman, 1961 — 1962.

7.    For example, see Herniter, Jerome, "Mathematical Designs of Marketing Systems," preceding paper in this session.

8.    See Beshers and Reiter, op. cit.

9.   See Heer, David M. , "The Trend of Interfaith Marriages in Canada,"
     American Sociological Review, 27, 245 — 250, (Apr. 1962), for data
     suggesting the influence of supply of eligible mates upon marriage
     preferences.

10.  See Beshers, James M. , "Birth Projections with Cohort Models,"
     Demography, 2, 593 — 599 (1965).

# DISCUSSION

Frederick F. Stephan
The Population Council

I share with you the excitement induced by some of the ideas developed in these two papers. It would have been nice had we had more time in which to explore freely the many possible applications of these ideas. In the case of the paper by Herniter, my comments are limited by the lack of specific information given about the subject of the research. It would have been helpful if we had known just what the product was, what brands were involved, what particular populations were involved; in other words, if we could have penetrated the veil cast over private commercial research by research agencies because release of information might benefit their clients' competitors.

At this meeting we are concerned with the interaction between computers and theorists, or perhaps with the interaction between many kinds of people, from computer specialists to ordinary human beings engaged in making generalizations from common experience. Some of our ordinary experience we organize into data acquisition systems. We have various systems of reporting. We conduct surveys. The information assembled by these systems merely supplements the everyday, informal observations by which our judgments, decisions, and actions are guided. Anyone who thinks about markets such as those discussed in the paper certainly has in the back of his mind a clear picture of what he sees when he walks into a supermarket. He remembers seeing a great deal of variation in the behavior of shoppers and in the rate at which a product is taken from the shelves. He remembers seeing the supply of some brands depleted and shoppers compelled to select another brand when their first choice was temporarily out of stock. Some of the brand switching reported in the paper, therefore, may be the result of these inventory phenomena. Likewise, he recalls the exogenous variables that econometricians recognize in their models: weather variations, holidays, and such seasonal phenomena as spring housecleaning, which may lead a housewife to buy the big economy size because she expects to use a large amount in a few days, instead of the little package. She may have visiting relatives who are using her washing machine continuously, especially if they have to wash diapers and children's clothes. Our common knowledge indicates other concrete factors that at times lead to a change in the size of package or the brand purchased.

The sentence ending the first paragraph of the paper jolted me a little; it states: "However, in practice, to obtain models that predict well, we generally find it necessary to describe the phenomena as realistically as possible." If I read it as literally as possible, it calls for the inclusion in the model of hundreds of variables that can be observed. It is clear to all of us, I suppose, that almost any variable, y, that we study is a function of a very large or even infinite number of variables, some of which we can recognize and specify, but others of which are yet to be discovered.

$$y = f(x_1, x_2, x_3, x_4, \cdots).$$

Because we can study only a few variables at a time, we ignore almost all of them and attempt to approximate y by a suitable function of the few we retain in our model, say $x_1$, $x_3$, and $x_4$. If we succeed, that is, if the model predicts well, it is because the aggregate effect on y of the many variables we ignore is very small compared with the effect of the few variables we retain, at least within a reasonable range of variation of those variables. In other words, we decompose the actual system, as we do in factor analysis, into a number of components and hope that the first few components we take out of this very complex system account for most of the variance of y. If we are shrewd or lucky, we succeed with a model that is not "as realistic as possible," but rather as effective as possible under the practical limitations of what we can do with the information we can get. Often we do not use all the information we have about relevant variables simply because we would so complicate the analysis that we could neither finish our work nor get any answers. One of the computer's greatest contributions is that it enables us to include more variables.

In many situations, the additional variables may not improve the prediction because they are so closely correlated with the other variables in the model and do not add much more information about y. But we do need data for additional sets of variables which introduce factors not already well represented in the set that we are using in our explanatory model. Potentially, the computer can enable us to include more variables, but if we are not sufficiently well informed nor sufficiently skillful in imagining which variables ought to be added, we find, as we did with the old desk calculator types of statistical analysis, that we are not raising the multiple correlation very much. This condition limits the usefulness of computers in representation of complex social systems. Unless we can get the kinds of data needed to cover the more important sources of variation, we shall be left with a large unexplained portion of variation. Basically, we are in a dilemma. We want to make our models realistic, but we also want to make them economical. Since we cannot do both completely, we must compromise on what I would call an "appropriate" model, considering all the restrictions on what we can do, considering our position in the real world as observers and data gatherers, and working out, under all the circumstances, what will best achieve the purpose we are trying to satisfy by setting up our model.

Characteristically, we find that as we increase the stress on realism and, therefore, the complexity of the models we build to represent markets and various social systems, we are driven into Monte Carlo procedures. Then we are very much at the mercy of the technical characteristics of the computer, especially speed and often the capacity of the memory. Monte Carlo tends to be very expensive when a high degree of accuracy is required in the results. For some social science models we shall have to wait 10 or 20 years or longer before progress in computer design and technology will make it feasible to work with them.

Another line of progress open to us is to get more and better information. We may refuse to accept the limitations of available information, seeking instead to improve the process of data acquisition and to obtain new types of information about the system. We can attempt to observe and measure directly what we want to know instead of inferring it from readily available correlates. In the market study, the interviewers could have asked each respondent why she changed brands, and they could have ascertained the actual situation in the store when the purchases were made. Which brands were prominently displayed? Were other brands out of stock? What else were you purchasing at the same time? Do you buy a smaller box when you have a heavy load of groceries to take home? The answers to these questions might eliminate most of the need for an elaborate model and for the usual indirect evidence about important factors in the choice of brand and size of package.

These two papers also raise a question about the conditions of observation and measurement under which our data are produced: how much error and bias is introduced at each step, and how much can we learn about propagation of these biases and errors in the computer processing of the data? We know that data are imperfect; we know that the input into the computer includes, along with actual information, a certain amount of noise. How much noise is there in the final result? In surveys, as Leslie Kish of the University of Michigan and others have pointed out, we are already distressed by the difficulty of estimating sampling errors for some of the calculations from the survey results made by the survey analysts. We can only imagine what additional noise is added by the further calculations made by users on the basis of the survey results. Clearly, we need to include in computer routines provision for estimates, not only of sampling error, but also response error and other types of noise in the input data. We will find in some instances that the output is predominantly noise. This may seem unduly pessimistic, but in processing data we encounter situations in which a small change in the amount of noise in the data fed in produces a large change in the numbers that we get in the output.

A parallel problem is what James Beshers referred to as linking up a computer model with the substantive theory of a social scientist. When we examine carefully the theory of the social scientist, we find that most of it is expressed in concepts and statements that are not well defined and that are ambiguous to some extent. Because of this "semantic latitude," individuals can interpret the words in different ways. If one tries to make their meaning precise so that they can be expressed rigorously in a model or computer program, different people reading the sentences come up with different formulations of the meaning in precise terms. Consequently, in the translation of theory into models, there is variability over which we have no control. Our models must be formulated in precise terms. One cannot simply take a book of theory, punch it on cards, and feed it into the computer. If, in meeting the more rigorous requirements of the computer language, the computer specialist or programmer neglects, revises, or distorts important aspects of the meanings of the theorist, then the theorist is fully justified in disowning the computer output.

We need a sensitivity analysis of our models to see to what extent the output of the model is affected by variation in the formulations of the initial theoretical concepts and assumptions in formally precise machine-readable terms. In some cases we find that they may be relatively insensitive to variations in some of the definitions and assumptions, very sensitive to others. One of the major assumptions ordinarily made in aggregative models is that the interaction between the microsystems is negligible or can be expressed in simple terms readily incorporated into the model. But if the purchases of a family are affected in many complex but important ways by the neighbors' purchases or by the purchases of another customer in the store at the same time, then we cannot aggregate households by merely adding up their behavior as independent microsystems. We have to consider the network influences that lead to mass phenomena such as fads, boycotts, general shifts in preferences, and changes in the style of consumer behavior. A different model and different computer program are required.

Another problem we face in representing social systems by computer models is the temptation to consider only the steady state or limiting distribution and to forget that for a long period the system may exhibit important transient phenomena. Suppose, for example, we start an advertising campaign, and then as Herniter indicated, the level of purchases rises. At the very beginning of the advertising campaign, it may increase very rapidly and then later subside. There may well be a period in which sales fall below their level before the campaign. And why? Because dealers and consumers stock up in response to their first experience with the advertisements, following which for a period of time they sell or use their purchases and are not ready to reorder or make additional purchases. This is a familiar phenomenon in marketing. Manufacturers find that they have to put a lot of product into the pipeline, into the distributor's warehouses, and on the dealer's shelves. Hence, sales are tremendous for the first few months, and then slack off and fluctuate for a time before stabilizing on a steady level or trend.

Finally, the biggest problem of all is "What psychological meanings can be appropriately and legitimately applied to the computer output?" Here the computer cannot help us because it operates on symbols, not on their meanings. The human race has evolved slowly as a race of intelligent organisms. Its artifacts and technical systems have evolved much more rapidly. There has not been a sufficient period of biological evolution to make the operation of the human brain match in its progress the operation of devices like our computers. At the present time the greatest emphasis should be placed on the education and cultivation of the human intellect so that the creation of models, especially those of large-scale social systems, will advance with the capabilities of computers.

## FREE DISCUSSION

Owing to time limitations, the open discussion was limited to three questions, all addressed to Mr. Herniter's paper.

The first asked whether any attempt was made to attach some psychological significance to the form of the fitted distribution function. The reply was that no attempt was made to give it any psychological interpretation; the function was chosen to describe what took place without giving any reasons for it. The actual formulation was selected because it described the data well and was easy to manipulate.

Since Markov models in these situations typically underestimate loyalty when played through several time transitions, the question was raised as to whether the model fits. Mr. Herniter stated that the model was found to fit, not only with the original data from Chicago but also with data from New England and the West Coast, which indicates that the model can be used to predict in other geographical areas as well. By dealing with individual consumers and using the semi-Markov process, one gets much less loyalty in a single transition in this application than would have been the case if gross models had been used; thus a better fit is obtained for loyalty defined this way. Over several transitions, however, loyalty is underestimated.

In response to a question regarding the use for such a model, Mr. Herniter said that it is used in sales forecasting: overshooting of market shares occurs following a big advertising campaign, and the model is used to predict this.

In conclusion, Mr. Herniter urged everyone to try to make models as realistic as possible. He stated that the value of a model should be measured by its ability to predict observable phenomena.

# V.    ESTIMATION OF PARAMETERS IN SOCIAL SYSTEMS

# ESTIMATION OF PARAMETERS IN SIMULATION MODELS OF SOCIAL SYSTEMS*

**Arnold Zellner**
**University of Wisconsin**

## Introduction

In this paper we review a range of techniques for estimating parameters in models of social systems. The estimation problem is only one part of the process of model construction, a process that generally involves initial exploration of the data, model information, estimation, testing and experimentation, reformulation, re-estimation, additional testing and experimentation, and so on. Ideally, we would like to have statistical techniques that are optimal, relative to the whole process of model construction. Since this difficult problem has not been solved as yet, we limit ourselves here to consideration of statistical techniques for estimating parameters in given models, a partial problem in the general process of model construction.

The plan of this paper is as follows: The next section, "Analysis of Regression Models," reviews estimation techniques for regression models. The section "Analysis of Models for Proportions" analyzes models involving proportions. The section "'Simultaneous-Equation' Econometric Models" briefly considers "simultaneous-equation" econometric models. The section "Some Special Problems" explores several problems resulting from inadequate data. Finally, the section "Concluding Remarks" lists areas requiring further work.

## Analysis of Regression Models

Single-Equation Techniques

We consider initially the situation in which we have multivariate observations for time periods $t = 1, 2, \ldots, T$ on a subject of interest — for example, a single household or firm, or a group of households or firms. We further assume that the model which "explains" these observations has M regression equations, the $\mu^{th}$ of

---

*Much of the work reported in this paper was performed with financial assistance from the National Science Foundation, Grant GS-151.

which is given in conventional matrix form

$$y_\mu = X_\mu \beta_\mu + u_\mu,$$
(1)

where $y_\mu$ is a T x 1 vector of observations on the $\mu^{th}$ "dependent" variable, $X_\mu$ is a T x $k_\mu$ matrix with rank $k_\mu$ of observations on $k_\mu$ nonstochastic "independent" variables, $\beta_\mu$ is a $k_\mu$ x 1 vector of regression coefficients, and $u_\mu$ is a T x 1 vector of unobserved random errors. Equation 1 is linear in the elements of $\beta_\mu$ but, of course, may be nonlinear in the variables. Further, we assume that the elements of $u_\mu$ have zero means; i.e., $Eu_\mu = 0$, and convariance matrix

$$Eu_\mu u'_\mu = \sigma_{\mu\mu} I_T,$$
(2)

where $I_T$ is a T x T unit matrix. Equation 2 implies that the elements of $u_\mu$ have common variance $\sigma_{\mu\mu}$ and are nonautocorrelated; i.e., $Eu_\mu(t) u_\mu(t') = 0$ for $t \neq t'$.

We now review some points arising in the estimation of the parameters associated with Equation 1, neglecting for the time being the fact that Equation 1 is one equation of an M-equation model. Application of the classical method of least-squares leads to the estimator for $\beta_\mu$

$$\widehat{\beta}_\mu = (X'_\mu X_\mu)^{-1} X'_\mu y_\mu.$$
(3)

It is well known that under the previous specifying assumptions this estimator is the minimum-variance estimator in the class of unbiased estimators which are linear in the elements of $y_\mu$. Further, if it be assumed that the elements of $u_\mu$ are normally distributed, the estimator $\widehat{\beta}_\mu$ is the maximum-likelihood estimator for $\beta_\mu$. Finally, with the normality assumption and with noninformative prior distributions for the parameters of the model, $\widehat{\beta}_\mu$ in Equation 3 is the mean of the posterior distribution of $\beta_\mu$ in the Bayesian approach (see References 1 — 4). Thus, when reliance is placed entirely on the sample information in making inferences, the quantity in Equation 3 has much to commend it as a point of the coefficient vector $\beta_\mu$.

As regards estimation of $\sigma_{\mu\mu}$, the error term variance, the estimator

$$s_{\mu\mu} = (T-k_\mu)^{-1} (y_\mu - X_\mu \widehat{\beta}_\mu)' (y_\mu - X_\mu \widehat{\beta}_\mu)$$
(4)

is an unbiased estimator.  The maximum-likelihood estimator is slightly different from Equation 4 in that the sum of squared residuals is divided by $T$ rather than by $T-k_\mu$.  In the Bayesian approach with noninformative prior distributions, the posterior distribution of $\sigma_{\mu\mu}$ is an inverted chi-square distribution with mean equal to the sum of squared residuals divided by $T-k_\mu-2$ (see References 2, 5).*

Use of the above techniques permits an equation-by-equation analysis of the model.  However, this equation-by-equation approach does not take into account the fact that in many circumstances different $y_\mu$, or alternatively different $u_\mu$, may be correlated.  For example, if one equation explains expenditure on autos and another installment debt, it is quite likely that these variables will have a nonzero correlation.  Or, if we are explaining investment outlays of firms in an industry, it is quite probable that outlays of different firms will be correlated, since firms are subject to similar random shocks.  Recognition of the fact that our variables are likely to be correlated is interesting and has implications for both estimation and testing procedures in whatever system of inference is being utilized.  With respect to estimation, it is generally possible to exploit these correlations to obtain more precise estimates of regression coefficients.  In testing, it is important to take account of the correlations mentioned above in deriving appropriate test procedures.  Neglect of such correlations can lead to tests of dubious validity.

We now turn to reviewing techniques that are designed specifically for analyzing models with such correlations present.

Joint Estimation and Testing Procedures

For convenience we write our $M$-equation regression model in the following form:

$$\begin{bmatrix} y_1 \\ y_2 \\ . \\ . \\ . \\ y_M \end{bmatrix} = \begin{bmatrix} X_1 & & & \\ & X_2 & & \\ & & . & \\ & & & X_M \end{bmatrix} \begin{bmatrix} \beta_1 \\ \beta_2 \\ . \\ . \\ . \\ \beta_M \end{bmatrix} + \begin{bmatrix} u_1 \\ u_2 \\ . \\ . \\ . \\ u_M \end{bmatrix} \tag{5a}$$

or

$$y = X\beta + u, \tag{5b}$$

where $y$ stands for the $MT \times 1$ vector on the left-hand side of Equation 5a, $X$ for the $MT \times k$ block diagonal matrix on the right-hand side of Equation 5a, with $k = \sum_{u=1}^{M} k_\mu$, $\beta$ for the $k \times 1$ coefficient vector, and $u$ for the $MT \times 1$ error

*See Reference 6 for additional analysis of residuals.

vector. As it stands, Equation 5b is in the form of a single-equation multiple-regression model. However, our specifying assumption regarding the covariance matrix for the error vector u will differ from that made in connection with $u_\mu$ in Equation 2. As before, we assume $Eu = 0$, but now

$$Euu' = \begin{bmatrix} \sigma_{11} & \sigma_{12} & \cdots & \sigma_{1M} \\ \sigma_{21} & \sigma_{22} & \cdots & \sigma_{2M} \\ \cdot & \cdot & \cdot & \cdot \\ \cdot & \cdot & \cdot & \cdot \\ \cdot & \cdot & \cdot & \cdot \\ \sigma_{M1} & \sigma_{M2} & \cdots & \sigma_{MM} \end{bmatrix} \odot I_T = \Sigma_c \odot I_T = \Sigma , \tag{6}$$

where $\odot$ denotes direct or Kronecker matrix multiplication. The form of Equation 6 implies the absence of serial correlation of any kind, but does permit non-zero contemporaneous covariances.

As explained in Reference 7, application of Aitken's generalized least-squares principle to the system in Equation 5 yields the minimum-variance linear unbiased estimator

$$b^* = (X' \Sigma^{-1} X)^{-1} X' \Sigma^{-1} y , \tag{7}$$

with covariance matrix given by

$$V(b^*) = E(b^* - \beta)(b^* - \beta)' = (X' \Sigma^{-1} X)^{-1} . \tag{8}$$

In addition to having the property of being a minimum-variance linear unbiased estimator, the estimator in Equation 7 has the following properties:

1.    The estimator $b^*$ is the estimator which minimizes the mathematical expectation of every positive definite quadratic form in the coefficient sampling errors or in the forecast errors (see Reference 8).

2.    With a normality assumption, $b^*$ is the maximum-likelihood estimator for $\beta$.

3.    With a normality assumption and noninformative prior distributions, $b^*$ is the mean of the posterior distribution of $\beta$ for given $\Sigma$ in a Bayesian analysis of the model (see Reference 5).

4.    In general, $b^*$ will differ from the single-equation least-squares estimator, which means that the single-equation estimator is inefficient. In References 7 and 8, the gain in efficiency is analyzed and found to be substantial, and greatest when independent variables in different equations are orthogonal — i.e., $X_\mu' X_{\mu'} = 0$, and when error terms of different equations are highly correlated.

5.    When either the $X_\mu$ matrices are proportional to each other (or equal as a special case) or all covariances are zero, $\sigma_{\mu\mu'} = 0$ for $\mu \neq \mu'$, or both, the estimator b* algebraically reduces to the single-equation least-squares estimator.

These properties commend the estimator b* in Equation 7 to us. However, it is the case that b* depends on the usually unknown matrix $\Sigma$ . In Reference 7, it is proposed that a consistent estimator of $\Sigma$ , say $\Sigma_e$, formed from single-equation least-squares residuals, be employed to construct the estimator.

$$b = (X' \Sigma_e^{-1} X)^{-1} X' \Sigma_e^{-1} y. \tag{9}$$

The following properties of the estimator b have been established. It is a consistent estimator of $\beta$ , i.e., plim $b = \beta$ ; $Eb = \beta$ to terms of order $T^{-1}$; b and b* have the same asymptotic normal distribution; and the moment matrix of b is given by $V(b) = (X'\Sigma_e^{-1}X)^{-1} + o(T^{-1})$, where $o(T^{-1})$ denotes terms of higher order of smallness than $T^{-1}$ in probability. In addition to these properties, an exact finite sample analysis of a two-equation model in Reference 9 revealed that for the model considered, large-sample properties "took hold" for moderate-sized samples.

With respect to testing procedures, the F statistic for testing the general linear hypothesis

$$C\beta = 0 \tag{10}$$

derived in Reference 10 is

$$F_{q, N-k} = \frac{N-k}{q} \frac{y'\Sigma^{-1}X(X'\Sigma^{-1}X)^{-1} C'\left[C(X'\Sigma^{-1}X)^{-1} C'\right]^{-1} C(X'\Sigma^{-1}X)^{-1}X'\Sigma^{-1}y}{y'\Sigma^{-1}y - y'\Sigma^{-1}X(X'\Sigma^{-1}X)^{-1}X'\Sigma^{-1}y}, \tag{11}$$

where $N = MT$, $k = \sum_\mu k_\mu$, and q is the number of restrictions implied by the hypothesis in Equation 10. In Reference 7 it is shown that this is a likelihood ratio test and that if $\Sigma_e$ is substituted for $\Sigma$ the resulting statistic, say $\tilde{F}$, has the following properties: $\tilde{F} = F_{q, N-k} + O(T^{-1/2})$, and $q\tilde{F}$ and $qF$ are both asymptotically distributed as chi-square with q degrees of freedom. These facts can be utilized to test hypotheses about the coefficients in individual equations and those appearing in different equations.

The statistical procedures described earlier have been programmed (see Reference 11) and applied in several studies (see References 12 - 14). To illustrate their application, we report the results of an analysis of some microinvestment data. The annual data pertain to individual corporations for the period 1935 — 1954. For each firm, in accord with a version of Grunfeld's investment theory (see Reference 15), gross investment $y_\mu$ (t) is made to depend on the beginning of year value of outstanding shares, a proxy for expected profitability, $x_{\mu 1}$ (t), and beginning of year real capital stock $x_{\mu 2}$ (t). That is,

$$y_\mu (t) = \beta_{\mu 0} + \beta_{\mu 1} x_{\mu 1} \cdot (t) + \beta_{\mu 2} x_{\mu 2} (t) + u_\mu (t) ,$$

with $t = 1, 2, \ldots, 20$, and $\mu = 1, 2, \ldots, 10$. In Table 1 are shown the single-equation least-squares estimates as well as several sets of joint estimates. The latter were computed using an estimate of the matrix $\Sigma$ based on single-equation least-squares residuals. The estimated correlation matrix for the system is one of the outputs of the program, shown in Table 2. It is seen that the standard errors associated with the joint estimates are quite a bit smaller than those associated with the single-equation estimates. Furthermore, Table 2 shows that some residual correlations are fairly high.

## Analysis of Models for Proportions

Single-Equation Techniques

In this section we briefly review some procedures for estimating parameters in an equation explaining the variation of a sample proportion, such as the proportion of consumers purchasing an automobile in a given time period. We assume that the sample proportion for the $t^{th}$ time period, $p_t$, based on $n_t$ cases, is given by

$$p_t = P_t + u_t \qquad t = 1, 2, \ldots, T, \tag{12}$$

where $P_t$ is the $t^{th}$ "true" proportion and the $u_t$'s are assumed independently distributed, each with a binomial distribution with mean zero and variance $P_t (1-P_t) /n_t$. Further, we denote the total number of cases by $N = \sum_{t=1}^{T} n_t$.

The models considered below differ in the choice of function to represent the variation of the $P_t$. In the "probit" or "normit" model, * $P_t$ is represented by the cumulative normal distribution function as follows:

$$P_t = F (\nu_t) = (2\pi)^{-1/2} \int_{-\infty}^{\nu_t} e^{-1/2 (z^2)} dz, \tag{13}$$

with

$$\nu_t = \beta_1 + \beta_2 X_{2t} + \beta_3 X_{3t} + \ldots + \beta_k X_{kt}, \tag{14}$$

*See References 16 - 21 for further discussion of the model.

TABLE 1

Single-Equation Least-Squares and Efficient Estimates of Grunfeld's Investment Equation*

| Corporation | Equations Estimated Individually by Least Squares | | | Equations Estimated Jointly by Efficient Regression Technique | | | | | | | | |
|---|---|---|---|---|---|---|---|---|---|---|---|---|
| | Const. | $x_1$ | $x_2$ | Const. | $x_1$ | $x_2$ | Const. | $x_1$ | $x_2$ | Const. | $x_1$ | $x_2$ |
| General Electric | -9.956 (31.37) | .02655 (.01557) | .1517 (.02570) | -28.16 (29.23) | .03864 (.01436) | .1385 (.02495) | -24.38 (25.48) | .04085 (.01207) | .1183 (.02282) | -11.190 (21.11) | .03324 (.009285) | .1241 (.02140) |
| Westing-house | -.5094 (8.015) | .05289 (.01571) | .09241 (.05610) | -1.318 (7.524) | .05791 (.01449) | .06259 (.05290) | .6850 (6.398) | .06162 (.01157) | .01009 (.04309) | 4.114 (5.089) | .05254 (.007945) | .04119 (.03474) |
| U.S. Steel | -49.20 (148.1) | .1749 (.07420) | .3896 (.1424) | ---- | ---- | ---- | -71.07 (97.51) | .2073 (.04837) | .2472 (.1187) | -18.56 (78.42) | .1698 (.03774) | .3195 (.1011) |
| Diamond Match | .1615 (2.066) | .004573 (.02716) | .4374 (.07959) | ---- | ---- | ---- | .8314 (1.297) | .001954 (.01757) | .3559 (.06280) | 2.200 (1.125) | -.01807 (.01508) | .3646 (.05783) |
| Atlantic Refining | 22.71 (6.872) | .1624 (.05704) | .003102 (.02197) | ---- | ---- | ---- | ---- | ---- | ---- | 26.46 (6.475) | .1312 (.04733) | .01024 (.01866) |
| Union Oil of Calif. | -4.500 (11.29) | .08753 (.06563) | .1238 (.01706) | ---- | ---- | ---- | ---- | ---- | ---- | -9.669 (9.010) | .1121 (.04558) | .1285 (.01553) |
| Goodyear | -7.723 (9.359) | .07539 (.03395) | .08210 (.02799) | ---- | ---- | ---- | ---- | ---- | ---- | -2.583 (7.588) | .07603 (.02019) | .06413 (.02291) |
| General Motors | -149.8 (105.8) | .1193 (.02583) | .3714 (.03707) | ---- | ---- | ---- | ---- | ---- | ---- | -133.0 (73.23) | .1133 (.01670) | .3857 (.03123) |
| Chrysler | -6.190 (13.51) | .07795 (.01997) | .3157 (.02881) | ---- | ---- | ---- | ---- | ---- | ---- | 2.454 (11.51) | .06720 (.01661) | .3059 (.02712) |
| IBM | -8.686 (4.545) | .1315 (.03117) | .08537 (.1003) | ---- | ---- | ---- | ---- | ---- | ---- | -5.565 (3.559) | .1310 (.01673) | .05713 (.05754) |

*The theory of the Grunfeld investment equation is discussed in Y. Grunfeld, "The Determinants of Corporate Investment," unpublished Ph. D. dissertation, University of Chicago, 1958, and in J. C. G. Boot and G. M. De Wit, "Investment Demand: An Empirical Contribution to the Aggregation Problem," International Economic Review, Vol. 1, 3 – 30 (1960). The data underlying the calculations, taken from the latter source, are annual observations, 1935–1954, on the following variables for each corporation:

Dependent variable: firm's deflated gross investment

$x_1$: value of firm's outstanding shares at beginning of year

$x_2$: firm's beginning of year real capital stock.

TABLE 2

Estimated Disturbance Correlation Matrix

| | General Electric | Westinghouse | U.S. Steel | Diamond Match | Atlantic Refining | Union Oil | Goodyear | General Motors | Chrysler | IBM |
|---|---|---|---|---|---|---|---|---|---|---|
| General Electric | 1.000 | .738 | .449 | .600 | -.016 | .019 | .431 | .288 | -.071 | .484 |
| Westinghouse | | 1.000 | .641 | .617 | .004 | .143 | .544 | .164 | .122 | .547 |
| U.S. Steel | | | 1.000 | .748 | .235 | -.296 | .301 | -.275 | .359 | .393 |
| Diamond Match | | | | 1.000 | .131 | -.232 | .281 | -.270 | .118 | .407 |
| Atlantic Refining | | | | | 1.000 | .151 | -.148 | -.323 | .061 | .220 |
| Union Oil of Calif. | | | | | | 1.000 | .200 | .533 | -.129 | .139 |
| Goodyear | | | | | | | 1.000 | .214 | .074 | -.182 |
| General Motors | | | | | | | | 1.000 | -.279 | .124 |
| Chrysler | | | | | | | | | 1.000 | .214 |
| IBM | | | | | | | | | | 1.000 |

where the X's are nonstochastic variables. The estimation problem is to estimate the $\beta$'s, given observations on the X's and the sample proportions $p_t$, $t = 1, 2, \ldots, T$. At least two approaches are available: the maximum-likelihood approach (see References 16, 17) and the minimum-normit $-\chi^2$ approach (see Reference 18). These methods yield estimators with the same asymptotic properties.* Here we consider just the minimum normit-$\chi^2$ method. In Reference 21 it is shown that the minimum-normit-$\chi^2$ estimator, b, of the vector $\beta' = (\beta_1 \beta_2 \cdots \beta_k)$ can be expressed as

$$b = (X' \Sigma_e^{-1} X)^{-1} X' \Sigma_e^{-1} v^0, \tag{15}$$

where X is a T x k matrix of observations on the X's; $v^0$ is a T x 1 vector of observed normits, the elements of which are given by $p_t = F(v_t^0)$, where F is the cumulative normal distribution function; and the matrix $\Sigma_e$ is a diagonal matrix with elements $p_t(1-p_t)/n_t [z(p_t)]^2$, where z represents the normal density function, $(2\pi)^{-1/2} e^{-1/2 (z^2)}$. The moment matrix of the estimator b is given by

$$V(b) = (X' \Sigma_e^{-1} X)^{-1} + o(n_t^{-1}), \tag{16}$$

which can be employed for computing standard errors, etc.

In the logit model the dependence of $p_t$ on $v_t$ is represented by use of the logistic function as follows:

$$p_t = \frac{1}{1+e^{-v_t}} = \frac{1}{1+e^{-(\beta_1 + \beta_2 X_{2t} + \cdots \beta_k X_{kt})}}. \tag{17}$$

Again the problem is to estimate the $\beta$'s, and several approaches with the same asymptotic properties are available. For example: maximum likelihood, minimum-$\chi^2$, and minimum-logit-$\chi^2$ (see References 23 — 25). In the minimum-logit-$\chi^2$ approach we compute sample logits, logit $(p_t) = \ln \left[ p_t/(1-p_t) \right]$, where ln stands for the natural logarithm. Representing the T x 1 vector of sample logits

*See Reference 22 for some work on the finite sample properties of alternative estimation techniques.

by logit (p), it is shown in Reference 21 that the minimum-logit-$x^2$ estimator of the $\beta$'s in Equation 17 can be expressed as follows:

$$b = (X'\Sigma_e^{-1}X)^{-1}X'\Sigma_e^{-1} \text{ logit } (p),\tag{18}$$

where $\Sigma_e$ is a diagonal matrix with elements $[n_t p_t(1-p_t)]^{-1}$. Also, this matrix appears in the moment matrix of the estimator,

$$V(b) = (X'\Sigma_e^{-1}X)^{-1} + o(n_t^{-1}).\tag{19}$$

Another model, the so-called "linear probability model," which has been employed extensively, is $P_t = v_t = \beta_0 + \beta_1 X_{1t} + \ldots + \beta_k X_{kt}$. Here the functional form for $P_t$ should not violate the bounds zero and one. Representing the observed T x 1 vector of proportions by p, we have

$$p = X\beta + u,\tag{20}$$

with $u' = (u_1 u_2 \ldots u_t)$. The least-squares estimator for $\beta$,

$$\widehat{\beta} = (X'X)^{-1}X'p,\tag{21}$$

is unbiased: i.e., $E^{\widehat{\beta}} = \beta$, and has covariance matrix given by

$$V(\widehat{\beta}) = (X'X)^{-1} X' \Sigma X (X'X)^{-1},\tag{22}$$

where $\Sigma$ is a diagonal matrix with elements $P_t(1-P_t)/n_t$. While the estimator $\widehat{\beta}$ in Equation 21 is unbiased, it is not efficient. An asymptotically efficient estimator is

$$b = (X'\Sigma_e^{-1}X)^{-1}X'\Sigma_e^{-1}p,$$

where $\Sigma_e$ is a diagonal matrix with elements $\widehat{p}_t(1-\widehat{p}_t)/-n_t$, and $\widehat{p}_t$ is the computed unweighted least-squares estimate of $P_t$.

## Joint Estimation of Relationships Involving Proportions

Just as with continuous variables, proportions may frequently be correlated. For example, the proportion of consumers buying durable goods is probably positively correlated with the proportions taking on installment debt. This correlation is of interest in itself and can be utilized to improve estimation precision. Below we indicate briefly how this can be done in terms of equations in the "linear probability form." (Note that the same approach can be utilized for equations involving normits, logits, etc.).

As in the section "Analysis of Regression Models," we write our model for the M-equations of the model in the following form:

$$
\begin{bmatrix} p_1 \\ p_2 \\ \vdots \\ p_M \end{bmatrix} = \begin{bmatrix} X_1 & & & \\ & X_2 & & \\ & & \ddots & \\ & & & X_M \end{bmatrix} \begin{bmatrix} \beta_1 \\ \beta_2 \\ \vdots \\ \beta_M \end{bmatrix} + \begin{bmatrix} u_1 \\ u_2 \\ \vdots \\ u_M \end{bmatrix} , \tag{23}
$$

or

$$
p = X\beta + u, \tag{24}
$$

where $p' = (p_1' \, p_2' \cdots p_M')$, $\beta' = (\beta_1' \, \beta_2' \cdots \beta_M')$, and $u' = (u_1' \, u_2' \cdots u_M')$, X denotes the block diagonal matrix in Equation 23, $p_\mu$ is a T x 1 vector of observed proportions for the $\mu^{th}$ characteristic ($\mu = 1, 2, \ldots, M$), $\beta_\mu$ is a $k_\mu$ x 1 coefficient vector, and $u_M$ is a T x 1 error vector. The variance-covariance matrix of the error vector in Equation 24 is given by:

$$
Euu' = \begin{bmatrix} \Sigma_{11} & \Sigma_{12} & \cdots & \Sigma_{1M} \\ \Sigma_{21} & \Sigma_{22} & \cdots & \Sigma_{2M} \\ \vdots & \vdots & \vdots & \vdots \\ \Sigma_{M1} & \Sigma_{M2} & \cdots & \Sigma_{MM} \end{bmatrix} = \Sigma , \tag{25}
$$

where the submatrices of the symmetric matrix $\Sigma$ are all diagonal with

$$
\Sigma_{\mu\mu} = \begin{bmatrix} P_{\mu 1}(1-P_{\mu 1})/n_1 & & \\ & \ddots & \\ & & P_{\mu T}(1-P_{\mu T})/n_T \end{bmatrix} ,
$$

and for $\mu \neq \mu'$

$$
\Sigma_{\mu\mu'} = \begin{bmatrix} \left[ p_{11}^{\mu\mu'}(1) - P_{\mu 1}P_{\mu'1} \right]/n_1 & & \\ & \ddots & \\ & & \left[ p_{11}^{\mu\mu'}(T) - P_{\mu T}P_{\mu T} \right]/n_T \end{bmatrix} ,
$$

where $p_{11}^{\mu\mu'}$ (t) is the probability that an individual will have both characteristics (denoted by $\mu$ and $\mu'$) in period T. Since $\Sigma$ can be estimated from the data, the following asymptotically efficient estimator can be calculated:

$$b = (X'\Sigma_e^{-1}X)^{-1}\Sigma_e^{-1}p, \qquad (26)$$

where $\Sigma_e$ is the consistent estimate of $\Sigma$ in Equation 25. The moment matrix of the estimator is given by

$$V(b) = (X'\Sigma_e^{-1}X)^{-1} + o(n_t^{-1}).$$

An illustrative calculation in which this and the above techniques are utilized is presented in Reference 21.

### "Simultaneous—Equation" Econometric Models

"Simultaneous-equation" models represent a broadening of the regression model considered in the section "Analysis of Regression Models." With regression models, there are M equations for M dependent variables, the $y_\mu$, with just one appearing in each equation.

In simultaneous-equation models with M equations, there are again M dependent or endogenous variables whose variation the model is designed to explain. However, in such models more than one endogenous variable may appear in equations (the so-called "structural equations") of the model. A typical equation takes the following form:

$$y_\mu = Y_\mu \gamma_\mu + X_\mu \beta_\mu + u_\mu, \qquad (27)$$

where $y_\mu$ is a T x 1 vector of observations on the $\mu^{th}$ endogenous variable, and $Y_\mu$ is a T x $m_\mu$ matrix of observations on $m_\mu$ endogenous variables, other than $y_\mu$, appearing in this equation with nonzero coefficients. $X_\mu$ is a T x $\ell_\mu$ matrix of "predetermined" variables appearing with nonzero coefficients. $\gamma_\mu$ and $\beta_\mu$ are $m_\mu$ x 1 and $\ell_n$ x 1 coefficient vectors, respectively, and $u_\mu$ is a T x 1 coefficient matrix.

Assuming that Equation 27 is identified, its parameters can be estimated by a variety of single-equation methods, including two-stage least-squares, limited-information maximum likelihood (see References 26-28 for an exposition of these techniques). Furthermore, several methods for estimating the parameters of all equations simultaneously are available, namely, "full-information" maximum likelihood (FIML), three-stage least-squares (3SLS), and linearized maximum likelihood (LML) (see References 29-31 for descriptions of these techniques). Much work has been done to establish the properties of alternative estimation techniques (see Reference 27). All of the above methods yield consistent estimators, while the FIML, 3SLS, and LML methods also produce estimators that are asymptotically equivalent and efficient. Thus, as with regression systems, there will usually be a gain in efficiency associated with simultaneous estimation as compared with single-equation estimation.

If we represent the system of equations as

$$Y\Gamma + XB = U ,\qquad\qquad (28)$$

where $Y = (y_1 \cdots y_M)$ , $X = (x_1 \cdots x_M)$ , $U = (u_1 \cdots u_M)$ , and $\Gamma$ and $B$ are coefficient matrices, we note that if $\Gamma$ is triangular, if the covariance matrix of contemporaneous errors is diagonal, and if these errors are not serially correlated, then we have a "fully recursive" model. For such a model, application of least-squares equation by equation yields consistent estimators which are maximum-likelihood estimators if an assumption of normality is introduced   (see, for example, Reference 28).

Bayesian techniques for the analysis of simultaneous-equation models are currently being developed (see References 32, 33). Also, it should be noted, as pointed out in Reference 1, that the likelihood function approximates the posterior distribution of parameters and thus can be utilized for making posterior inferences in large samples.

## Some Special Problems

In the preceding sections the properties of estimation techniques have been reviewed under the assumptions that models are perfectly specified and that the data used for estimation are exactly what the investigator desires. As everyone knows, these assumptions are, at best, approximately satisfied in practice. Such problems as departures from independence, omitted variables, use of incorrect functional forms, errors of measurement, incomplete data, etc., frequently arise. In this section we analyze a few of these problems, which seem particularly important in efforts to produce meaningful parameter estimates for simulation models and which have a direct relationship to the way in which data are collected.

## Aggregation Problems

To illustrate several aspects of the aggregation problem, assume that we are interested in estimating regression coefficient vectors in the following set of regression equations: *

$$y_\mu = X_\mu \beta_\mu + u_\mu \qquad \mu = 1, 2, \ldots, M,\qquad\qquad (29)$$

*The notation is the same as employed in the section "Analysis of Regression Models."

but have only the following simply aggregated data available:

$$\bar{y} = \sum_{\mu=1}^{M} y_{\mu} \quad \text{and} \quad \bar{X} = \sum_{\mu=1}^{M} X_{\mu}. \tag{30}$$

If we posit a regression equation connecting $\bar{y}$ and $\bar{X}$, namely, $\bar{y} = \overline{X\beta} + \overline{U}$, and estimate $\bar{\beta}$ by computing the least-squares estimator

$$\bar{b} = (\bar{X}'\bar{X})^{-1} \bar{X}' \bar{y}, \tag{31}$$

we may ask, as is done in Reference 34, what it is that $\bar{b}$ estimates? The mathematical expectation of $\bar{b}$ is given by

$$E\bar{b} = \sum_{\mu=1}^{M} B_{\mu} \beta_{\mu}, \tag{32}$$

where $B_{\mu} = (\bar{X}'\bar{X})^{-1} \bar{X}' X_{\mu}$. We see, as Theil points out in Reference 34, that the expectation of a particular element of $\bar{b}$, say $\bar{b}_i$, involves corresponding $(\beta_{\mu i})$ and noncorresponding $(\beta_{\mu j}$ $(j \neq i))$ microcoefficients in general. This implies that the "macroestimator" $\bar{b}$ has an aggregation bias, which makes its interpretation quite difficult. One sufficient condition for this not to be so is that

$$\beta_1 = \beta_2 = \cdots = \beta_M, \tag{33}$$

namely, that the "micro" coefficient vectors be equal, as can be seen from Equation 32, since $\Sigma B_{\mu} = I$. Thus, when it is necessary to use aggregated data, as defined in Equation 30, it would be helpful to have such data relate to relatively homogeneous microunits to avoid aggregation bias and the associated difficulties of interpreting what it is that has been computed.

To clarify this point further, it is useful to write $\beta_{\mu} = \beta + \delta_{\mu}$, where $\beta$ is the vector mean of the $\beta_{\mu}$, and $\delta_{\mu}$ is a vector of deviations from the mean. Then by simply adding up the equations in Equation 29, we are led to

$$\bar{y} = \bar{X} + \sum_{\mu=1}^{M} X_{\mu} \delta_{\mu} + u, \tag{34}$$

where $u = \sum_{\mu=1}^{\mu} u_{\mu}$. Equation 34 illustrates rather well that in estimation using the aggregated data, $\bar{y}$ and $\bar{X}$, we are assuming, hopefully, that the $\delta_{\mu}$ are negligibly small. If they are not, computational results may be marred by aggregation bias. Further, as has been emphasized by Orcutt on many occasions, aggregating data involves an important loss of sample information which could be exploited for testing hypotheses and for increasing the precision of estimation.

Above, we have considered aggregation in a single dimension, for example, aggregation over individuals. We note that in general, data may be aggregated over individuals, commodities, time, and space, with the difficulties mentioned above generally compounded (see Reference 34 for an analysis of "multiple" aggregation). In particular, temporal aggregation is bothersome when we are interested in establishing the short-run dynamic properties of models. An example is provided in Reference 35 where the following "monthly" model is considered:

$$q_{tj} - q_{tj-1} = \beta (q^*_{tj} - q_{tj-1}),$$

or

$$q_{tj} = \beta q^*_{tj} + (1-\beta) q_{tj-1}, \tag{35}$$

where $q_{tj}$ represents an observation for the $j^{th}$ month of the $t^{th}$ year, $q^*_{tj}$ is a desired level, and $\beta$ is a parameter. Letting $Q_t = \sum_j q_{tj}$ and $Q^*_t = \sum_j q^*_{tj}$, it is straightforward to establish that

$$Q_t = Q^*_t - \frac{1-\beta}{\beta} (q_{t,12} - q_{t-1,12}), \tag{36}$$

an equation that is in a form quite different from Equation 35. Thus, if an investigator were to analyze annual data with a model in the form of Equation 35, he could be led to completely erroneous inferences about the dynamics of the system. If only annual data are available and if Equation 35 is believed to be an appropriate model, the investigator should be bringing these data to bear on Equation 36. For example, if $Q^*_t = \gamma Z_t$, where $Z_t$ is an observable variable, he might try estimating

$$Q_t = \gamma Z_t + \left( \frac{1-\beta}{\beta} \right) R_t,$$ where $R_t$ is an estimate of $q_{t;12} - q_{t-1,12}$.

Of course, this procedure is not nearly as satisfactory as proceeding with an analysis of monthly data. With such data, the form of Equation 35 can be investigated much more thoroughly than with annual data. And if the model is found satisfactory, estimates with greater precision can be obtained from the monthly data.

Much of the work on aggregation has been concerned with linear aggregation; that is, analyzing the effects of aggregating models linear in the parameters. If models are nonlinear in the parameters, the effects of aggregation remain to be analyzed. However, we note the following result, which sheds some light on the nature of the problem. Suppose that our model to explain observations on the $i^{th}$ individual $(i = 1, 2, \ldots, N)$ is

$$y_i(t) = f[x_i(t), \theta_i] + u_i(t), \tag{37}$$

where $t$ denotes time, $x_i(t)$ is a vector of explanatory variables, $\theta_i$ a vector of parameters, and $u_i(t)$ a random disturbance. Now if we expand the function $f$ about the means of $x_i(t)$ and $\theta_i$, $\bar{x}(t)$ and $\theta$, respectively, we obtain

$$y_i(t) = f[\bar{x}(t), \theta] + [x_i(t) - \bar{x}] \frac{\partial f}{\partial x_i(t)} + (\theta_i - \theta) \frac{\partial f}{\partial \theta_i} + \ldots + u_i(t), \tag{38}$$

where the partial derivatives are evaluated at $(\bar{x}(t), \theta)$. Then, on aggregating over individuals, we have, neglecting terms of order higher than the first,

$$y(t) = \sum_i y_i(t) = N f[\bar{x}'(t), \theta] + U(t),$$

or

$$\bar{y}(t) = f[\bar{x}(t), \theta] + \bar{U}(t), \tag{39}$$

where $\bar{y}(t) = N^{-1} \sum_i y_i(t)$, and $\bar{U}(t) = N^{-1} \sum_i u_i(t)$. Thus as long as higher-order terms in Equation 38 can be neglected, Equation 39 can be used with macrodata to estimate the parameter vector $\theta$ in the nonlinear function f, with $\theta$ being interpreted as the mean of the microparameter vectors, the $\theta_i$. This approxima-

tion of course depends upon the extent to which higher-order terms in Equation 38 can be neglected, a point that cannot be extensively explored when only macrodata are available.

Another problem that arises often in practice is that of missing observations. Suppose, for example, that we are interested in estimating the parameters of the equation

$$y(t) = \rho y(t-1) + X(t)\beta + u(t), \tag{40}$$

where $X(t)$ is a $1 \times k$ vector of nonstochastic explanatory variables at time $t$; $\beta$ is a $k \times 1$ coefficient vector, $y(t)$ is the dependent variable, $y(t-1)$ the same variable lagged one period, $\rho$ is a scalar parameter, and $u(t)$ is a nonautocorrelated error term. Now suppose that we have observations on the variables in $X(t)$ for all $t$, but only the following $T+1$ observations on $y(t)$: $y(0)$, $y(4)$, $y(8)$, . . . , $y(4T)$. The problem then is to use these observations to make inferences about $\rho$ and $\beta$. To solve this problem, we see that Equation 40 implies the following relationship for the observations that we do have:

$$y(t') = \rho^4 y(t'-4) + [X(t') + \rho X(t'-1) + \rho^2 X(t'-2) + \rho^3 X(t'-3)]\beta + w(t'),$$

$$\tag{41}$$

where $t' = 0, 4, \ldots, 4T$, and $w(t') = u(t') + \rho u(t'-1) + \rho^2 u(t'-2) +$

$\rho^3 u(t'-3)$. Both maximum–likelihood and Bayesian procedures for estimating the parameters in Equation 41 are developed in Reference 36. Significantly, the form of Equation 41 is quite different from that of Equation 40, and thus an uncritical use of Equation 40 for analysis of the observations at hand can easily lead to confused inferences.

Finally, we take up, rather briefly, one additional problem arising in the analysis of cross-section data. Such data relate to different individuals at a point in time, t. If we assume that individuals have different regression coefficient vectors, a regression model for the data would be

$$
\begin{bmatrix} y_1(t) \\ y_2(t) \\ \vdots \\ y_N(t) \end{bmatrix} =
\begin{bmatrix} X_1(t) & & & \beta_1 \\ & X_2(t) & & \beta_2 \\ & & \ddots & \vdots \\ & & X_N(t) & \beta_N \end{bmatrix} +
\begin{bmatrix} u_1(t) \\ u_2(t) \\ \vdots \\ u_N(t) \end{bmatrix}, \qquad (42)
$$

where $N$ is the number of individuals in the cross section, $X_\mu(t)$ is a $1 \times k$ vector of independent variables for the $\mu^{th}$ individual; $\beta_\mu$, a $k \times 1$ vector of regression coefficients; and $u_\mu(t)$, the $\mu^{th}$ disturbance term. The problem with Equation 42 is that with $N$ observations we cannot estimate all the $\beta$'s, $Nk$ in number, since there are not enough degrees of freedom. Usually in cross-section work we assume $\beta_1 = \beta_2 = \cdots = \beta_N = \beta$ and estimate the common $\beta$ in the following model:

$$
\begin{bmatrix} y_1(t) \\ y_2(t) \\ \vdots \\ y_N(t) \end{bmatrix} =
\begin{bmatrix} X_1(t) \\ X_2(t) \\ \vdots \\ X_N(t) \end{bmatrix} \beta +
\begin{bmatrix} u_1(t) \\ u_2(t) \\ \vdots \\ u_N(t) \end{bmatrix}, \qquad (43)
$$

or

$$ y = Z\beta + u. $$

The least-squares estimator for $\beta$, $\hat{\beta} = (Z'Z)^{-1}Z'y$, has expectation $\beta$ if the assumption $\beta_1 = \beta_2 = \cdots \beta_N$ is valid. If this assumption is invalid, the mathematical expectation of $\hat{\beta}$ is given by

$$ E\hat{\beta} = (Z'Z)^{-1} \left[ X_1'(t) X_1(t) \beta_1 + \cdots + X_N'(t) X_N(t) \beta_N \right], $$

which is a rather complicated function of the microcoefficient vectors, the $\beta_i$. As with aggregation over individuals, the expectation of a single element of $\hat{\beta}$ will depend on "corresponding" and "noncorresponding" microcoefficients (see References 28, 37 for additional analysis bearing on this problem). Practically, what is suggested from these observations is that if we have to work with cross-section data, it is important to use models whose parameters can reasonably be taken to be the same for different individuals, and to group individuals whose parameters are likely to be the same.

**Concluding Remarks**

In the preceding sections we have briefly reviewed a range of techniques for estimating parameters of models. While the arsenal of multivariate statistical tools for implementing the construction of models is indeed a formidable one, it must be recognized that there are problems that require further research. A few of these are as follows:

First, there is the age-old problem of measurement error. Additional techniques for analyzing sets of data to determine properties of measurement error would be very welcome. Also, it would be desirable to have better methods for estimating parameters with imperfect data.

Second, there are problems arising when we work with small samples of data. Some techniques have desirable asymptotic properties but unknown finite sample properties. This is particularly disturbing in analyzing time-series models with small samples of data, since usually convergence to asymptotic results is rather slow. It appears that Bayesian techniques will provide useful results on this problem (see Reference 38).

Third, there are the problems associated with the use and formulation of prior information in the analysis of data. We would like to have good procedures for combining information from various sources with current sample information in order to improve the precision of estimation and to produce better predictions. Study of techniques for accomplishing this is underway, and further results for multivariate statistical models will be forthcoming.

Fourth, there is a whole range of problems associated with the analysis of "mixed" models, that is, models involving both continuous and discrete random variables.

Fifth, there is the thorny problem of broadening the distributional assumptions underlying statistical techniques (see References 39, 40 for important contributions on this problem). Rather than assume normality initially, we need techniques that would enable us to utilize the data in making inferences about distributions of variables in multivariate situations.

Sixth, there is more work needed on the sensitivity of statistical techniques to specification errors. By studying further the robustness of statistical procedures, we are generally able to use them more intelligently.

There is thus much more work to be done in improving statistical techniques. However, in order to reap the potential payoff that results from applying them, we require extensive data of good quality. Most of the serious problems mentioned in the preceding section, "Some Special Problems," arise because of inadequate data. While procedures can sometimes be invented to circumvent some of these problems, they are usually founded on additional specifying assumptions, assumptions which in most cases can not be thoroughly investigated. In a large model, a compounding of such imperfectly studied assumptions leads to doubts about the general quality of the model. Good researchers, in such a situation, will press demands for better data. It is to be hoped that data-generating organizations will be responsive to such demands.

**References**

1. Jeffreys, H. , <u>Theory of Probability</u>, 3rd ed. , Clarendon Press, Oxford, 1961.

2. Raiffa, H. , and R. Schlaifer, <u>Applied Statistical Decision Theory</u>, Graduate School of Business Administration, Harvard University, Boston, 1961.

3. Savage, L. J. , "Bayesian Statistics, " in <u>Decision and Information Processes</u>, R. Machel, Ed. , The Macmillan Co. , New York, 1962.

4. Tiao, G. C. , and A. Zellner, "Bayes' Theorem and the Use of Prior Knowledge in Regression Analysis, " <u>Biometrika</u>, <u>51</u>, 219 — 230 (1964).

5. Tiao, G. C. , and A. Zellner, "On the Bayesian Estimation of Multivariate Regression, " <u>Journal of the Royal Statistical Society</u>, Series B, <u>26</u>, (1964).

6. Anscombe, F. J. , "Examination of Residuals, " in <u>Fourth Berkeley Symposium on Mathematical Statistics and Probability</u>, Vol. I, University of California Press, Berkeley, 1961.

7. Zellner, A. , "An Efficient Method of Estimating Seemingly Unrelated Regressions and Tests for Aggregation Bias, " <u>Journal of the American Statistical Association</u>, <u>57</u>, 348 — 368 (1962).

8. Zellner, A. , and D. S. Huang, "Further Properties of Efficient Estimators for Seemingly Unrelated Regression Equations, " <u>International Economic Review</u>, <u>3</u>, 300 — 313 (1962).

9. Zellner, A. , "Estimators for Seemingly Unrelated Regression Equations: Some Exact Finite Sample Results, " <u>Journal of the American Statistical Association</u>, <u>58</u>, 977 — 992 (1963).

10. Roy, S. N. , <u>Some Aspects of Multivariate Analysis</u>, John Wiley & Sons, New York, 1957.

11. Stroud, A. , and A. Zellner, "Program for Computing Efficient Regression Estimates and Associated Statistics, " Systems Formulation and Methodology Workshop Paper 6204, Social Systems Research Institute, University of Wisconsin, Madison, 1962.

12. Barten, A. P. , "Consumer Demand Functions under Conditions of Almost Additive Preferences, " <u>Econometrica</u>, <u>32</u>, 1 — 38 (1964).

13. Feige, E. L. , <u>The Demand for Liquid Assets:  A Temporal Cross-Section Analysis</u>, Prentice-Hall, Englewood Cliffs, N. J. , 1964.

14. Hardin, E. , "Michigan's Employment Problem and the Elasticity of Substitution, " manuscript, 1964.

15.    Grunfeld, Y. , "The Determinants of Corporate Investment, " unpublished
       Ph. D. dissertation, University of Chicago, 1958.

16.    Finney, D. J. , Probit Analysis, 2nd ed. , Cambridge University Press,
       Cambridge, 1952.

17.    Anscombe, F. J. , "On Estimating Binomial Response Relations, " Biometrika,
       43, 461 — 464 (1956) .

18.    Berkson, J. , "Estimate of the Integrated Normal Curve by Minimum Normit
       Chi-Square with Particular Reference to Bio-Assay, " Journal of the American
       Statistical Association, 50, 529 — 549 (1955) .

19.    Tobin, J. , "The Application of Multivariate Probit Analysis to Economic
       Survey Data, " Cowles Foundation Discussion Paper No. 1, Yale University,
       New Haven, 1955.

20.    Zellner, A. , and T. H. Lee, "Joint Estimation of Relationships Involving
       Discrete Random Variables, " Econometrica, 33, 382 — 394 (Apr. 1965) .

21.    Cramer, E. M. , "Some Comparisons of Methods of Fitting the Dosage
       Response Curve for Small Samples, " Journal of the American Statistical
       Association, 59, 779 — 793 (1964) .

22.    Berkson, J. , "Application of the Logistic Function to Bio-Assay, " Journal of
       the American Statistical Association, 39, 357 — 365 (1944) .

23.    Berkson, J. , "A Statistically Precise and Relatively Simple Method of
       Estimating the Bio-Assay with Quantal Response Based on the Logistic
       Function, " Journal of the American Statistical Association, 48, 565 — 599
       (1953) .

24.    Berkson, J. , "Maximum Likelihood and Minimum $\chi^2$ Estimates of the Logis-
       tic Function, " Journal of the American Statistical Association, 50, 130 — 162
       (1955) .

25.    Cornfield, J. , and N. Mantel, "Some New Aspects of the Application of
       Maximum Likelihood to the Calculation of the Dosage Response Curve, "
       Journal of the American Statistical Association, 45, 181 — 210 (1950) .

26.    Goldberger, A. S. , Econometric Theory, John Wiley & Sons, New York, 1964.

27.    Johnston, J. , Econometric Methods, McGraw-Hill Book Co. , New York, 1963.

28.    Klein, L. R. , A Textbook of Econometrics, Row, Peterson & Co. , Evanston,
       Ill. , 1953.

29.    Koopmans, T. C. , Statistical Inference in Dynamic Economic Models, John
       Wiley & Sons, New York, 1950.

30.  Rothenberg, T. J., and C. T. Leenders, "Efficient Estimation of Simultane-
     ous Equation Systems," Econometrica, 32, 57 — 76 (1964).

31.  Zellner, A., and H. Theil, "Three-Stage Least Squares: Simultaneous Esti-
     mation of Simultaneous Equations," Econometrica, 30, 54 — 78 (1962).

32.  Dreze, J., "The Bayesian Approach to Simultaneous Equations Estimation,"
     O. N. R. Research Memorandum No. 67, The Technological Institute, North-
     western University, Evanston, Ill., 1962.

33.  Rothenberg, T. J., "A Bayesian Analysis of Simultaneous Equation Systems,"
     Report 6315, Econometric Institute, Netherlands School of Economics,
     Rotterdam.

34.  Theil, H., Linear Aggregation of Economic Relations, North-Holland Publish-
     ing Co., Amsterdam, 1954.

35.  Mundlak, Y., "Aggregation over Time in Distributed Lag Models," Inter-
     national Economic Review, 2, 154 — 163 (1961).

36.  Zellner, A., "On the Analysis of First Order Autoregressive Models with
     Incomplete Data," Systems Formulation and Methodology Workshop Paper
     6405, Social Systems Research Institute, University of Wisconsin, Madison,
     1964.

37.  Zellner, A., "Estimation of Cross-Section Relations: Analysis of a Common
     Specification Error," Metroeconomica, 14, 111 — 117 (1962).

38.  Zellner, A., and G. C. Tiao, "Bayesian Analysis of the Regression Model
     with Autocorrelated Errors," Journal of the American Statistical Association,
     59, 763 — 778 (1964).

39.  Box, G. E. P., and D. R. Cox, "An Analysis of Transformations (with Dis-
     cussion)," Journal of the Royal Statistical Society, Series B, 26 (1964).

40.  Box, G. E. P., and G. C. Tiao: "A Further Look at Robustness via Bayes's
     Theorem," Biometrika, 49, 419 — 432 (1962).

# COHORT ANALYSIS OF ATTITUDE DATA*

**William M. Evan**
**Massachusetts Institute of Technology**

In a recent inventory of findings in several fields of social science, Berelson and Steiner note that these sciences have very little to say about

. . . central human concerns: nobility, moral courage, ethical torments, the delicate relations of father and son or the marriage state, life's way of corrupting innocence, the rightness or wrongness of acts, evil, happiness, love and hate, and even sex. [1]

Assuming that this assessment is true, it appears that these "central human concerns" — comprising as they do the drama of life — are very elusive and tend to be insusceptible to analysis by means of prevailing social science theories and methodologies.

One such element of the drama of life is the formation, stability, and change in the values and attitudes of people as they pass through the life cycle. The dynamics of attitude change and attitude stability involve a multidetermined process, an understanding of which often falls to the lot of the poet, novelist, and philosopher, rather than to that of the social scientist. This situation exists even though the discovery and analysis of changes in the values, attitudes, and opinions of a generation, or of several contemporaneous generations, would seem to be a basic problem in social science.

---

*Prepared for the Conference on Computer Methods in the Analysis of Large-Scale Social Systems, Joint Center for Urban Studies of M.I.T. and Harvard University, Cambridge, Mass., October 19 — 20, 1964. I would like to express my gratitude to the American Philosophical Society for a grant that made this study possible, to the Roper Public Opinion Research Center for making available the vast quantity of data necessary for this investigation, and to Mrs. Rita Weisbrod and Corey Fair for invaluable assistance.

## Theoretical and Methodological Problems

Notwithstanding the recent literature on the beat generation and on angry young men, there have been few efforts to explore the dynamics of attitude change for as long a period as a generation. In fact, there is little consensus as to how long a generation is. [2] Biologically, a generation may range from 20 to 30 years, the length of time it takes for a son to become a father. In terms of political or economic climates, a generation may be only 15 years. For example, the transition from the depression thirties to the prosperous postwar forties was a very sharp one indeed. In some fields of science and engineering, a generation may be 10 years or even less.

In the face of such ambiguities, one may well wonder whether social science ought not leave this subject to the poet, novelist, and philosopher. However, if social science is to develop a predictive and explanatory theory of social change, it will have to include the dynamics of macrosocial change as well as the dynamics of microsocial change, such as the antecedents, concomitants, and consequences of changes in the mentality of one or more generations. Let me cite but one example of the necessity for such knowledge. Whenever a law is passed, which is an example of a macrosocial change, public opinion in favor of the law in question tends to increase. [3] Thus, the desegregation decision of the U. S. Supreme Court was followed by a gradual increase in favorable attitudes towards social integration among Northern and Southern whites. [4] This shift in favorable attitudes is by no means the only microsocial consequence of this particular macrosocial change. However, the illustration points to the proposition that if a macrosocial change is to succeed in any realm, whether political, legal, economic, or technological, it must trigger microsocial changes, including attitude changes. In short, the concept of a generation, which has been of considerable interest to European social theorists, [5] deserves theoretical and empirical study by American social scientists if we are to progress in our understanding of the processes of social change. [6]

The twin problems of theory and methodology have impeded progress in research on generations. First, we do not yet have a sufficiently comprehensive theory of either the structure of attitudes or of mechanisms whereby they change or remain stable. To be sure, Festinger, [7] Heider, [8] members of the Yale program of experimental studies in attitude change, [9] and others, [10] have made significant contributions toward the goal of constructing a comprehensive theory.

As for methodological difficulties, they are equally substantial. Cross-sectional surveys of attitudes make it difficult to isolate processes of change. Some trend studies, using successive cross-sectional surveys, have made valuable contributions in documenting attitude changes, but not necessarily in explaining them. There are virtually no longitudinal studies of public opinion and attitudes over any substantial period of time. To initiate a 20- to 25-year longitudinal study of attitudes is obviously an enterprise fraught with many problems, theoretical and practical. To mention but a few: repeated interviews may affect the respondent's attitudes and subsequent responses; sample mortality can bias the results; and, last but not least, the investigator's own life expectancy can influence the conduct of the research. [11]

Because of the limitations of past cross-sectional and longitudinal studies for research on generational changes in attitudes, it occurred to me that the demographer's procedure of cohort analysis[12] was a potentially fruitful substitute for a long-term panel or a longitudinal investigation.[13] Such an analysis has since been applied by others[14] and becomes ever more fruitful as survey "data banks" at the Roper Survey Research Center and elsewhere grow larger.[15] With the help of computers, the task of processing and analyzing huge quantities of data has now become feasible.

### Procedure

It was in light of these considerations that a cohort analysis was undertaken of a set of public opinion questions asked approximately 20 years apart — a crude operational definition of a generation in view of the nature of the available data — to facilitate a study of intragenerational and intergenerational shifts in attitudes. After a fairly extensive search of the archive at the Roper Center to develop a time series of similar or identical opinion questions, we identified 20 pairs of questions, drawn from 40 different public opinion polls conducted by the American Institute of Public Opinion. In examining the data, we shall look at decennial cohorts as they age over an interval of time between two successive surveys which, with one exception, were 20 years or more apart. An example of the cohort classification of data from successive cross-sectional surveys is shown in Table 1.

TABLE 1

Cohort Classification of Data from
Successive Cross-Sectional Surveys

| Year of Cross-Sectional Survey | Age of Cohort A | Age of Cohort B | Age of Cohort C | Age of Cohort D |
|---|---|---|---|---|
| 1935 | 20-29 | 30-39 | 40-49 | 50-59 |
| 1955 | 40-49 | 50-59 | 60-69 | 70-79 |

The hypotheses that we shall explore deal with the relative effects of aging and historical situation on the various cohorts.[16] Aging has generally been viewed as having a conservatizing influence because of increasing psychological rigidities, a deceleration in the learning rate, and a fear of the unfamiliar or the novel.[17] In addition, aging may be viewed sociologically as having a conservatizing effect due to changes over time in the status-set and reference groups of an individual. As a person grows older, his status-set — that is, his complement of statuses in various institutional spheres — diminishes, his network of social interactions shrinks, and, in general, he undergoes a process of disengagement from his social environment.[18]

Regarding the effects of history on the attitudes of a generation, I hypothesized that some historical situations, such as depressions, have a liberalizing effect on political opinions, particularly if the members are adversely affected by the economic conditions; other historical situations, such as wars and prosperity, have a conservatizing effect on political opinions.   Note that I referred to the effect of historical situations on political opinions; non-political opinions may be influenced by aging and by historical forces other than those of a political and economic type represented by wars and fluctuations in the business cycle.   Since a generation, by definition, involves the interaction of aging and exposure to historical events, a cohort analysis of attitudes is guided by the logic of analysis of variance in seeking to measure the relative effect of the component factors on opinions.

In classifying a particular response to a survey question as to whether it reflects a liberal or a conservative attitude, we relied on whether the responses to the question correlated with voting behavior in the last Presidential election in order to avoid subjective judgments as to what opinions are liberal or conservative.   For example, expressing a favorable opinion regarding the government's breaking up of monopolies can be currently construed as a liberal attitude — although it is contrary to the nineteenth-century conception of liberalism — because a significantly higher proportion of those who favor this opinion voted Democratic in Presidential elections than those who were opposed to this opinion.   Conversely, a significantly lower proportion of those favoring this opinion voted Republican than those who were opposed to this opinion.   Ideally, we would have also wanted to apply Guttman scaling or factor analysis in discriminating between liberal and conservative opinions, but neither was possible because the set of repeated opinion questions we identified were not asked of the respondents in any of the 40 surveys.

Of the 20 pairs of similar or identical questions, only 6 were found to be significantly associated with voting behavior in the Presidential election at the time of both surveys.   Hence, these 6 pairs of items will be interpreted on a liberalism-conservatism attitude dimension based on voting behavior.   The items in this set pertain to social security:  medicare legislation, the government's role in the breaking up of monopolies, labor unions, membership in the League of Nations and the United Nations, political self-identification, and preference for a liberal or conservative party.

Of the 14 remaining pairs of questions that did not correlate with voting behavior, 6 pertain to receptivity or opposition to a new pattern of behavior affecting a prevailing cultural norm.   Thus, opposing the death penalty, favoring government dissemination of birth control information, advocating a small family, approving of women wearing shorts in public, not attending church, and favoring equal pay for women performing equal work are opinions reflecting a willingness to modify prevailing practices and their underlying cultural norms.   We shall thus interpret the responses to these 6 items as indexing a traditionalism-modernism attitude toward the culture.

The other 8 pairs of questions were not analyzed in this phase of the research.   In subsequent analyses, we shall ascertain whether the relationships involving these items resemble either of the two sets of questions — those falling on the political liberalism-conservatism dimension or those on the cultural traditionalism-modernism dimension — or whether they differ from both of them.[19]

**Results**

In examining the responses to the 12 questions in Tables 2 — 13, we shall first inquire whether there are <u>intracohort</u> and <u>intercohort</u> increases in conservatism for all four cohorts. If the data conform to this pattern, then the aging hypothesis would be confirmed. On the other hand, if we observe that there is both <u>intracohort</u> and <u>intercohort</u> variation in conservatism, i.e., increases as well as decreases in conservatism, then this would suggest the effects of historical situations. In other words, <u>intracohort</u> and <u>intercohort</u> increases in conservatism indicate aging is the major source of the attitude change, particularly if the level of conservatism in the cohort at the time of the second survey is not significantly different from the level of conservatism of an equivalent age group in the first survey. On the other hand, <u>intracohort</u> stability or decrease in conservatism and <u>intercohort</u> stability or variation in conservatism indicate the effect of historical situations. If, however, we observe either <u>intracohort</u> stability or decrease in conservatism together with <u>intercohort</u> increase in conservatism, we would infer that aging and historical experience have interacted in producing conservatism.

An examination of Tables 2 — 13 suggests that regardless of the category of the question, whether political or cultural, the historical situation seems to have more effect than does aging. In 6 of the 12 questions, the historical hypothesis was confirmed, whereas the aging hypothesis was supported in only 2 of the 12 questions. In the remaining 4 questions, there is evidence of an interaction effect of aging and historical situations. These findings would suggest, surprisingly, that the dynamics of generational attitude shifts are not different for our two types of questions.

To explore other factors potentially affecting the responses to the political and cultural sets of questions, we analyzed some structural sources of attitude differentiation within a cohort, such as occupation, rural-urban residence, sex, and geographic location. The present state of the analysis of the data permits a brief consideration of the effects of rural-urban residence and occupation on cohort attitude changes.

Are attitude changes similar for both the rural and the urban subcohorts and with respect to the cultural and political questions? Concerning the effect of rural-urban residence on the responses to the political questions, rural as well as urban subcohorts, in all four cohorts, as shown in Table 14, underwent a decline in mean conservatism. This decline in conservatism is slightly greater for urban than for rural subcohorts in all but the oldest cohort. For the latter, exposure to the diversity and heterogeneity of political opinion in an urban environment had the effect of liberalizing attitudes, but somewhat less so than for the rural subgroup in this cohort.

As regards the effect of rural-urban residence on cultural attitudes, all subcohorts — except for the rural in the next-to-the-oldest cohort — underwent a slight increase in mean traditional responses (see Table 15). In other words, rural-urban residence does not have a differential effect on cultural attitudes, but it does tend to have a differential effect on political attitudes. Evidently, cultural attitudes not only change more slowly than political attitudes, but are also more multidetermined. This difference between the two sets of questions was apparently masked in examining the attitude shifts in the cohorts undifferentiated by socially structured subdivisions.

TABLE 2

Per Cent of Conservative Opinions
of Four Cohorts and Equivalent
Age Groups in Early Survey

Early question:  Should the
government attempt to break
up large business organizations? (1937)

Recent question:  What is
meant by the term monopoly?
Do you think there are any
monopolies in this country
at this time? (1956)

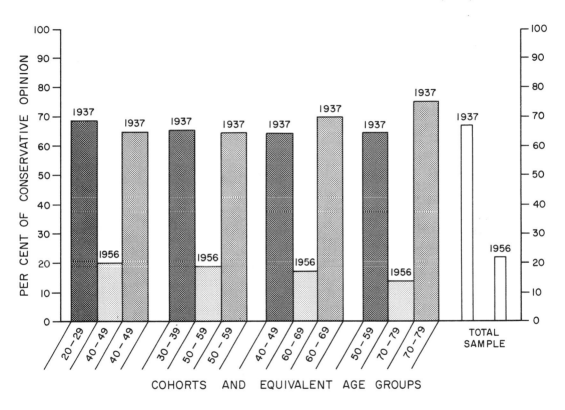

COHORTS  AND  EQUIVALENT  AGE GROUPS

With reference to the effect of occupation on political attitudes, manual as well as
nonmanual subcohorts, in all four cohorts, manifest a decline in mean conservatism (see Table 16). The decline in conservatism was greater for the nonmanual
subcohorts in all but the youngest cohort. Nonmanual workers are more exposed
to formal education, mass media, and other types of social experiences, which
may have a liberalizing effect.

The effect of occupation on cultural attitudes, as shown in Table 17, appears to be
very slight indeed as well as inconsistent. Manual as well as nonmanual workers,
in the next-to-the-youngest and in the oldest cohorts, show a slight increase in

TABLE 3

Per Cent of Conservative Opinions
of Four Cohorts and Equivalent
Age Groups in Early Survey

Early question:   At present, the Social
Security System provides benefits for
old age, death and unemployment. Would
you favor changing the program to include
payment of benefits for sickness, dis-
ability, doctor and hospital bills? (1943)

Recent question:   Would you
favor or oppose having the
social security tax increased
in order to pay for old age
medical insurance? (1961)

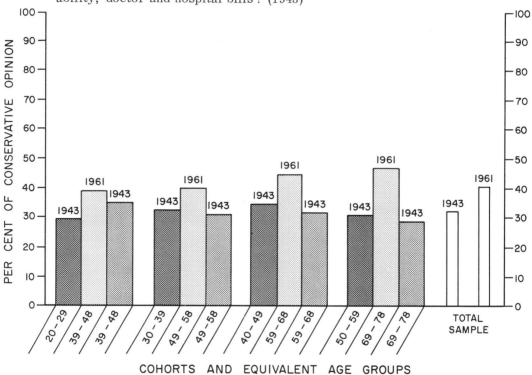

mean traditionalism; in the youngest cohort, there is a very small increase in
mean traditionalism of manual workers and no change in the attitudes of nonmanual
workers; in the next-to-the oldest cohort, both manual and nonmanual workers
underwent a slight decrease in mean traditionalism. Clearly, occupation has a
different impact on political than on cultural attitudes; although it tends to liberal-
ize political attitudes,  especially those of nonmanual workers,  it has a negligible
and inconsistent effect on cultural attitudes.

TABLE 4

Per Cent of Conservative Opinions
of Four Cohorts and Equivalent
Age Groups in Early Survey

Early question:  Are you in favor
of labor unions? (1938)

Recent question:  In general
do you approve or disapprove
of labor unions? (1959)

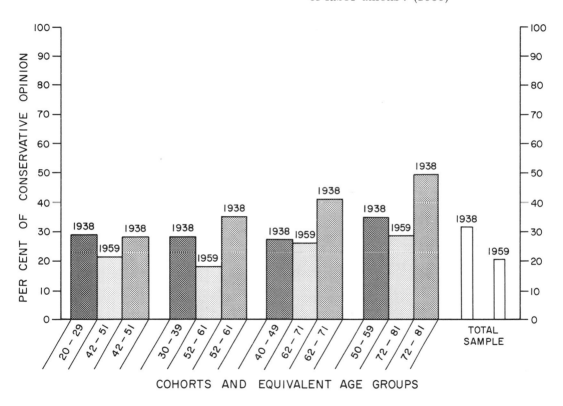

The subcohort analysis using the variables of rural-urban residence and occupation suggests that attitude changes do vary by type of question, a fact obscured in examining the attitude shifts in the undifferentiated cohorts shown in Tables 2 — 13.  In general, it is surprising that the attitude changes with respect to the political and cultural questions were not more extensively affected by occupation and rural-urban residence.  Does this reflect an increasing process of additudinal homogenization in an urban industrializing society in which large organizations and mass media may be exerting increasing influence on the opinions and attitudes of people? Or are some of the occupational differences masked by the need to treat this variable dichotomously because of the small N's?

TABLE 5

Per Cent of Conservative Opinions
of Four Cohorts and Equivalent
Age Groups in Early Survey

Early question:  Would you like to see
the United States join the League of
Nations? (1938)

Recent question:  Do you think the
United States should give up its
membership in the United Nations
or not? (1961)

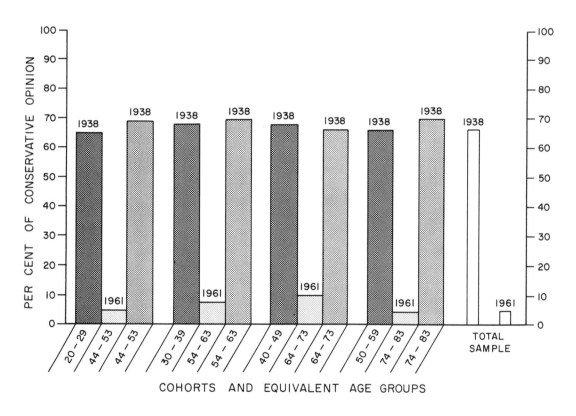

COHORTS  AND  EQUIVALENT  AGE  GROUPS

### Limitations of the Data

The limitations of the data we have presented are legion.  Not only are some of the
pairs of questions not identical in wording, but even identical questions may have
different meanings to the sample of respondents in two historical periods.  Hence,
observed opinion shifts within a cohort could be due, in part, to changes in cultural
meanings of the questions and changes in verbal patterns.  In addition, it should be
noted that changes in the sampling procedure of the American Institute of Public
Opinion and of other polling organizations — from the use of quota samples in the

TABLE 6

Per Cent of Conservative Opinions
of Four Cohorts and Equivalent
Age Groups in Early Survey

Early question: In politics,
do you regard yourself as a
liberal or a conservative?
(1938)

Recent question: Taking
everything into account,
would you say that you
yourself are more of a
liberal or more a con-
servative in politics?
(1957)

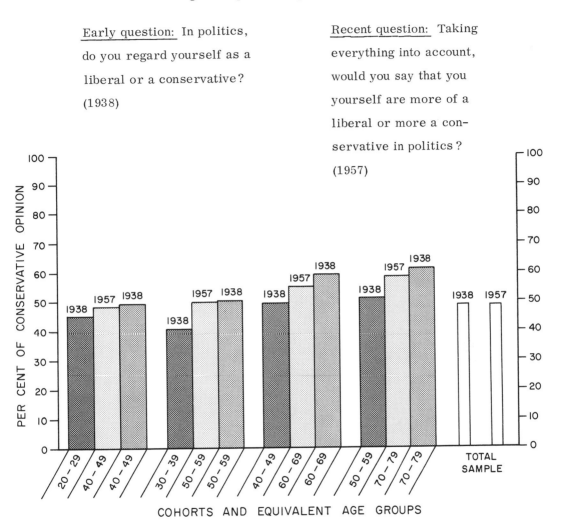

thirties and forties to a modified type of area probability sampling in recent years
— could yield results accounting for some of the opinion changes. [20]

Yet another problem I discovered in undertaking a cohort analysis of public opinion
data is the need to develop a correction factor that would take account of cohort
attrition, whether due to geographic mobility, occupational mobility, or death.
Such a correction factor is necessary in order to ensure that cohort opinion shifts
are not due to social structural or ecological changes.  For example, some blue-
collar workers in 1940 could very well be performing white-collar jobs in 1960,
not only because of their upwardly mobile aspirations, but also because the

TABLE 7

Per Cent of Conservative Opinions
of Four Cohorts and Equivalent
Age Groups in Early Survey

Early question: If there were
only two political parties in
this country, one for conservatives and one for liberals,
which one would you join? (1937)

Recent question: Suppose there
were only two major parties in
the United States, one for liberals and one for conservatives,
which one would you be most
likely to prefer? (1961)

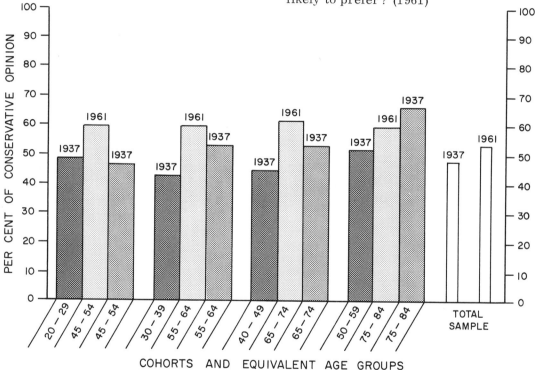

occupational structure of American society has undergone change. In examining
subclassifications within a cohort, it is especially necessary to rule out shifts of
an occupational, geographic, or other sort, which could be affecting the direction
and magnitude of opinion change. For instance, in Table 18 we notice that on the
average, approximately 17 per cent of rural liberals who were 20 to 29 years of
age in the 1937 survey have become conservative in the 25-year time span, that is,
in the survey in 1961, and that 19 per cent of urban liberals in this cohort have
become conservative. However, in estimating the impact of aging in the urban
context, we must take account of census data on rural-urban mobility over the 25
years. The extent of conservatization of urban liberals must be discounted

TABLE 8

Per Cent of Traditional Opinions
of Four Cohorts and Equivalent
Age Groups in Early Survey

Early question: What do you consider
is the ideal size of family — a husband,
wife and how many children? (Actual
number of children?) (1941)

Recent question: What do you
think is the ideal number of
children for a family to have?
(1962)

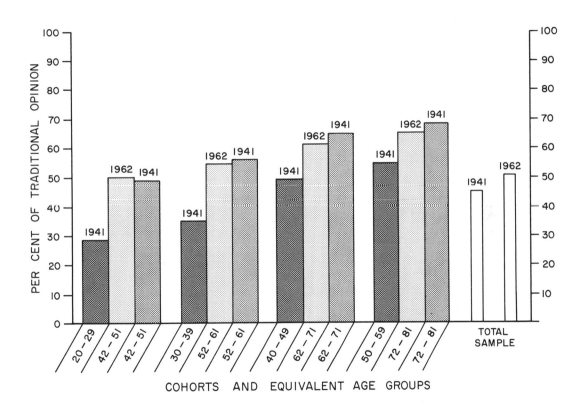

somewhat because the 1961 urban cohort contains 1937 rurals who were more conservative at the start. To make these adjustments would require the use of census
data for urban-rural and occupational mobility shifts of the various age groups.
The work of developing and applying correction factors to the results of our cohort
analysis is still in progress. [21]

TABLE 9

Per Cent of Traditional Opinions
of Four Cohorts and Equivalent
Age Groups in Early Survey

<u>Early question:</u>  Do you think
it is all right for women to
wear shorts on the street? (1939)

<u>Recent question:</u>  Do you approve
or disapprove of women wearing
shorts in public? (1961)

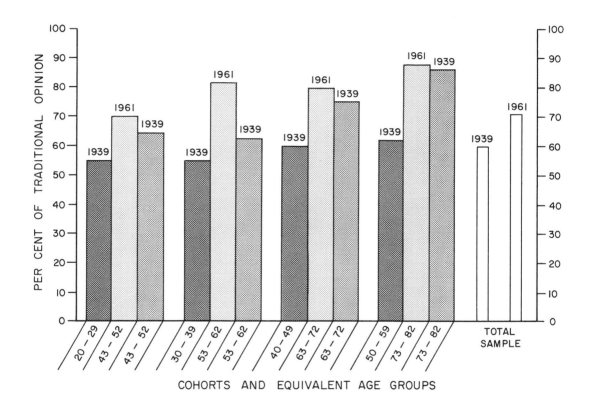

COHORTS AND EQUIVALENT AGE GROUPS

## Conclusion

Our findings, tentative as they are because of the limitations of the data discussed above, point to the impact of historical situations and of such variables as occupation and rural-urban residence on the attitudes of different generations. A more accurate estimate of the effects of socioeconomic factors on individual attitude shifts in various cohorts will be made possible with the aid of correction factors.

Taking as a point of departure the findings of cohort analyses, such as the one presented in this paper, and the growing body of experimental findings on attitude

TABLE 10

Per Cent of Traditional Opinions
of Four Cohorts and Equivalent
Age Groups in Early Survey

Early question:   Did you happen to
go to church last Sunday? (1939)

Recent question:   Did you yourself
happen to attend church in the last
seven days? (1959)

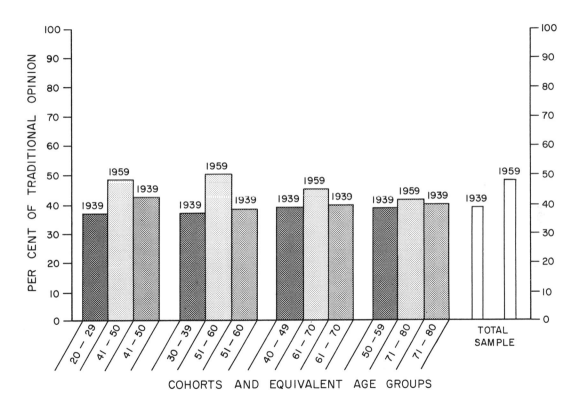

change, it would be worth exploring the utility of devising various computer simulation models of generational changes in attitudes akin to the "prognostic" model of Pool and Abelson [22] and the "process" model of Abelson and Bernstein. [23] The complexities of such an undertaking would suggest a need for initial experiments with simulations at the community level — in both homogeneous and heterogeneous communities — before making the transition to the level of the total society. Thus, cohort analysis as well as other types of attitude studies could provide the input for simulation models of generational shifts in attitudes. And these in turn might pave the way for a longitudinal study to verify the results of both cohort analyses and

## TABLE 11

Per Cent of Traditional Opinions
of Four Cohorts and Equivalent
Age Groups in Early Survey

Early question:  Would you like to
see a government agency furnish birth
control information to married people
who want it? (1938)

Recent question:  In some places in the
United States it is not legal to supply
birth control information.  How do you
feel about this — do you think birth
control information should be made
available to anyone who wants it, or
not? (1959)

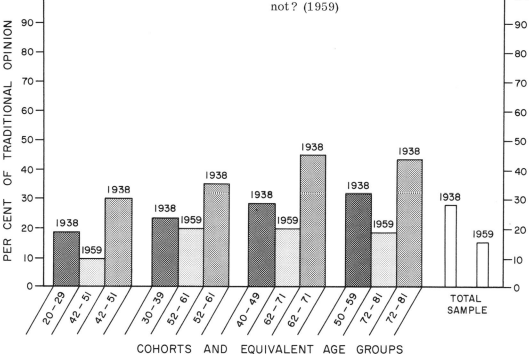

simulation models.  Since the cost of a long-term longitudinal study is very great
in both time and treasure, a quasi-longitudinal inquiry is of considerable promise
as an intermediate type of investigation.  A noteworthy example of such a study is
the G. E. Consumer Research Project of Reuben Hill at the Family Study Center at
the University of Minnesota. [24]  Hill and his colleagues selected a sample of families of three-linked generations, including grandparents, parents, and children who
were themselves young adults and married.  This kind of quasi-longitudinal study
with retrospective questions to isolate the effects of age and historical experiences
would be a relatively inexpensive way of verifying the results generated by cohort
analyses as well as by simulation models of generational changes in attitudes.

TABLE 12

Per Cent of Traditional Opinions
of Four Cohorts and Equivalent
Age Groups in Early Survey

Early question:  Are you in
favor of the death penalty
for murder? (1937)

Recent question:  Are you in favor
of the death penalty for persons
convicted of murder? (1960)

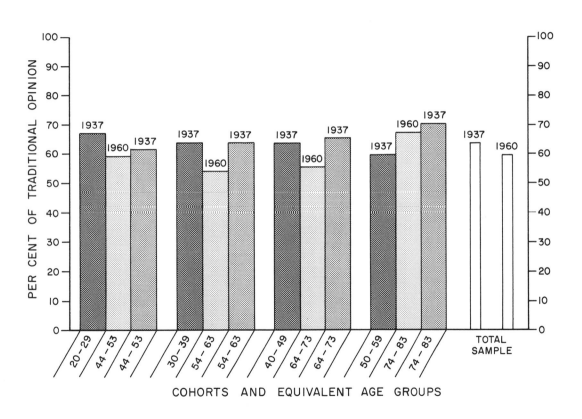

These strategies for tracing attitudes through the life cycle address themselves to a
basic problem in the theory of social change.  For as Ryder puts it, ". . . social
change occurs to the extent that successive cohorts do something other than merely
repeat the patterns of behavior of their predecessors."[25]  And in developing the
methodology and theory of studying generational changes in attitudes, social scientists may also contribute to our understanding of a "central human concern."

TABLE 13

Per Cent of Traditional Opinions
of Four Cohorts and Equivalent
Age Groups in Early Survey

Early question:  If women take the
place of men in industry,  should
they be paid the same wages as
men?  (1942)

Recent question:  Do you approve or
disapprove of paying women the same
salaries as men,  if they are doing
the same work?  (1962)

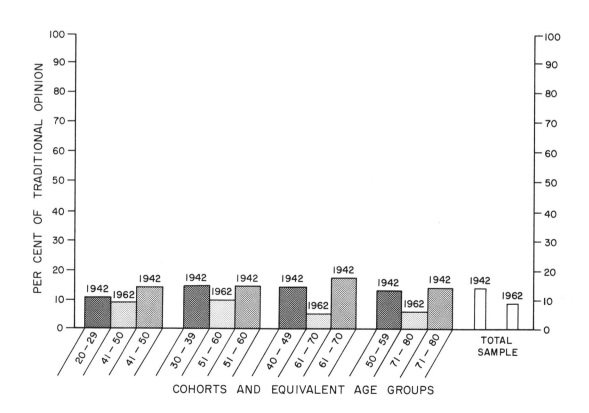

TABLE 14

Per Cent of Conservative Opinions of Four Cohorts, Classified by
Rural-Urban Residence, on Six Political Questions

| Questions | Cohort 20-29/40-49 | | | | Cohort 30-39/50-59 | | | | Cohort 40-49/60-69 | | | | Cohort 50-59/70-79 | | | |
|---|---|---|---|---|---|---|---|---|---|---|---|---|---|---|---|---|
| | R | U | R | U | R | U | R | U | R | U | R | U | R | U | R | U |
| Join liberal or conservative party | 53 | 47 | 62 | 57 | 45 | 42 | 61 | 59 | 53 | 44 | 75 | 57 | 56 | 51 | 69 | 56 |
| Government action on monopolies | 73 | 68 | 17 | 23 | 67 | 68 | 21 | 20 | 67 | 65 | 21 | 19 | 71 | 64 | 8 | 15 |
| Liberal or conservative in politics | 48 | 46 | 47 | 49 | 45 | 41 | 67 | 44 | 52 | 47 | 68 | 50 | 60 | 47 | 44 | 60 |
| Labor unions | 32 | 30 | 32 | 18 | 36 | 27 | 28 | 16 | 33 | 26 | 25 | 28 | 47 | 31 | 31 | 25 |
| Social Security-Medicare | 30 | 31 | 45 | 37 | 37 | 32 | 43 | 39 | 36 | 35 | 40 | 40 | 40 | 29 | 44 | 51 |
| Join/stay in League/UN | 64 | 67 | 5 | 5 | 67 | 70 | 10 | 8 | 70 | 68 | 4 | 15 | 69 | 66 | 9 | 3 |
| Mean Conservative Response: | 50 | 48 | 36 | 31 | 50 | 47 | 38 | 31 | 52 | 48 | 39 | 35 | 57 | 48 | 34 | 35 |

TABLE 15

Per Cent of Traditional Opinions of Four Cohorts, Classified by
Rural–Urban Residence, on Six Cultural Questions

| Questions | Cohort 20-29/40-49 | | | | Cohort 30-39/50-59 | | | | Cohort 40-49/60-69 | | | | Cohort 50-59/70-79 | | | |
|---|---|---|---|---|---|---|---|---|---|---|---|---|---|---|---|---|
| | R | U | R | U | R | U | R | U | R | U | R | U | R | U | R | U |
| Capital punishment | 74 | 66 | 62 | 59 | 71 | 62 | 51 | 57 | 66 | 63 | 51 | 58 | 65 | 57 | 70 | 67 |
| Birth control | 27 | 16 | 10 | 12 | 25 | 24 | 20 | 22 | 32 | 28 | 16 | 25 | 38 | 31 | 28 | 13 |
| Church attendance | 35 | 38 | 52 | 47 | 39 | 37 | 54 | 49 | 35 | 40 | 46 | 46 | 34 | 43 | 37 | 46 |
| Women's dress | 60 | 54 | 80 | 65 | 60 | 55 | 90 | 78 | 68 | 57 | 88 | 76 | 63 | 63 | 90 | 85 |
| Family size | 38 | 23 | 57 | 46 | 43 | 33 | 59 | 53 | 52 | 47 | 64 | 61 | 66 | 48 | 71 | 65 |
| Women's wages | 10 | 14 | 6 | 12 | 15 | 17 | 10 | 12 | 17 | 14 | 9 | 4 | 12 | 17 | 8 | 6 |
| Mean Traditional Response: | 41 | 35 | 47 | 40 | 42 | 38 | 47 | 45 | 45 | 42 | 37 | 45 | 49 | 43 | 51 | 57 |

TABLE 16

Per Cent of Conservative Opinions of Four Cohorts, Classified by
Occupation (Manual vs. Nonmanual) on Six Political Questions

| Questions | Cohort 20-29/40-49 | | | | Cohort 30-39/50-59 | | | | Cohort 40-49/60-69 | | | | Cohort 50-59/70-79 | | | |
|---|---|---|---|---|---|---|---|---|---|---|---|---|---|---|---|---|
| | M | NM | M | NM | M | NM | M | NM | M | NM | M | NM | M | NM | M | NM |
| Join liberal or conservative party | 45 | 45 | 49 | 64 | 32 | 49 | 38 | 63 | 35 | 53 | 86 | 52 | 42 | 57 | 50 | 50 |
| Government action on monopolies | 73 | 68 | 22 | 24 | 61 | 64 | 17 | 25 | 66 | 65 | 18 | 16 | 69 | 65 | - | 14 |
| Liberal or conservative in politics | 39 | 50 | 25 | 48 | 43 | 44 | 43 | 51 | 47 | 56 | 42 | 52 | 35 | 51 | 25 | 38 |
| Labor unions | 26 | 29 | 13 | 24 | 21 | 26 | 16 | 22 | 20 | 22 | 13 | 36 | 17 | 25 | 60 | 50 |
| Social Security-Medicare | 22 | 34 | 52 | 45 | 27 | 36 | 52 | 54 | 29 | 42 | 40 | 50 | 23 | 40 | 25 | 57 |
| Join/stay in League/UN | 65 | 75 | 4 | 8 | 69 | 84 | 12 | 9 | 70 | 77 | 20 | 3 | 65 | 83 | - | - |
| Mean Conservative Response: | 45 | 50 | 27 | 36 | 39 | 50 | 30 | 37 | 45 | 52 | 37 | 30 | 41 | 53 | 40 | 41 |

## TABLE 17

Per Cent of Traditional Opinions of Four Cohorts, Classified by
Occupation (Manual vs. Nonmanual) on Six Political Questions

| Questions | Cohort 20-29/40-49 | | | | Cohort 39-39/50-59 | | | | Cohort 40-49/60-69 | | | | Cohort 50-59/70-79 | | | |
|---|---|---|---|---|---|---|---|---|---|---|---|---|---|---|---|---|
| | M | NM | M | NM | M | NM | M | NM | M | NM | M | NM | M | NM | M | NM |
| Capital punishment | 69 | 75 | 68 | 61 | 63 | 73 | 53 | 61 | 66 | 67 | 61 | 35 | 58 | 67 | 81 | 100 |
| Birth control | 26 | 17 | 12 | 10 | 26 | 21 | 26 | 19 | 29 | 29 | 21 | 17 | 30 | 31 | 20 | 38 |
| Church attendance | 29 | 38 | 41 | 44 | 30 | 40 | 47 | 55 | 38 | 40 | 56 | 38 | 30 | 42 | - | 43 |
| Women's dress | 36 | 60 | 51 | 68 | 50 | 49 | 84 | 82 | 54 | 60 | 48 | 83 | 64 | 56 | 100 | 89 |
| Family size | 29 | 29 | 45 | 42 | 35 | 35 | 56 | 50 | 50 | 43 | 54 | 41 | 50 | 55 | 100 | 64 |
| Women's wages | 21 | 20 | 17 | 8 | 28 | 21 | 15 | 6 | 20 | 22 | 10 | 7 | 27 | 19 | 11 | - |
| Mean Traditional Response: | 35 | 40 | 39 | 40 | 39 | 40 | 47 | 46 | 43 | 43 | 42 | 30 | 43 | 45 | 52 | 56 |

TABLE 18

Illustration of Problem
of Cohort Attrition and
Need for a "Correction Factor"

Per Cent Conservative Response to Question:

"Suppose there were only two major
parties in the United States, one for
liberals and one for conservatives,
* which one would you be more likely
to prefer?"

Age 20-29, 1937 Survey | | | Age 45-54, 1961 Survey | |
---|---|---|---|---
 | Urban | Rural | | Urban | Rural
Conservative | .47 | .54 | Conservative | .57 | .62
Liberal | .53 | .46 | Liberal | .43 | .38

## References

1.   Berelson, Bernard, and Gary A. Steiner, Human Behavior:  An Inventory of Scientific Findings, Harcourt, Brace & World, New York, 1964, p. 664.

2.   Berger, Bennett M., "How Long is a Generation?," British Journal of Sociology, 11, 10 — 23 (Mar. 1960).

3.   Lazarsfeld, Paul F., "Public Opinion and the Classical Tradition," Public Opinion Quarterly, 21, 46 — 47 (1957), and Hadley Cantril, Gauging Public Opinion, Princeton University Press, Princeton, 1944, p. 228.

4.   Hyman, H. H., and P. B. Sheatsley, "Attitudes on Desegregation," Scientific American, 195, 35 — 39 (Dec. 1956), and "Attitudes Toward Desegregation," Scientific American, 211, 16 — 23 (July 1964).

5.   See, for example, Berger, op. cit.; Karl Mannheim, Essays on the Sociology of Knowledge, Routledge and Kegan Paul Ltd., London, 1952, pp. 286 — 320; Rudolph Heberle, Social Movements, Appleton Century Crofts, New York, 1951, pp. 118 — 127; and S. N. Eisenstadt, From Generation to Generation, The Free Press of Glencoe, Illinois, 1956.

6.   Ryder, N. B., "Notes on the Concept of a Population," American Journal of Sociology, 49, 453 — 461 (Mar. 1964).

7.   Festinger, Leon, A Theory of Cognitive Dissonance, Harper and Row, New York, 1957.

8.   F. Heider, The Psychology of Interpersonal Relations, John Wiley & Sons, New York, 1958.

9.   Rosenberg, Milton J., et al., Attitude, Organization, and Change, Yale University Press, New Haven, 1960; Sherif, Muzafer, and Carl I. Hovland, Social Judgment, Yale University Press, New Haven, 1961; and Rosenberg, M. J., "A Structural Theory of Attitude Dynamics," Public Opinion Quarterly, 24, 319 — 340 (Summer 1960).

10.  Kelman, H. C., "Processes of Opinion Change," Public Opinion Quarterly, 25, 57 — 78 (Spring 1961); Schein, Edgar H., with Inge Schneier and Curtis H. Barker, Coercive Persuasion, W. W. Norton & Co., New York, 1961, pp. 117 — 139, 269 — 282.

11.  Jones, H. E., "Problems of Method in Longitudinal Research," International Journal of Human Development, 1, 93 — 99 (1958); Goldstein, J., "The Relative Advantages and Limitations of the Panel and Successive-Sample Techniques in the Analysis of Opinion Change," Journal of Social Psychology, 50, 305 — 320 (1959); Goldfarb, Nathan, An Introduction to Longitudinal Statistical Analysis, The Free Press of Glencoe, Illinois, 1960, pp. 55 — 73; Kodlin, D., and D. J. Thompson, An Appraisal of the Longitudinal Approach to Studies of Growth and Development, Society for Research in Child Development, Lafayette, Ind., 1958.

12. See, for example, Ryder, op. cit., pp. 453ff; Jaffee, A. J., Handbook of Statistical Methods for Demographers, Preliminary Edition, U. S. Department of Commerce, Bureau of the Census, U. S. Government Printing Office, Washington, D. C., 1951; Whelpton, P. K., Cohort Fertility: Native Women in the United States, Princeton University Press, Princeton, 1954; and Eldridge, Hope T., "A Cohort Approach to the Analysis of Migration Differentials," Demography, 1, 212 — 219 (1964).

13. Cf. Evan, William M., "Cohort Analysis of Survey Data: A Procedure for Studying Long-Term Opinion Change," Public Opinion Quarterly, 23, 63 — 72 (Spring 1959).

14. Cf. Crittenden, John, "Aging and Party Affiliation," Public Opinion Quarterly, 26, 648 — 657 (Winter 1962); Hyman, H. H., and P. B. Sheatsley, "Attitudes Toward Desegregation," Scientific American, 211, 16 — 23 (July 1964).

15. Hastings, P. K., "The Roper Public Opinion Research Center: A Review of its First Three Years of Operation," Public Opinion Quarterly, 25, 120 — 126 (Spring 1961); and "The Roper Center: An International Archive of Sample Survey Data," Public Opinion Quarterly, 27, 590 — 598 (Winter 1963).

16. Cf. Evan, op. cit., pp. 68 — 69.

17. Toch, H., "Attitudes of the 'Fifty Plus' Age Group: Preliminary Considerations Toward a Longitudinal Survey," Public Opinion Quarterly, 17, 391 — 394 (Fall 1953); Hinshaw, Robert S., The Relation of Attitudes and Opinion to Age, Ph. D. dissertation, Princeton University, 1944; Harry Kay, "Theories of Learning and Aging," in Handbook of Aging and the Individual: Psychological and Biological Aspects, J. E. Birren, Ed., University of Chicago Press, Chicago, 1960, pp. 614 — 654; and Jerome, E. A., "Age and Learning — Experimental Studies," in J. E. Birren, Ed., op. cit., pp. 655 — 699.

18. Cf. Cumming, Elaine, and W. E. Henry, Growing Old: The Process of Disengagement, Basic Books & Co., New York, 1961.

19. For a further analysis of the data, see Evan, William M., Rita R. Weisbrod, and Corey Fair, "Intra-Generational and Inter-Generational Attitude Change: A Cohort Analysis of Public Opinion Data," forthcoming.

20. Stephan, F. F., and P. J. McCarthy, Sampling Opinions: An Analysis of Survey Procedure, John Wiley & Sons, New York, 1958, pp. 38 — 40; Mosteller, Frederick, et al., The Pre-Election Polls of 1948, Social Science Research Council, New York, 1949, pp. 83 — 118; Moser, C. A., Survey Methods in Social Investigation, William Heinemann Ltd., London, 1958, pp. 100 — 108.

21. Evan, Weisbrod, and Fair, op. cit.

22. Pool, Ithiel de Sola, and Robert P. Abelson, "The Simulmatics Project," Public Opinion Quarterly, 25, 167 — 183 (Summer 1961).

23.    Abelson, Robert P., and Alex Bernstein, "A Computer Simulation Model of Community Referendum Controversies," Public Opinion Quarterly, 27, 93 — 122 (Spring 1963).

24.    Hill, Reuben, "Patterns of Decision-Making and the Accumulation of Family Assets," in Household Decision-Making: Consumer Behavior, Nelson N. Foote, Ed., 5, New York University Press, New York, 1961, pp. 57 — 80; and "Judgment and Consumership in the Management of Family Resources," Sociology and Social Research, 47, 446 — 460, (July, 1963).

25.    Ryder, op. cit., p. 461.

## FREE DISCUSSION

In response to the discussant's query on autocorrelated errors, a paper was cited that deals with the problem of autocorrelation in regression analysis from the Bayesian point of view. This paper appeared in a recent issue of the <u>Journal of the American Statistical Association</u>. It was agreed that the problem of estimating procedures when one is working with the wrong model is an area in which research is needed. Computations of residuals ordered in different ways are sometimes used to check the model. One is then able to investigate departure from functional forms.

A different approach to this problem of finding the right model has been tested at the University of Michigan. Here a step-regression technique is coupled with a simple learning device. This procedure enables one to select a model that fits the observed data in a maximal form. In an objection to this procedure, however, a paper was cited that demonstrated how just such an iterative process for finding models generated completely misleading results. Such an outcome is possible since one is using the same data both for testing and for estimation, in a framework which is not well defined. One suggested solution to this problem is to find the model that seems to fit the original data and then apply it to a new set of data.

It was pointed out that finding the right model was only a first step; such a model must then be tested against further observations, whether they be in the form of projection or prediction. The basic limitation to this approach is the sluggish rate of change that characterizes human life. While one is waiting for this change to occur, however, the computer can be used to speculate and to elaborate one's theoretical framework.

The discussion then turned to the problem of determining the right statistical procedure for estimating the parameters of a model thought to be correct. The computer enables one to solve such a model, to simulate it, and to come out with predictions or explanations that can then be compared with the actual data. The validity of the model's parameters cannot be evaluated, however, since various <u>ad hoc</u> procedures were used to estimate them in the first place. Someone suggested that this problem might eventually be solved through statistical analysis of the output from the model. Although no easy solution was offered, it was proposed that two models might be compared by setting up the problem so that one model collapses into the other.   In this case, if a given coefficient were zero, the hypothesis would be accepted, and we would choose model A; if, however, the hypothesis were rejected, we would choose model B.

The discussion closed with the comment that the conference should attempt to switch to the causative level, rather than remain at the descriptive level, where it seemed to be focused.   Issue was taken with this point because the inadequacies of our present time-series data and the compound nature of causal relationships seem to make such an approach untenable.

# VI.    SIMULATION MODELS

# THE USES OF SIMULATION

Aaron Fleisher
Massachusetts Institute of Technology

Most of the papers read at this conference treat of matters which are procedural rather than substantive, and the techniques they describe are related, in varying intimacies, to simulation. It seems appropriate, therefore, to ask what simulations are and where they might lead.

Let me take up the second question first. What might the social sciences look like after, say, 25 years? One frequently hears it said of physics — because its structures are so accurate and so comprehensive — that it is the ideal toward which other sciences must trend if they are to register progress. One hears this more often from social scientists. I think that this longing mistakes both the nature of physics and of the social sciences. It has done nothing but make mischief.

Compared to human affairs, physical phenomena are simple. Electrons are not distinguished by socioeconomic class; the properties of matter are independent of history — most of the time. The theories that account for many physical affairs are described by simple sets of partial differential equations that require only the first two derivatives and are linear in both.

Physics does not even resemble other physical sciences. I used to make my living doing research in meteorology. Its difficulties smell of the social sciences. The atmosphere is stratified; describe it as an initial value problem and you will need about $10^4$ data. If you should decide to replace dynamics with statistics, then an extensive history of each of these data must be added.

Linear approximations are not good; the atmosphere is thermodynamically open and chemically reactive, and its composition and phase vary with time and place. Meteorology still is much simpler than the social sciences, merely because it does not have to take account of purpose. There are no issues of national or metropolitan policy which can influence the path or occurrence of hurricanes. Physics is a wonderful source from which to document the formal process of research. It is not a sampler for the morality of science.

187

Having ventured what the social sciences will not resemble, I need only consider
the complement of the picture to guess what they may look like.  At worst, I commit the same mistake.

I think that the social sciences will never be thoroughly systematic.  They will be
composed of fragments, made ad hoc.  I do not know the size, spacing, and number
of these fragments.  The size may well be small and the spacing large.  I take comfort from thinking that the number will be substantial.  Issues of policy can only
make matters more difficult, for validities, which in any case have transients, will
then become almost capricious.

Let me turn now to the first question:  What is simulation?

Science without an empirical base is impossible, and where theory is weak, the
strength of the science is largely measured by its capability in making accurate,
intelligent observations.  It seems to me that simulations can contribute much to
this capability.  However, I have in mind only part of the range of activities which
have been called simulations.

At one end of this range are numerical solutions to sets of equations that might
model physical or social systems.  The future state of the atmosphere, obtained by
solving its dynamic equations, is such an example.  The numerical results can be
applied either to predict the weather or to verify the model's accuracy.  The solution of a problem in linear programming is another example.  In this case the
results are applied to policy.  Both these examples show the use of strongly constructed models.

The bulk of the simulations contrived in the social sciences are located at the other
end of the scale, problems for which no model in any decent sense exists; only
conjecture — vague, tentative, and intuitive.  In these circumstances, simulation
means squeezing consequences out of a crude structure put together from supposi-
tions.  The computer is necessary to this process precisely because the structure
is crude and the analysis labored.  Simulations are never terse, and rarely elegant.

By itself this exercise helps, because it forces the simulator to confront his simulation at every detail.  The simulation itself may also sharpen the problem by suggesting what other data may be relevant and what other relations to look for.
In a world where everything appears to be somewhat related to everything else, a
means for sorting relevances can be a great comfort.

This kind of simulation is essentially empirical.  It does take its start from a model
of sorts.  But every experiment is a choice, and therefore no experiment is purely
empirical.  It is experiment with an important qualification.  A simulation can say
nothing about the real world.  It can neither generate a datum nor uncover an empirical law.  A formal structure only is taken into the laboratory.  The best that
simulation can do is explore the consequences of that structure.

They will, almost always, depend on a set of n-parameters.  One hopes that n can
be made small, for the result of each run of the experiment is one point in the n-
dimensional space of the parameters.  The figure generated by the results of all

possible runs describes the properties of the structure simulated. To fill out the figure sufficiently may require, even when n is small, many more points that can be afforded, despite the size of the memory, the speed of the computer, and the affluence of the economy. The fine art of designing experiments is not yet dispensable.

Simulators make a deep obeisance to realism; the impedimenta carried by their simulations, therefore, are often enormous. Now that the Bureau of the Census has made available the 1-1,000 tape, it is easier to increase the baggage. I should think that one might be more interested, at first, in the penalty that unrealism exacts, and therefore seize upon simulation as the chance to try the outlandish conjecture and the pathological case. The penalty might not be large, and if it is, the insight gained may compensate. A big simulation is not necessarily better. It is difficult to account for the results no matter how they come out. I am not arguing that all elaborations are unnecessary. I do urge that a sharp question is more important than a detailed facsimile.

The computer's ability to manipulate vast, vague structures is occasionally confused with personal theorizing. Simulation is no substitute for systematic structures. It is the beginning of theorizing, not the end. Contrariwise, simulation can help to avoid some excesses of theorizing. A particular formalism in which to cast a problem is chosen sometimes more for its ease in manipulation than capability at representation. Such practice is not without justification. Manipulation, after all, is one important purpose of theory. Simulation requires explicit rules but not a formal apparatus; moreover, these rules need not be numerical — wherein lie its principal advantages. And the computer is capable of executing these rules, numerical or not, with great despatch — wherefore are the two so intimately coupled. These circumstances have generated the sentiment that simulation has advantages because "you don't need to know any mathematics." It is likely that occasions can arise when a knowledge of mathematics, however deep, is useless. It is equally likely that there exists some simulation that would have been unnecessary but for a knowledge of a little mathematics. A good pianist need not know how to read music, but it is rare that he does not.

I have kept my remarks short, for I did not want, as it has been said, "to speak like a missionary preaching to cannibals." However, because it is a short paper it needs a summary even more than a long one. I have argued that in the near future the social sciences will remain largely empirical and that simulation can serve as a device for making experiments in vitro. I think that this use is more important, at this time, than the massive making of models and that the principal contribution of simulation lies in the direction of intelligent, vivacious empiricism.

# SIMULATION METHODOLOGY*

Martin Greenberger

**Project MAC and Sloan School of Management**
**Massachusetts Institute of Technology**

I never intended to simulate my house-heating problem and indeed, I never did. But in a casual study of the problem, I noticed a few simple truths which seem to apply to a great deal of simulation work. That is why I am taking the liberty of discussing this personal story of my heating system in a serious talk on simulation methodology. [†]

Three and a half years ago my wife and I purchased a very large, old, three-story, 16-room, uninsulated house. It was clear to us from the start that heating the house would be a major expense. [‡] The heating plant consists of two gas furnaces, one blowing hot air to 19 registers, and the other circulating hot water to 10 radiators. Each furnace is controlled by its own clock-thermostat.

During our first winter in the house, partly in order to divert my attention from the growing gas bills and partly in the hope of finding ways to alleviate the cost burden, I began to collect daily figures on gas consumption. The data collected over a period of 40 days exhibited considerable variance, fluctuating from a daily high of

---

*Work reported herein was supported in part by Project MAC, an M.I.T. research program sponsored by the Advanced Research Projects Agency, Department of Defense, under Office of Naval Research Contract Number Nonr-4102(01). Reproduction in whole or in part is permitted for any purpose of the U. S. Government.

[†] In adapting the talk for this reissued volume, I have chosen the abbreviated form (see Reference 1) rather than the original longer (and now somewhat obsolete) form (see Reference 2).

[‡] As a matter of information, I believe that Boston gas rates are among the highest in the world. In 1961, 300 ccf (hundred cubic feet) of gas cost $49.10 in Boston, $47.67 in New York City, and $21.23 in Pittsburgh.

35 ccf to a daily low of 17 ccf.   A spread of this magnitude gives the optimist some hope of finding measures to keep consumption as low as possible without sacrificing comfort.

Let us view the matter as an eager student of simulation might have done.   The system consists of the house and the assorted apparatus for producing, distributing, and controlling heat.   The manipulable or instrument variables include storm windows, room and furnace thermostats, an aquastat, radiator valves, air registers, and dampers.   There are also 9 fireplaces, but they are not in active use   The target variables are the temperatures in each of the rooms, maintenance and service costs, and the monthly gas bills.   Altering the number, location, or setting of any of the instrument variables is a means of adjusting the target variables.

To simulate this system, we must decide which variables deserve inclusion, and we must determine relationships that link the variables.   An obvious variable to include is outdoor temperature, since we know it directly affects the heat loss radiated from the house.   In the parlance of the model-building trade, outdoor temperature is an exogenous variable of decided importance.

Figure 1 displays the 40 daily gas consumptions, each one plotted against the mean outdoor temperature on the corresponding day.   As would be expected, the gas consumption depends inversely on the mean temperature.   The lower the temperature, the more gas consumed, and conversely.

On the first try we might fit a straight regression line to the points of Figure 1, as shown.   This line provides an initial relationship for the model.   Incidentally, it is not a bad fit as regression lines go.   It yields a numerical correlation coefficient of just a shade under .90.   But with more information, we can do better.

My wife and I both go to work on weekdays, and during the first winter we did not have children to keep warm.   I therefore formed the habit of turning the settings of the two thermostats down $10^{o}$ when we left in the morning; they automatically reverted to normal for our return in the evening.   Let us call this policy A.   On the weekends, when we were home, and on Wednesdays, when a lady came to clean, I kept the thermostats on the same settings throughout the day   Let us call this policy B.   In both policies, I lowered the settings overnight.

If we now separate the points of Figure 1 into those associated with policy A (Figure 2) and those associated with policy B (Figure 3), and neglect the remaining points, we obtain surprisingly close fits to each of two smooth curves.   In Figure 2, only the three hollow points are substantially off the curve.   All three lie above the curve and correspond to Tuesdays.

The points of Figure 3 show slightly more variation.   The three hollow points falling beneath the curve all correspond to Wednesdays, and two of these three Wednesdays happen to be the day after two of the three Tuesdays cited above.   Since the latter have larger consumptions than their curve would predict, while the former have smaller consumptions, my guess is that I made incorrect meter readings on the corresponding two Tuesday nights.

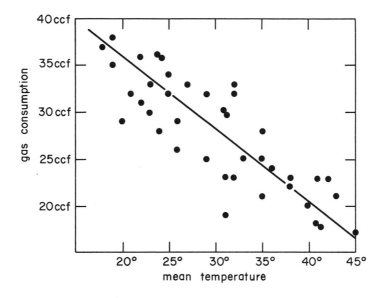

Figure 1.   Daily gas consumption on all days during December 1961
            and January 1962 for which a record was taken:  (gas
            consumption measured in 100 cubic feet, temperature
            in degrees fahrenheit).

If we superimpose the curves of Figures 2 and 3 upon each other, as in Figure 4,
we notice that they have opposite concavities; they bend toward each other at the
ends (20° and 45°), and they depart from each other at the middle (30° to 35°).
This is not the appropriate place to speculate on the physical reasons for this behavior, but we can note the economic implications, as given in Figure 5.   The greatest potential saving obtained from using policy A rather than policy B occurs in the
middle range of temperature, and this saving decreases steadily as either of the
extreme temperature ranges is approached.   At temperatures below 15° and above
50°, we might conclude that both policies cost about the same.

The finding of opposite concavities is interesting from an academic point of view,
and turns out to be of practical interest as well.   Without overdoing its importance,
and without stretching the analogy with a simulation study too far, I believe we can
extract a few simple lessons from the story.

First, careful analysis of available data can serve a simulation study both as a
guide and as a check.   A model of my heating system would have to produce the
characteristic of opposite concavities to be convincing.   Other peculiarities of the
model would be considered suspect if not evidenced by the data.

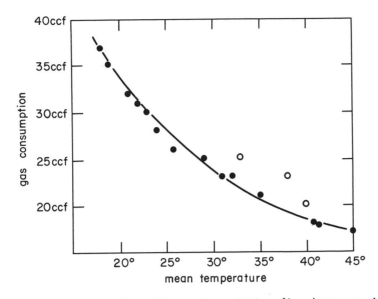

Figure 2.   Days from Figure 1 on which policy A was used.

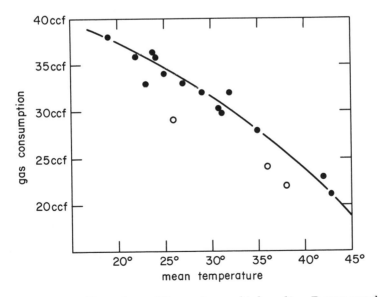

Figure 3.   Days from Figure 1 on which policy B was used.

Frequent and easy communication between model and data is important throughout the development of a simulation model.   Too often data analysis and model development are isolated in separate, prolonged efforts.   Only when the model is complete, if then, do we have the interest and resources to return to the data for verification. By then it may be too late.   The final complexity of the model can make serious validation impractical.

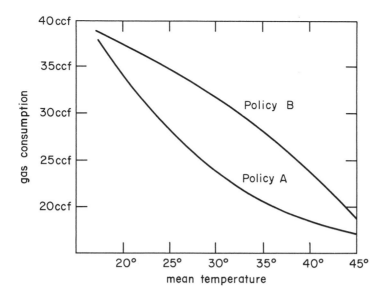

Figure 4.   Superposition of Figures 2 and 3.

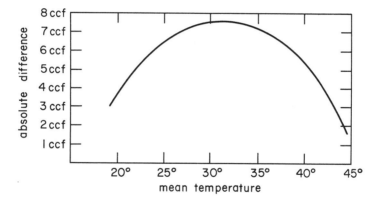

Figure 5.   Absolute difference between consumptions resulting
from policies A and B.

We would prefer to construct our model incrementally, running each new piece singly and in combination with other pieces before proceeding. This allows us to build an understanding of the model as we build the model itself. It guards against unnecessary arbitrariness, and pinpoints deficiencies both in the model and in the data. If sensitivity runs indicate that certain deficiencies are critical, we gain valuable guidance for further research and data collection efforts.

The incremental approach also provides resistance to overcomplexity. Ideally, a simulation is never more complicated than it need be for the ends it is to serve.

The temptations toward overcomplexity are related to the computer's versatility. It is so simple to be literal about the way things happen in the real system when modeling the system on a computer. Stochastic effects are easy to copy, nonlinearities and interaction offer no particular problem, and behavior can be portrayed at any level of detail, no matter now fine. Superficially, the only reason to exercise any restraint at all is to keep the formulation within the space and time capabilities of the machine.

Complexity that cannot be unraveled obstructs understanding the validation. This is already a problem in research applications, and will become a problem in a practical context as well when the results of simulations begin to be used routinely to support business, military, and legislative decision. How do we mediate between two conflicting sets of results when we are unable to understand the models that produced them?

The development of a simulation model must be by persons intimately familiar with the subject matter. This principle has been violated in the past by excessive delegation of responsibility to mathematicians and programmers interested primarily in questions of structure and style. To use the house-heating problem as an example, only someone with a firsthand knowledge of the meaning of the heating data could have resolved Figure 1 into Figures 2 and 3. Nor could anyone else have spotted the probable sources of error in data collection.

These simple lessons may be summed up as follows. The simulation process should be characterized by (1) easy access to data during model building; (2) incremental construction of the model with frequent testing and verification of partial results; (3) avoidance of unnecessary arbitrariness and overcomplexity; (4) retention of proxy by the research worker at the computer. Such requirements are difficult to satisfy under the constraints imposed by traditional ways of using a large computer. The mode of operation has been too impersonal and too inflexible.

The development of time sharing within the past several years is a significant step forward. A research worker can now have immediate and continuous access to a computer, while a community of other users enjoy equally good service at the same time. Interactive systems that employ this new mode of computation point ultimately to a greatly improved relationship between research worker and computer. At M.I.T.'s Project MAC, we have been building and using such systems for the past 4 years.[3, 4, 5] As these systems continue to get better and a wide assortment of research workers start to use them in earnest, the computer will graduate from dogged workhorse to nimble research assistant. It will spend less time grinding out lengthy simulations and performing tedious calculations, and more time organizing information and helping the worker to build and test models.

The research process is essentially a loop whose phases are data collection, analysis, model formulation, model testing, and model alteration. In the future, the computer will participate along with the research worker in each of these phases. A single integrated system will allow him to move gracefully and flexibly from one phase to another, and back again. The worker will suffer some discomfort during the initial period of adjustment to his new assistant but the expansion of creative powers that results will provide ample recompense.

**References**

1.    Greenberger, M., "Simulation and a House-Heating Problem," <u>Behavioral Science,</u> <u>11</u>, 143 — 147 (Mar. 1966).

2.    Beshers, J. M., Ed., <u>Computer Methods in the Analysis of Large-Scale Social Systems</u>, Joint Center for Urban Studies, M. I. T. and Harvard University, Cambridge, Mass., 1965.

3.    Greenberger, M., M. M. Jones, J. H. Morris, Jr., and N. D. Ness, <u>On-Line Computation and Simulation:   The OPS-3 System,</u> The M.I.T. Press, Cambridge, Mass., 1965.

4.    Greenberger, M., and M. M. Jones, "On-Line Simulation in the OPS System," <u>Proceedings of the 21st National Conference of the Association for Computing Machinery</u>, Thompson Book Company, Washington, D. C., 1966.

5.    Jones, M. M., <u>On-Line Incremental Simulation,</u> Ph. D. dissertation, M.I.T., 1967.

## DISCUSSION

### J. C. R. Licklider
### International Business Machines Corporation

Thanks very much for the opportunity to make these remarks of concurrence and endorsement. Some of my friends tell me that I must be getting old, that my behavior in discussion situations of this sort is milder now, and that I tend to agree and approve instead of controverting, but the fact is that the world is just behaving so much better. This will be my mildest or most positive performance.

I can subscribe to everything but one thing that Professor Fleisher said. The exception is what he said when he was so outspoken about the importance of the empiric quality. I do not want him to make that a derogation of the theoretical, but being greedy, I want the tools and techniques and the simulation and modeling that let us have either the empirical or the theoretical, and indeed let us have both in combination. I think there is no reason why not.

Martin Greenberger's discussion makes me joyous inside. I thank him for the kind remark about my small connection with the beginning of Project MAC. I am increasingly happy with it as it goes on.

Now, I have learned something substantive from Greenberger's methodological discussion. I have just moved into a house with almost as many fireplaces as his own. I need to use his method. As a name for the method, I like the term "dynamic modeling," and I want to say why I like it and what I think it encompasses. Note, first, that my chairman has a last name that stands for dynamic modeling. (Editor's note: Charles H. Dym presided at this session.) To me, dynamic modeling includes simulation in its most empirical sense — what we do when we are just trying to understand a complex situation and are playing with local parts of it and putting them together in various ways so that we can appreciate what is implied about the behavior of the whole. For me, dynamic modeling subsumes also formal mathematical models that are reduced to computer programs. The main thing I want a dynamic model to be is dynamic — I want it to unfold before my eyes and show me the implications of what I have set down, and I want it to do this in the way Martin Greenberger stressed, the way that will let me make and correct mistakes without great trauma, that will let me interact with data and observation and conduct

197

experiments in the realm of thought.  Often it is less expensive to do experiments in the domain of thought than it is to do experiments that involve observation of the world, and there is a kind of strategy that says:  "Let's do most that which is the fastest or the most economical. "  When data are expensive and fragmentary, we often want to see what configuration of ideas, when projected against the data, best accounts for them, and it may be more efficient and productive to play around with the ideas, watching the projection as we play, than to wait for more data.

Nostalgia requires that I say that I spent a long time, a few years ago, in the basement of this building working with analog computers.  (Editor's note: Sloan Building, M. I. T. )  I did that before I saw the light and learned about digital ones.  With analog computers one works with oscilloscopes hooked onto various places in his circuit, and with nobs and switches and plug boards.

He literally stands there, jiggling and trying to make the apparatus implement the thoughts that are in his head.  He can tell when the traces on the scope are getting better, and when they are right.  Then he can look and can see what structure he has produced in his analog simulation that causes the behavior he observes.  It is at last possible to do that now, with digital computers.  I want to project a little beyond what Martin Greenberger talked about.  I want to get the oscilloscopes hooked up to digital computers in the way we used to connect them to analog computers.  Indeed, parts of Project MAC are involved in doing almost precisely that. It is a little expensive, currently, but the cost of everything in the information-processing technology, the real cost to manufacture, is going down fast.  If the actual cost to the student will go down as rapidly, then we shall soon probably be able to have simulation models unfolding before our eyes.

The name for the foregoing should be, as I suggested, "dynamic representation. " The idea is to represent our ideas in a way that lets them come to life when we press the button, that makes them dynamic so that we can see their implications and their behavior.  It is not too much to say that dynamic modeling is a new departure in the representation of things.  Always before, except for the analog computers which were highly constrained in their scope of applicability, we have had to represent things in a static form on paper.  When we wanted to do something with them, we had to get them back out of the static form, process them in our heads, and then put them back onto paper.  Mathematical models have that character; they are just static things.  These models that we are talking about now have a static form, of course — the representation that you can pass on to posterity — but they also have the dynamic one.  For the first time, I think, we are getting a sufficiently good representation with both qualities to make it possible for an intellectual community to focus a large effort in a coherent way on a problem that is too complicated for any one individual to handle for himself.

I want to interject here some thoughts about the preparation of very large computer programs.  That is an intellectual effort too great for any one person.  In fact, some of the very large programs developed for the Defense Department have required hundreds of people for their production — computer programs of as much as a half-million machine instructions.  Although almost anybody can sit down and and in the course of an afternoon generate and debug a program 100 machine instructions long — I have seen people do 400 — the very large programs cost as much as $30 per machine instruction, which amounts to something when there are 500,000 machine instructions. The incremental cost, in fact, goes up to $100 per machine instruction. That is what happens when you try to get many human beings to focus their efforts on a large problem. A "breakthrough" in this intellectual realm (dealing with large quantities of information and very complex processes) is beginning to show in Project MAC. Project MAC now has something approaching 500,000 instructions in its "public" file of programs and data. The significant points are: (1) the programs were prepared on-line with much help from the computer itself, and (2) preparation cost only a fraction — in fact, the whole of Project MAC cost only a fraction — of 500,000 times $15. It is very obvious that here is the way to produce programs inexpensively. It is also a way to achieve coherence, to make sure that all the programs work together.

Finally, let me tell you some of the things on my list here, that I will not talk about because the time has flown:

Analysis by synthesis:  At last it is possible to analyze a situation by experimenting with the synthesis of revelant ideas — with the creation and modification of models — until we get them to work correctly and produce the observed data. Then we know what it might have been that gave rise to the situation under study.

The opposition of procedure orientation and problem orientation, or field orientation:  Almost all of the languages so far developed for communication with computers have been oriented toward the preparation of procedures rather than toward the solving of problems. But real power is achieved when the jargon and the semantic support of the particular problem area get into the language in such a way that they bear directly on the problem to be solved, when the data structures, and operations, of the language are those in terms of which the people — the substantive workers in the field — naturally think. Now, to develop such languages of course requires an interaction between such substantive-oriented people and information and computer scientists. That can happen only in the context that we have been talking about.

Graphic languages:  Finally, let me mention Ivan Sutherland's Sketchpad program and developments along that line that have been continuing here at M.I.T. Let me say only that if you are not familiar with the concept of Sketchpad, you should get familiar with it. It opens a new and very significant door to dynamic modeling and computer simulation.

## FREE DISCUSSION (I)

The discussion began when someone asked whether complexity is always needless, particularly when a problem itself might be complex. It was suggested that with the possibilities inherent in the computer, the whole principle of parsimony needs to be rethought. "Needless complexity" was originally used to describe complexity that gets in the way of validation. One way to make a model that is both complex and valid might be to build the model up in pieces, either from the outside in or in a hierarchical combination. The advantage of this approach is that it allows one to stay close to the real-world data.

A plea was made for simplicity whenever possible. The advantages are obvious: (1) It leaves less room for logical error; (2) Its product is likely to be more acceptable to the nontechnical consumer. Certainly what constitutes an adequate degree of richness in a model can only be answered in terms of the goals of the experimenter.

An analogy was drawn between a problem in biological research and an application of simulation models. In biological research it is often stated that what is true of rats is not necessarily true of monkeys, and what is true of monkeys is not necessarily true of humans. Is there not a similar problem in determining when one can generalize from the simulation to the reality it is supposed to represent? The response to this query stressed that model builders clearly do not aim at a complete description of the system. Thus the biological problem might be restated: Do particular properties of the rat correspond to other properties in the monkey? The concern is with extracting properties that are consistent both internally and with the empirical data.

The applicability of this solution for a model with several independent variables was questioned. This type of model would involve testing within a multidimensional space, and it is not clear how much of this space has to be spanned in order to determine its applicability.

The discussion stressed that more and more energy is being devoted to just this problem. Attempts are being made to develop techniques, some algorithmic and some heuristic, for searching in very complex spaces. Researchers concerned with artificial intelligence are presently very much involved in this area.

A final comment was made about the imaginative aspect of simulation modeling that occurs at the conceptual stage.   At this stage of model building one is more concerned with the internal consistency of ideas and the derivation of secondary-order effects from an initial set of assumptions than with the model's correspondence with empirical data.   The computer may then be an aid in refining the more nebulous thoughts.

# ATTITUDINAL VARIABLES IN LARGE-SCALE SOCIAL SYSTEMS

**Ithiel de Sola Pool**

**Massachusetts Institute of Technology**

The absence of good time-series data concerning the distribution of beliefs, opinions, and attitudes in society is a major restriction on the effectiveness of current social research. Demographic and economic data, collected routinely, form the basis for a large part of the calculation and planning that make possible the operation of a great society. We take it for granted that the Bureau of the Census and various economic agencies will collect and make available data about the location and characteristics of the population, their income and expenditures, and the production and flow of goods. But routinely available time-series data about what people think, or about their morale, or about their satisfaction and dissatisfaction with the government, or about their desires, is almost nonexistent. This lack of regularly compiled attitudinal data has frequently been deplored. The Ford Foundation, when it was launched about 15 years ago, announced this as a problem it proposed to work on. But it made little progress in doing so, and has since dropped the matter.

A few more or less satisfactory attitudinal time series are already available. Voting statistics have been used as an index of attitudes far more extensively than they really deserve. They are a rather artificial measure. Although voting is significant in political outcome, the voter is constrained by so many conditions, such as the choice of candidates offered or his party loyalty, that his vote is not a very accurate indicator of his attitudes. Nonetheless, since his attitudes are one of the best indices we have, much use has been made of them.

Since the 1930's, thanks to the emergence of recurrent public opinion polls, we have had the potentiality for developing a much better type of index of attitudes prevailing in large social systems. Some work on time series in poll results was published in the early 1940's. Hadley Cantril collected many of the Gallup Poll results on attitudes toward the war in Europe, toward American intervention, toward the British, and toward the major issues of the day — isolationism and internationalism. [1] He produced a significant barometer that revealed important patterns of American attitude change as Nazi aggression spread. Each Allied defeat resulted in an initial adverse reaction, coupled with an increase in persons undecided about what American policy should be but followed by an increase of anti-Nazi feeling.  This rather isolated example of systematic time-series reporting on public opinion was not effectively followed up.

In that early period, the Public Opinion Quarterly published the results of the Quarters Polls in each issue, thus providing the kind of standard data service that government publications provide in other fields; but soon, as the volume of poll data became too great for a private journal to handle, that feature was dropped. Until fairly recently, a good many public opinion poll organizations simply discarded their old cards.  Under such circumstances, the general use of public opinion polls was analogous to the case of books if no libraries existed and if publishers, after putting out a single edition, destroyed the plates and never produced a second edition.  Few people in the opinion survey field made use of previously collected information.  Each time anyone wanted information he had to commission a new survey.

This was, obviously, a ridiculous state of affairs.  Clearly, our understanding of new data about attitudes prevalent in any social system could be much improved if the new data were put into the context of previous information.  So the notion of a survey archive, a library for opinion polls, developed quite naturally.

The ideal archive scholars dream about is completely universal; it collects data from all over the world; its data is freely accessible to anyone who wants it. These desiderata, however, are not easy to achieve, for national pride and proprietary considerations intervene.  The original data producers, or data suppliers, have legitimate vested interests in the material they have bought or collected. To some degree, they tend to want to control its use by other persons, particularly when possible commercial implications are involved.  With the exception of the situation in economics and demography, little attitude data is collected by the government.  Raw data collection, as well as research with it, is largely in private hands.  Nonetheless, despite difficulties, the development of survey archives is progressing.  Many are being formed, of which by far the most important is the Roper Public Opinion Research Center in Williamstown, the depository for such large American survey organizations as Gallup and Roper.  It also contains a very considerable international collection.  Its objective is to be a universal survey archive; all others are specialized.  The Roper Center has recently initiated a practice of depositing copies of its material with other organizations belonging to what it calls an International Survey Library Association.  We hope that in the years to come every major social research center will form a depository.

Currently at M.I.T. we are trying to develop a system for handling large amounts of old poll data — a system that would make them easy to store, easy to retrieve, easy to manipulate and report.

I became aware of some of these problems in the course of an election study done in 1960. [2]  We used cards from the Roper Center covering approximately 130,000 respondents to election surveys over roughly a decade, 1950 to 1960; up to that time this study was perhaps the most massive example of bringing together large amounts of attitudinal material from a variety of sources for use in a single analysis.

The problems arising from this kind of composite survey analysis are largely analogous to those in other kinds of massive data operations under discussion here, though perhaps with different emphases.   Difficult problems in the survey field may be less difficult in other fields, and vice versa.   While no problems are unique, the profiles of those in attitudinal and nonattitudinal data bases are a little different.

### The Problem of Dissimilar Source Data

Students of public opinions and attitudes are compelled to use extremely varied types of information, derived from a variety of sources and incomplete in many ways.   We are not in the position in this field of using a census file which, if incomplete, is incomplete in an established, uniform, standardized way and for which the decisions on methodology are made in a centralized fashion.   In the field of public opinion we use studies done here, there, and everywhere, for this client and that client, designed without consideration of the interests of the secondary user.   As you look through survey code books you will find diverse definitions of all the major social classifications, or face sheets data.   The items included vary, and the questions used to measure any particular attitude change from survey to survey. If you are interested in relating three variables, on one survey you may find only two of them; on another survey, another two; and on another survey, another two; and on another survey one of these pairs differently measured.   This is a severe problem.   It can be addressed, however, partly by standardizing questionnaires and also by resorting to ecological correlations.

The development of standards, conventions, and accepted practices for the conduct of surveys is a first step.   It is quite feasible to standardize some of the questions on background information, though not the actual attitudinal questions themselves. No one, for example, ought to do an American political survey without including a question on religion.   It is a question which has often been omitted in the past because it is embarrassing to ask and creates some difficulty for the interviewer. Nevertheless, it should be included.   There are a number of such categories that pollers regard as necessary.   But the amount of standardization that can be established by convention is rather limited.

To a very considerable extent, the problem of ragged incomplete data sets must continue to be met by making ecological rather than individual correlations.   Our 1960 election study provides an illustration.   Robert Abelson and I collected data on voter attitudes on some 50 issues.   We classified all voters into a series of voter-types.   For each voter-type we calculated the percentage adhering to each side on each issue, partially because we were working on a ragged data set with some information on certain individuals and other information on others, and also because we were using computers slower than those now available.   If we were programming the job from the beginning today, we would do it quite differently. Given modern technology, we would not have lost the initial complete information on each of the 130, 000 respondents.   We would still have had to resort to ecological correlations, since the information on the individuals was ragged, but we could have made our ecological cells at will, varying them from problem to problem and experimenting with different cuts.   For example, for one purpose we might have distinguished voter-types of different age levels, while for another we might have distinguished by education but not by age.   In 1960, however, we set up 480 rigid voter-types, and after the information was sorted into these types the original data was lost.

Incidentally, in 1964 we are replicating the 1960 research, but it is not a major study and is unsponsored. Since its sole purpose is to discover whether the 1960 success was a matter of luck or whether the same approach will work a second time, we are simply reusing the programs from last time, which accounts for the fact that we have not broken away from our previous rigidity. Our objective, however, is simplicity of replication, which we have achieved by adopting a rule against changing the system and by using the extraordinary facilities of Project MAC.

If we were starting from scratch, as perhaps we shall in 1968, we would store the original data in full. We would then create a correlation matrix of all the variables being used, calculating the correlations across individuals either by finding subsets of individuals who had been queried about both variables or by using a Goodman kind of approach to estimate individual correlations from ecological correlations. The approach requires flexible definition of voter-types. Actually, the correlations we need to calculate are those remaining within voter-types, which will almost always be much smaller than the correlations in the population as a whole. Most often two attitudes are typically found together because people of a certain type hold both attitudes. (Anti-Catholicism and Republicanism were correlated in 1960 but only because Protestants were inclined toward both those views. Within various Protestant voter-types these attitudes were often uncorrelated.) With flexibly defined voter-types, and with estimates of the individual correlations of attitudes within them, we should be able to produce a substantially more powerful simulation.

## The Problem of Lack of Panel Data

By no means unique to attitudinal data but crucial to working with it, is the fact that very few opinion surveys use panels; that is, the time series are all based upon interviews with different samples of people each time. The solution to this problem is to use more panels, but that is hardly feasible. On a large scale, panels are expensive, they are difficult to maintain intact, and in replies to attitude questions there is significant panel effect. Replies regarding certain other kinds of data, such as demographic data or economic data, probably are not changed much by repeatedly interviewing the same people. Attitudes, however, probably are changed by such enquiries. But more important, if you have reinterviewed a panel you cannot be sure whether you have panel effect or not. Your results may be completely reliable, but you will not know. Various solutions to the problem include the use of rotating panels, or partial panels, in which you retain some people but constantly change others. This process, however, soon creates the need to equate individuals either by finding respondent-types or by some other means.

## The Problem of Coding Errors

An apparently trivial problem in secondary analysis of attitude data has become very important practically. Since we deal with data coming from a variety of sources, each collected for its own purposes, we receive cards in unclean condition. We spend a large part of our research time discovering other people's mistakes. We have been working on this problem at M.I.T., as have a number of other places. It can be dealt with effectively by the development of cleaning programs that look for identifiable and frequent kinds of errors, most notably punches that are not possible under the rules in the code book.

## The Problem of Data Retrieval

A significant problem in handling survey data on a massive basis is that of information retrieval. Essentially it consists of indexing the archive, a problem not unique to attitudinal data but vastly more difficult than that of indexing census data, which though they are massive data, are grouped into a quite limited set of categories. Attitude data are also massive, but since the data are collected with questions independently written by different persons, there arise vast numbers of different codes, questions, and indices. To find those that bear on your problem is a horrendous task.

For example, suppose one is interested in political alienation, a subject on which the literature contains many time-series assertions. Many people believe there is growing alienation in American industrial society. I personally do not believe it, but that is my prejudice — I can not now prove it. Unquestionably, it exists. Maybe it has always been present, maybe it is declining, maybe it is growing. In principle, we should be able to establish good trend data by scanning the vast research files that bear on this question. Of course, in order to accomplish this we must define alienation and decide what measures it. Scores of different kinds of data that appear in public opinion polls could be used as measures of alienation. One example is nonvoting. Another is an inclination to say in elections surveys, "Both candidates are bad," as distinct from "Both are good men." Another is agreement with such statements as "Everybody is looking out for number one," or "If there's a problem in this community, there's nothing I can do about it." Notice that neither statement uses the word alienation. It is an act of high-order abstraction to translate any one of these responses into alienation. No mechanical indexing system that simply looks for key words in survey questions is going to reveal the fact that all of those just mentioned deal with alienation.

Clearly we need some kind of tagging system. Dr. Philip Stone at Harvard University, who has been much interested in this problem, has been working on survey indexing by use of the General Inquirer.[3] Any tagging system is dependent on the intelligence of some human indexer. As long as he sees problems the way you do, it works, but there is always the possibility of the interrogator asking for a new concept.

The difficulty of indexing survey archives is particularly great because, in contrast to the way in which articles or abstracts are labeled, the intent of the man who writes the questions for an attitude survey is to disguise his purpose. An author puts a title or abstract on a text to make it easy for the user to know what it is about. He tries to communiate his idea; he tries to be clear. The author of a survey question, on the contrary, tries to devise ingenious ways of getting at an attitude, often without letting the respondent know it. Survey questions, furthermore, must be couched in ordinary language without technical jargon. They employ words like "Do you think that things around here are better than they were a year ago or worse than they were about a year ago?" No distinctive key words stand out to indicate what the question is about. "Things," "here," "better," "worse" are not very helpful words for retrieval. Thus the problem of finding material in survey archives is an extremely severe one; nobody has been conspicuously successful in coping with it.

## The Problem of Context

In designing an archive for attitudinal data, the user may want data in complex combinations. There are so few obviously important series to report; there is nothing that stands out in attitude research as GNP or unemployment does in economics.

In attitude research we usually deal with very sparsely populated, extremely large multidimensional factor spaces. Many behaviors are possible. The interesting ones are not single attitudes but combinations of several. For example, the order in the answers may make a difference; the same verbal statement coming before may differ from the same verbal statement coming after. To illustrate: it is far from simple to look for white backlash in election survey questions. One can not ask about it directly. One must look for indicators of how a person intends to vote, plus indicators of how he usually votes, plus indicators of prejudice. The combination may lead us to infer the presence of backlash. First, we are interested only in people over 21, which is one survey question. Second, we are interested only in citizens eligible to vote, which is another question. Third, we are interested in whether the person is likely to vote at all. Fourth, we are interested in him only if he is a Democrat. When we have established these four points, we want to ascertain his attitudes toward civil rights. If he says that he is in favor of integration, the statement may or may not be indicative, depending on whether he has also at some point mentioned it as a problem in his community. In other words, it is quite different to support or oppose civil rights in the abstract than it is to respond to integration in his own neighborhood. Thus one must explore a long series of conditional statements before one can identify the phenomena of backlash in an interview.

In the election simulation we ran in 1964, we considered the most plausible model to comprise responses to three main campaign issues concerning which attitude survey data exist. These were nuclear responsibility, social welfare legislation, and civil rights. We approximated the election outcome by assuming that shifts from normal party affiliation were determined by these. We postulated that a Republican would switch if he agreed with the Democratic candidate on at least two out of three issues. Thus, if a Republican was in favor of civil rights but favored Goldwater's views on nuclear weapons and social welfare, he would probably not bolt. But if he disagreed with Goldwater on two out of three of these issues, he became a switcher in the model. Democrats in the 1964 campaign simulation behaved differently. They switched only on civil rights and only if they strongly opposed them.

This gives an idea of the kinds of complicated contingencies among survey responses that we want to be able to retrieve from the archive. They sound simpler than they actually are, for I have left out any cataloguing of combinations in the factor space that are not immediately helpful in explaining the main dynamics of the election. For example, the Independents: I have described how Republicans and Democrats switch, but another set of rules governs people who refuse to classify themselves in that way. Furthermore, we must account for those who say, "Don't know" or who give peculiar answers to the issue question. So the full set of decision rules for predicting 1964 election choices from old attitude data becomes rather complicated.

Computer programs now being developed make it easier than in the past to search a file of survey data for rather complex conditional combinations of responses.  At a national conference to be held at M.I.T., the main subject will be comparison of computer programs for attitude survey analysis.  The recent improvements are many.

For example, the problem just described did not involve looking at the order in which the replies appeared in the interview, an important possibility for survey analysis not yet explored.  In general, today, when an interview is completed, a human coder completely destroys the original structure of the interview.  He re-codes the data onto cards in which any given column refers to a particular category of response wherever that response may have appeared in the sequence of the interview.  In short, the data are recorded by a punch in a certain position on the card, that position being predetermined for any particular response rather than being a function of the sequence of the responses as they came out in the interview.  This process is no longer necessary with more modern technology.  With tapes instead of cards, we can efficiently move from using a positional notation to using a list of code labels in the order in which they occurred.   The human coder may now translate the questions into a more rigid and stylized language of code categories as they appeared in the interview.  The record then becomes a series of mnemonic words (instead of the original words) stored in the computer with the original structure of the conversation.  The coded interview is then subject to computerized content analysis in languages like COMIT or by the General Inquirer of Philip Stone. [3]

### Problem of Inefficiency of Tapes

The inefficiency of tapes is a problem I must leave to the many people more competent than I to discuss the technologies for random and associative access in large files.  And not only access is needed; a survey archive is a live file subject to repeated additions.

The ability to keep files live is a particularly important factor in handling panel data, since one follows particular individuals through time.  One needs to keep updating data on panel members.  In that respect the record-keeping operations appropriate to panels are similar to those used on personnel files or on students.  Over a 4-year period a university, for example, collects new information about a student's examinations, grades, consultations, payments, and course selection.  His file is subject to constant change and growth.  Similarly, a panel member is a unit for sequential record keeping of various kinds.

In closing, I might illustrate some unsuspected advantages of using a survey archive by referring to our election study.  The basic index of political tendency in our 1960 study was reported Congressional voting, using data collected from 1950 to 1960.  It occurred to us that maybe this was a mistake.  After all, the things that were going on in 1950 and 1952 and 1954 were not really very much like the things going on in the election of 1960.  Maybe we should have used as our basic index only the most recent data.  We tried that, only to learn that what we gained by recency and the elimination of secular trends was more than offset by what we lost in the stability and, therefore, the reliability of the data.  That is to say, we got better prediction using a data file which was 10 years long and which therefore washed out in the course of its fluctuations all kinds of conjunctural and random variations than we did using the most up-to-date part of that file. An interesting implication is that the attitudinal system is stable, despite the fact that attitude data have always been considered a matter of whim, since people are changing. How can you predict from it? we are often asked. There is no doubt that attitudes change. The attitude system is a highly mobile one, but the system itself has a surprising degree of continuity. The distinction is like the one between the weather and the climate. The weather changes enormously from day to day, but the basic parameters of the weather system are extremely stable. Measurements obtained over a long period of time, averaging out temporary fluctuations and so on, enable us to make reasonable estimates of the outcome of the system. We can predict the temperature in Boston on December 30, 1984, with a fair degree of accuracy. We will be able to do only modestly better if we postpone our prediction until November 30, 1984. Similarly with attitudes; once we know the parameters — the analogue of the month and day in the weather prediction — we can predict the attitudes with modest accuracy, even though attitudes, like weather, are very changeable. This fact of the basic stability of the structure of the attitudinal system, at least given its parameters, despite its extreme variability of state from moment to moment, needs to be better appreciated. It suggests reasons why it is important to collect long-term attitude-series data.

Some work has been done on all of the problems I have discussed. For example, at M.I.T. we have spent much time developing programs for cleaning, packing, storing, labeling, and editing. Further, we are getting tabulations on demand from the MAC console so that we do not have to get 300 tables, wait a week, get 300 more, and then not know what to do with them. But many difficult problems remain. Of these the indexing and retrieval problem is the worst. Five or ten years from now I hope that it will not be necessary to introduce a speech by saying that we do not have attitude series of any significance. By that time, perhaps, when statements are made about growing alienation, we may be able to look up the evidence; similarly with statements about morale, or happiness, or the support for an administration, or the changing desires of consumers. I hope we shall be able to determine factually such important issues as whether we are becoming more conformist or not, or whether antisocial attitudes are increasing. These kinds of questions can be fruitfully dealt with if we handle correctly the basic data that have become increasingly available.

## References

1.  Cantril, Hadley, Donald Rugg, and F. W. Williams, "America Faces the War: Shifts in Opinion," Public Opinion Quarterly, 4, 651 — 656 (Dec. 1940); and Cantril, Hadley, "Opinion Trends in World War Two," Public Opinion Quarterly, 12, 30 — 44 (Spring 1948).

2.  Pool, Ithiel de Sola, and Robert P. Abelson, "The Simulmatics Project," Public Opinion Quarterly, 25, 167 — 183 (Summer 1961).

3.  Stone, Philip J., Dexter D. Dunphy, Marshall S. Smith, Daniel M. Ogilvie et al., The General Inquirer: A Computer Approach to Content Analysis, The M.I.T. Press, Cambridge, Mass., 1966.

## FREE DISCUSSION (II)

The discussion opened with a question on the three issue categories: whether they had information on how voters break down in each of these categories, and how the three categories are intercorrelated.

Dr. Pool replied in the negative, stating that this was one of the problems in using the 1960 programs in which the individual respondent data were lost. Dr. Pool's group now has only ecological correlations among these three variables. The problem could, however, be partially solved by going back to the original surveys from which an estimate of the correlations between these three categories could be obtained. Since their present correlation represents at best only a good guess, this will be one of the parameters to be played with, if the first simulation results are unsatisfactory.

When asked about measuring nuclear responsibility, Dr. Pool replied that most of the data were taken from questions having to do with the test ban.

The question was raised as to what part the contemporary communications media play in the simulation, and, more particularly, how events like the Chinese atomic explosion are handled, events which might conceivably change the results of an election. Dr. Pool replied that his concern was with a simulation of the election, not a prediction. Toward this end, any number of simulations might be run, depending on what the real issues of the campaign are perceived to be. The only limitation on this strategy is the data files and whether they contain the needed information. Thus the Chinese bomb issue could be handled, while the Jenkins affair could not, since public opinion pollers do not normally deal with morals questions.

Someone asked whether the increasing use of survey materials has made those conducting surveys more responsive to the secondary analyst's needs. Dr. Pool replied with a qualified "Yes," even though improvement is a slow process. The important step is getting pollsters to agree to put their materials in archives. Once the scholar has access to this material, he will discover the inconsistencies and the inadequate sample populations. The resulting constructive criticism should have, and is having, a very healthy effect.

**VII. PRESERVING ANONYMITY IN SOCIAL DATA SYSTEMS**

# SOCIAL RESPONSIBILITY AND COMPUTERS*

Oliver G. Selfridge
Massachusetts Institute of Technology

I am a computer man, I am on the side of computers, I am identified with Project MAC, a computer project at M.I.T., I like computers, and I think they like me. But, most important, I am a man. It seems to me that being a man carries with it certain responsibilities that being a computer does not. As the rising torrent of technological devices, with all their implications of power and control, threatens to overwhelm us, we must, as men, begin to exercise our own responsibilities in dealing with the dangers the technology brings.

We already are in the business of selling new powers to those who do not really understand them. These powers are valuable tools for civilization; they are also inevitable. The question I raise here is the proper constraints on their use in exchange for the values they bring.

Let us suppose that an inspector from the Bureau of the Budget comes to visit Project MAC. What do we show him? First, we show him that we can give him access to a computer through a teletypewriter. He is impressed, but not much. Next, we show him that it is possible through that teletypewriter to discover the values of the variable components needed to build a certain kind of electrical filter. He is not so much impressed as mystified.

Then we read in a program that handles a personnel file to show him that within a few seconds he can find all the relevant facts about an individual's history. That is, he can find out exactly what has been put into the computer about that individual. His eyes light up. (Of course, we do not include very much in our program, because it is only a test model, but even a layman can see the point.) As more and

---

*The work reported herein was supported by Project MAC, an M.I.T. research program sponsored by the Advanced Research Projects Agency, Department of Defense, under Office of Naval Research Contract Nonr-4102(01). Reproduction in whole or in part is permitted for any purpose of the U.S. Government.

more information is routed through the computer for every purpose, more and more information will be included in that file.

Finally, we show him some of the monitor programs already running in the computer. They keep track of literally hundreds of variables, storing away times, usages, names of people, and their programs, and displaying all these data in a way management can inspect. This he understands; the computer will one day be able to tell him exactly what is going on and who is doing what to whom.

Most businesses today do not make decisions even remotely based on the information that is known and stored within those businesses. It is simply not possible for all the information that should affect a decision to be presented at the place where the decision is made. Staff work, I believe, includes collating, summarizing and presenting information already documented within a business system; it is a job hard enough for people to do. But, of course, computers do not care how hard they work; also they can work a good deal faster than people at many kinds of tasks, especially those that do not involve the kind of judgment in which people excel.

The man from the Bureau of the Budget sees from our demonstration that at least we are beginning to learn how to control systems and people by means of a supply of adequate information. He knows it is valuable for the limited task that he sees as his own responsibility. It is up to us here to look a little further ahead.

At Project MAC all of the data and procedures, that is, everybody's numbers and programs, are kept in bulk storage on two disk files. They hold about 20 million computer words and are now dangerously crowded at about 97 per cent capacity. Every user of the system is assigned a certain number of tracks on which he must store all of his data and programs. Since the assigned number of tracks exceeds the actual capacity of the disks by about 50 per cent, we frequently distribute urgent pleas for users to discard their files of old, unused, or surplus programs and data.

It has been suggested that as a way of keeping down the disk loading, system programmers, who are responsible for the maintenance of the MAC time-sharing system, might inspect users' files and clean up for them. I am happy to say that this suggestion has been successfully resisted. In the present MAC system a user's files are sacrosanct. The master file directory authorizes access to his files only through his particular password and programmer number. It is a good sign, it seems to me, that the present users trust the system so well that they never question the reliability of the master file directory or the trustworthiness of the system programmers.

But there is one way in which the absolute rule has been broken. Within the MAC system a console can be made to act as a slave console of another console, so that the first does exactly what the second does. That can be valuable in helping a student, for example. It can be set up by system programmers, some of whom have the necessary profound access to the system, and it does not inherently need the permission of the person using the second console. It is this that concerns me.

Last week I invited a professor in the Electrical Engineering Department at the Institute to try some programming on the MAC computer. "It's very easy," I said. "I know that you have never in your life done any programming, but that doesn't matter. Come and sit down at a console and try a few things. Make all the mistakes you want, and you will find that you can learn to program very quickly. Nobody is going to inspect your programs, because nobody can get to your files without your password, which is your secret."

Of course, what I said was not true. It would have been very simple to set up a monitor program and a slave console to follow his. How we would have chuckled over his foolish mistakes! That is my point. Whether we are vain or proud, all of us have idiosyncracies; some of us do not mind exposing them to public inspection, but most of us do. Privacy is, for almost everyone, absolutely basic to a reasonable life.

If I go out for a walk late at night in Beverly Hills, California, where everyone drives a car, the police stop me, look at me with suspicion, and invite me to ride with them to the police station. But why should I explain that I like to walk? It is not that I have something to hide but simply that they are prying. And even if I do have something to hide, why shouldn't I be able to hide it? Of course, it is the job of the police to pry, just as it is the right of a person not to be pried into too much. And clearly the lines between the job of the police and the right of a person are changing and will continue to change. Where should this line be placed as the powers of the computer technology become appreciated and applied?

"But," you say, "if we are running a business, our employee has no right having something to hide, particularly on company time." (I dispute that, first of all.) But of course I am not talking about running a business but about running a society, a country, and a civilization. We do not realize how much the system is in fact keeping track of us even now. Our privacy depends on the fact that the system has no efficient way of collating all the information and displaying it. We give our names when we buy airline tickets. If we use certain airlines, that information is already centralized.

Clearly, it is becoming daily more attractive to use the computerized services that the system now offers. Although credit cards are useful and convenient (and any day now I expect to have to pay extra for the privilege of using cash), to use a credit card is to put information into the system. Even though that information is not collated, it soon can be, with the aid of the technology that we are helping to develop. In the future only the eccentric will not avail himself of the system so that his every movement and decision can be traced and followed.

I asked before: Even if I have something to hide, why shouldn't I be able to hide it? The standard answer is that only the guilty have something to hide, and they shouldn't be allowed to do so. But what is a sin to one man, or to the system, is not necessarily a sin to another. (I also confess that I am not sure that I am unalterably opposed to sin.) Even so, there are skeletons in every closet.

We should understand that, as computerized information processing becomes more prevalent, as the data bases spread throughout society, as the processing becomes speedier and more accurate, it may become very difficult to keep a skeleton in the closet.  I think the human race would be the worse for that.

We have already seen to what improper, even terrifying lengths the notion of  security can drive otherwise pleasant and reasonable citizens.  I am frightened when I consider the powers that will be available through the computer to the security officers in a decade or so.  We have seen excesses already, but they will seem mild besides what will be possible.

We must not suppose that the collection and forwarding of data on which decisions are based are inherently distinct from the decision-making process itself.  Whoever controls the information that a decision-maker sees is, in effect, the decision-maker.  Worse, the man who thought he was making the decisions before thinks that he is still making them.

In connection with the decision-making process, it seems to me that two more dangers emerge.  The first is that although the machine may not perform especially well, it may be easy for the man using it to protect himself and advance himself by using it improperly.

To illustrate:  a great number of examinations today are composed of multiple-choice questions, a type frequently unsuitable but widely used because of the ease with which it can be processed.  Personnel directors use such examinations on the ground that they supply unchallengeable evaluations to support their decisions.  For some of the decisions that they must make, reliance on the outcome of standardized tests processed by machine is perfectly appropriate, but it is obviously inappropriate in other cases.

I think that we should make a practice of questioning decisions made by the machine, especially when it is making decisions for which we must be responsible.  This questioning is one of the responsibilities of being a man.  "It was the best butter" is the reply to "I told you butter wouldn't suit the works."  We must be very careful not to make that reply ourselves.

The second danger is that the machine may perform its duties so well that man surrenders his responsibilities to it.  Quite possibly the computer will be doing too good a job, will consistently make the right decisions, and will make them so effectively that we come to rely on it.  It may well outperform us in other aspects.  In many ways the process of decision-making must evolve with the computer technology, and we must evolve with it. We shall be tempted to leave too much to a computer that will have shown its competence in limited problems, but the responsibility for the decisions is always ours.  Instead of being satisfied that the computer is doing as well as we have been doing, we should be trying to do better.

You will note that I refer to the individual man and the individual machine.  In a sense this is fantasy, because the system itself gives the orders.  Most decisions now being made are not arrived at single-handedly; they are made jointly, sometimes by men, sometimes by men and machines.  And at Project MAC, we are striving to help men make good decisions by their effective interaction with the computer.  But whatever the nature of the joint decision, it reduces the sense of individual responsibility for the individual decision. It is too easy to accept the decision made jointly, especially if we are not entirely aware of exactly who made it. Many kinds of people, however, have learned to question order and decisions, whether they come from dogma or morals or politics or ideal decision-makers or whatever. I think that lesson will have to be learned by more and more of the citizenry. It is no excuse to say that we surrender to the system because we were in effect instructed to do so.

We must look with a certain distrust on the role that computers will play in our society because they are potentially so powerful. "Ye shall know the truth and the truth shall make you free." But the truth in somebody else's hands can be used to enslave. If information is power, then total information is absolute power. I am frightened at the prospect. It is not enough to be aware, to understand, to set up standards. We must be directing study to the questions we can see arising. What are the social needs of a man for privacy? How can we set up public records on computers that are trustworthy enough to be trusted? The trustworthiness of computers to some extent depends on how trusted they are. Our file system at Project MAC is happily trusted, but the general public certainly does not trust computers or their technology. There are surely some problems, both social and technological, worth studying here. What will be the social and technological environment of decision-making in the future? How broadly will these questions affect every level of society? I notice that the fundamental attitudes of society towards computers are widely discussed these days but without any apparent consensus. Presumably one of our first tasks is to find out what public attitudes are and what affects them.

One question that ought to be raised at this point is whether it is better and faster to teach computer technologists a little sociology or to teach sociologists a little computer technology. Whatever the answer, it is surely necessary to encourage participation by sociologists.

Some years ago when I was becoming interested in artificial intelligence, I was often asked why I thought it a profitable subject to pursue. I used to answer that I believed the second half of the twentieth century would be remembered not for the conquest of space, which I regard as a kind of exciting game, but for the advance of information technology, that is, for computers.

Professor B. F. Skinner, at Harvard, has often discussed the extent to which behavioral control should be exercised on various sectors of society. Now there is no doubt that behavioral control, even if it is not noticeably powerful as yet, is growing more so. Skinner has correctly pointed out that absence of overt control is as much a form of control as is dictatorship; it is perhaps just as little responsive to the identified or real needs of the society. If we do not choose to choose, we are nevertheless making a choice. The difficulty is that sudden and enormous increments in the power wielded by those in control may be irreversibly dangerous to the rest of us. For that reason I should prefer that until we have learned how to handle it gently and appropriately, we should avoid the overt control that our technology can bring. We must not think that that is enough. We must then learn to handle the inevitable power gently and appropriately; if we do not live up to our responsibilities, somebody else may do it for us.

I believe that the dangers are closer than we realize, though we have been hearing the signals for some time.  I also believe that the urgency of our duties is greater than we may realize.  We must find a way to make decisions jointly with other men and with machines without diminishing our responsibility for making those decisions.  We must find out the real needs of society in an environment modified by computers.

I remind you at this point that although I do not sound much like one today, I am a computer man who works with computers.  When I say I am a computer man, it is the second word that is the important one.  We are all men, and I hope that none of us ever forgets it.  Our responsibility lies in learning to control our technology before it controls us.

# DISCUSSION

Joseph Weizenbaum

Massachusetts Institute of Technology

There are two points in Oliver Selfridge's rather gloomy but completely convincing talk on which I would like to comment. The first concerns the matter of "having something to hide." At the present time security agencies are able to find out almost everything about any given individual. But the chief reason legitimate investigations on a large scale are either not initiated or not carried out in ultimate detail is that such undertakings are simply not economically feasible. Selfridge suggests that investigation in total detail and at low cost is becoming possible.

In my view, one of the bases for the security of the individual in a democratic society is his prerogative to hide, even to hide from his government and its authorities. Once this prerogative is encroached, I believe we are threatened. In developing a technology which may impair an individual's ability to hide, we are threatening that individual's freedom. During the course of these meetings our visitor from Hungary, in discussing punch-card files on individuals, remarked quite matter of factly that much of his data came from the police. I regard that as frightening. All of us here, computer men and behavioral scientists, recognize a danger. The question is: What can we do about it? I agree with Selfridge that we must assume responsibility. But how can we translate a sense of responsibility into action?

It seems to me that computer people today are roughly in the same position as were the atomic scientists in 1945. At some point, perhaps at Almagordo, they were seized with the feeling that they had done something they wished they had not done, something that they wished could be undone. As Oppenheimer put it: "They had known sin." It was only later that they began to publish The Bulletin of the Atomic Scientists. I cannot escape wondering whether some time in the future we will publish a journal called The Bulletin of the Computer Scientists, also with a clock on the cover. Hopefully, with the example of the atomic scientists before us, we can anticipate their regret so apparent in the pages of their bulletin and avoid doing things which bring such regret about.

Of course it is impossible to halt the advance of science, to refrain from hypothesizing, searching, investigating, and experimenting. But it may be possible to

219

attack the problem in another way. If the small group of computer men who develop systems for use by the government can be inculcated with the same sense of responsibility we feel here, they may be able to control their technology; they may be able to keep it out of the hands of those who either do not understand it or who want to abuse it. This matter bears a great deal of further study and exploration.

My second point concerns the matter of questioning decisions made by the machine. Selfridge noted two dangers: the first, that the machine may not behave well enough; the second, that it behaves so well people will come to depend too strongly on its decisions. In both of these circumstances decision-making power is lost. I would like to mention a third factor that presents us with still another danger; it involves the bases of decisions. In order to question a decision, one has to know the reasons why it was made. But as computer programs grow more and more complex, as they grow larger and larger, and as they become more and more reliable, authors often no longer understand their programs. In a number of physical systems a variety of checks and balances make it irrelevant and unnecessary to know exactly how a certain number is computed. But in some circles real abuses can be observed. For example, an engineer with a set of differential equations to solve goes to the computer center and says: "Please solve these for me." The computer man replies: "What method do you want me to use?" The engineer answers: "I don't care; any method is fine." Such behavior is not only irresponsible, but the method used may be of second or third order of accuracy, making a difference in the result of which the engineer will be altogether unaware.

Similarly with social systems, one can easily predict that census data can be used to generate all kinds of information for the benefit of, for example, the Department of Agriculture, on the basis of which large government allotments are made to subdepartments and ultimately to farmers. In the beginning, decisions based on such data may be completely rational and carefully checked. But the computers themselves, the language of computers, and the people who have worked on the programs will in all probability have changed in due course; the information on which the decisions were originally based thus becomes obsolete. Nevertheless the computer continues to grind out decisions that no one is in a position to question because no one understands the bases upon which they were made. It seems to me that this all too familiar process has become another real danger.

# VIII. DATA PRODUCTION AND DISSEMINATION

# NEW METHODS FOR DISSEMINATING CENSUS RESULTS

**Conrad Taeuber**
**Assistant Director**
**U. S. Bureau of the Census**

The rapid increase in the availability of computers to government, planning, research, and business institutions has brought with it an increase in the demand for
census data in a form that can be handled by computers. Cross tabulations that
were not possible before, combinations of census-tract or block data into new units,
the collation of census-tract data with data from local sources, and extensive analyses, model building, and simulation have become feasible on a scale that seemed
impossible when the analysts were dependent on smaller and less effective tabulating
equipment.

The Census Bureau's standing offer to prepare special tabulations at cost has often
met with the retort that this would require the expenditure of funds not readily
available, since the Bureau must make a charge for this service. Moreover, the
efficient use of the Bureau's equipment requires the prospective customer to specify
the desired tabulations in advance. In many cases the research worker develops
these as the project goes forward with each step dependent on the results of preceding steps. Equipment at his home base is frequently available without an outlay
of funds on his part. Programming as well as the running of tabulating equipment
might be done under circumstances which require little direct expenditure for the
hours used. Similar considerations were often raised when card-tabulating equipment was widely used. The management problems involved in handling files as
large as the Census files is often overlooked. Manipulating records for 180 million
individuals, or even 180, 000, is considerably different from dealing with the
smaller number of records that are the norm for sample surveys.

The Bureau has always had a strong interest in making its data available for use on
the broadest possible basis. Virtually all of them are collected at public expense
and the public is entitled to a full measure of results.

Conventional publication allows widespread dissemination of the data that are put
into that form. Even though the 1960 Census of Population resulted in 141, 000 pages

of printed reports, this represented only a fraction of the information that has been or might be tabulated.  Publication in the form of the printed page can at best meet only the more general needs — it rarely can meet all of the needs of the specialist, whether he concentrates on some subject matter or on some geographic area.

By the middle of 1961, long before the tabulations were completed, the Bureau issued a report summarizing the published and unpublished data which were expected to result from the 1960 Census.  The published data included those for states, counties, SMSA's, cities, minor civil divisions, census tracts, and city blocks.  Some information was tabulated by enumeration districts, but none of this was published.  It is available in unpublished form.  The tabulations that provided most of the census-tract statistics were also done for small areas for which no census tracts had been established, and the unpublished data for the "pseudo-tracts" are available on an unpublished basis.  Virtually every report from the 1960 Census points out that in addition to the published information, there is usually other summarized information which was not included in the publication.  In some instances the tabulations were done for all cities or SMSA's, not only for those that were shown in the report.  Some tabulations are available in more detail than the summarized form that was used for publication.

Such information is available in the form of magnetic tape and often in the form of punch cards.  Summary reports such as the County and City Data Book or County Business Patterns are available in the form of cards or tapes as well as in printed form.

Special tapes have been created, stripping off from the basic file only those items which are of primary interest to the potential user.  Since the resulting file is considerably smaller than the original, processing costs are substantially reduced.  Under Bureau control, such a file can be made available to users for further processing.  Much more can be done along these lines.  Better planning and equipment is expected to result in shortening the time required to tabulate the data collected in future censuses.  This should reduce to some extent the need for special arrangements to provide data during the period of tabulation.  New equipment is expected to give flexibility, which may make it possible to provide for special purpose tabulations with minimal interference to the main census tabulations.

Providing statistical summaries in a form that can be handled by computers meets only part of the need.  It does not meet the need of the analyst who feels that he must have access to the data for each of a large or a small number of individuals, for the relationships which he wishes to study tend to be obscured by the use of summary data, no matter how numerous or small the areas might be.

No discussion of this topic can proceed very far without running into the question of confidentiality of census data.  The decennial census is conducted under the provisions of the basic Census law, which requires that the questions in the census be answered fully and accurately to the best of the ability of the individual, and assures him that the information he gives will not be disclosed to unauthorized individuals.  The Census law (Title 13, U.S.C., Sec. 9) provides that

(a)    Neither the Secretary, nor any other officer or employee of the Department of Commerce or Bureau or agency thereof, may, except as provided in section 8 of this title--

> (1)    use the information furnished under the provisions of this title for any purpose other than the statistical purposes for which it is supplied; or

> (2)    make any publication whereby the data furnished by any particular establishment or individual under this title can be identified; or

> (3)    permit anyone other than the sworn officers and employees of the Department or Bureau or agency thereof to examine the individual reports.

Section 214 of Title 13 provides that violators "shall be fined not more than $1,000 or imprisoned not more than two years, or both."

In addition, in March 1960, the President of the United States issued a proclamation relating to the forthcoming census in which he included the following:

> The sole purpose of the Census is to secure general statistical information regarding the population, its characteristics, and its homes. Replies are required from individuals only to enable the compilation of such general statistics. No person can be harmed in any way by furnishing the information required. Individual information collected in the taking of the Eighteenth Decennial Census will not be used for purposes of taxation, investigation, or regulation, or in connection with military or jury service, the enforcement of school attendance, the regulation of immigration, or the enforcement of any national, state, or local law, or ordinance. There need be no fear that disclosure will be made regarding any individual person or his affairs. For the due protection of the rights and interests of the persons furnishing information, every employee of the Census Bureau is prohibited, under heavy penalty, from disclosing any information which may come to his knowledge by reason of his employment.

The provisions of confidentiality which apply to information collected under compulsion apply also to information which is collected by the Bureau in its voluntary surveys, such as the Current Population Survey.

The public confidence that information can safely be given to the Census Bureau is one of the Bureau's most valuable assets. Accordingly, the Bureau goes to great lengths to justify this confidence. It is no more possible to be a little bit unconfidential than it is to be a little bit pregnant. If there should be widespread doubt about the Bureau's position in regard to confidentiality, or if it should be generally assumed that it does not strictly observe the rules of confidentiality, the Bureau's effectiveness would be significantly impaired. Administrative rulings and procedures have been developed over the years to aid in guaranteeing confidentiality. It has been held, for example, that it would not be proper to release a list of names and addresses of firms giving simple information about type of business and size of operations, such as is published in directories issued by some states and private firms. Names and addresses of householders or any category of individuals may not be released. Obviously, it would not be possible to release a list of individuals with particular characteristics, as, for example, all heads of households with incomes above a specified level.

It is not generally appreciated that direct disclosure is not the only type that must be prevented. Indirect disclosure would be involved if, through the comparison of two sets of numbers, as by subtraction, it would be possible to gain information about a case which would not have been published directly. As a simple though by no means complete guide, the Census Bureau normally will not publish statistics other than counts for any area if fewer than a specified number of units are involved. In industrial or business statistics it is further necessary to avoid the situation in which one of the units is so large that it dominates the cell, and thus publication would effectively constitute disclosure even though the minimum number of cases were included.

There is no provision in the present law which would exempt persons or agencies whose intent in seeking individual records clearly does not involve any potential injury to the persons whose records would be used. Nor is there any provision that recognizes that magnetic tape can be read only through the use of complex machines and highly technical procedures and therefore is not as open to potential misuse as schedules or punch cards which could be read with relative ease if they fell into the hands of unauthorized persons.

One other important aspect deserves mention. The data in the possession of the Bureau cannot be made available to any party on an exclusive basis. The person or organization with the imagination and the funds to make some new use of census materials cannot obtain exclusive rights to the product. The Bureau's facilities and services must be available equally to all potential users. Thus, a special service in the form of data collection or tabulation would be deemed to be available generally. The first purchaser may have some advantage simply because he is first. But he cannot exclude others from gaining access to the results. Later purchasers may be asked to pay a fair share of the costs of preparing the materials in question. Alternatively, the Bureau may elect to publish the results or otherwise make them generally available.

Within this framework the Bureau has sought to assist research workers and others in making effective use of the materials collected by the Census Bureau, both in the censuses and in regular or special surveys. The simplest procedure is of course that which involves making information available in the form of statistical totals. These may in turn be the raw materials which the analyst uses in more refined work or they may be in the form of the finished product, which he wants.

A considerable number of users have received the results in the form of tapes. Sales of tapes resulting from the 1960 Censuses of Population and Housing have exceeded $200,000.

The 1-1, 000 sample represents a new effort to meet the need of research workers who have access to computer or tabulating equipment.  At the time of this writing, 44 copies of the 1-1, 000 tapes had been placed, and 21 sets of the 1-10, 000 cards had been placed.  It was felt to be important that there be full public disclosure of the plans and the information that was to be made available in this form.  Although the sample is a very small fraction of the population, it was believed to be necessary to remove small area identification in order to avoid any possible disclosure. This has imposed a limitation which some persons have felt to be a major handicap to the full utilization of these materials.  It was also believed to be necessary to assure that the fact of the availability of these materials should be made known generally to the people who might have an interest in them and thus to assure equal access to them.  Although the Bureau stands ready to assist holders of these tapes in their utilization, the Bureau assumes no responsibility for or control of the uses that are made.  This is a new venture on the Bureau's part, and the conclusions of this Conference will help the Bureau decide what it ought to do along similar lines in the future.  Parenthetically, it may be noted that a number of other national census offices are making similar arrangements.

One variant of this approach has been found useful for some limited purposes.  Some of the data collected in the Economic Censuses were scrambled in such a way that there was no possibility of disclosure of individual operations, but the resulting data inputs were usable for the limited purposes for which they were prepared.  It may well be that there ought to be further exploration of the possibility of extending this approach, recognizing that the scrambling might make the resulting records useless for the study of certain types of relationships.

Another variant is the release of a copy of one of the 5 per cent tapes for use in a specific research project at the expense of the project sponsor.  An employee of the Census Bureau works on the project and he alone has access to these tapes. He arranges for tabulations to the specifications of the research agency involved; and he is responsible for returning the original tapes to the Bureau or having them blanked at the expiration of the agreement.  There are direct benefits to the government in that one of the tabulations the Bureau had proposed to make from these tapes is to be combined with the work to be done on the research project.  This represents another approach to the problem of making the census materials available for significant research in a situation in which a large sample is required.  At the same time the arrangements for the preservation of confidentiality of the materials meet all requirements.

A valuable provision of the law is the one that permits the Bureau to enter into co-operative relationships with nonprofit organizations for the conduct of projects of mutual interest.  Costs are to be shared on a mutually agreeable basis.  The Bureau has entered into a number of such arrangements, some of which have involved the use of records that required confidential treatment.  In these cases the representatives of the co-operating party who need to have access to confidential census records are appointed as special agents of the Bureau.  They take the same oath of confidentiality to which all regular Census Bureau employees subscribe. This is not a loophole to escape the limitations that were mentioned earlier, but it is a useful arrangement for the conduct of projects which are of bona fide mutual concern.  Normally the Bureau's interest would need to be expressed in its ability to provide staff and funds for its share of the project.

In a number of instances it has been found useful for a co-operative research project to have a worker from the co-operating organization stationed at the Bureau for an extended period. This has fostered close working relationships with the Bureau staff and has facilitated the planning for and execution of special tabulations. Such arrangements have not been used as fully as they might be.

It would not be fair to conclude without mentioning some of the operational problems that have already been encountered. The need to provide adequate documentation of the tapes has been made abundantly evident, and steps have been taken to make such information more readily available. Conversion to make the tapes compatible with another computer system has presented some problems. With the growing development of computer languages, the problems of making programs available in a form for general use are coming much closer to solution. The Bureau has learned, as others have, that one cannot simply provide a tape and have no further contact with it, but that it is necessary to stand ready to provide consultation on the format and use of these tapes. Control totals may represent a problem. In the case of the 1-1,000 sample, the Bureau processed the tapes to develop the rim totals that any user might expect to get from tabulations he might make with this file. Establishing control totals for sample surveys may also represent a problem. In the CPS, for example, the weighting that is applied to the regular tabulations may be too involved to be used in other tabulations of these materials, or it may not be relevant to the particular problem in hand. Editing or adjustments that are introduced in a late stage of processing have not always been carried back to the original records. If, then, the original records are to be used for other tabulations, there are problems of reconciling the totals secured from these with the published totals.

The Bureau has watched with considerable interest the developments which are generally subsumed under the heading "data banks." Making published or unpublished information for census tracts, blocks, or other small areas available for use in such a way that records which are developed locally can be related to the census information is a development that holds great promise. But record linkage that involves bringing other information into the records for the person, family, or firm, which were collected by the census, is feasible only to the extent that the resulting record remains in the hands of the Census Bureau. There are legal and technical problems in carrying out such a proposal. But there are also important public relations problems and the possibility that the special arrangements may be misconstrued in a way that might erode public confidence in the Census Bureau and its maintenance of confidentiality.

In summary, the topic under discussion is one that is of major interest to the Bureau. A number of conferences have been held with users of data to explore the problems and possibilities of taking advantage of the opportunities for the dissemination of information which have been opened up through the availability of computers. This Conference is a significant step in the further exploration of this topic. The Bureau intends to continue an active interest in the matter, with a high priority. For that purpose it has recently appointed a senior staff member to help appraise the needs and to stimulate the development of procedures that will best meet the needs and the opportunities that exist now, as well as those which can be anticipated for the future. The major activities of this assignment will center on the improvement of census data access.

Between now and the next decennial census there will undoubtedly be major advances in computer technology. No doubt there will also be substantial changes in the manner in which census results are made available to users. The 1960 Census saw significant gains in the time required to publish census results. Further gains can be confidently expected. With more advance planning and more attention to the needs of other users, procedures can be developed that would simplify the supplying of results tapes, as well as the provision of information for small areas or small subgroups of the population. Establishing small input files of restricted length during the regular processing would facilitate customer-specified cross tabulations at minimum machine cost and within minimum time. Much more attention could be paid to geographic location, and tabulation for special purpose areas would no doubt be considerably simplified. Greater geographic specificity with regard to such an item as place of work would contribute in a major way to some needed analysis. More geographic detail would also facilitate studies which involve the matching of external records to those in the census file.

If these and other gains are to be realized, there must be continued study of all phases of data collection and processing; and there must be the co-operation of the organizations primarily concerned with computer technology. Much depends on the users of census data themselves, and their willingness and ability to formulate their needs in sufficient time and detail to permit effective recognition of them at the time when the procedures for the census are being developed.

# DATA NEEDS FOR COMPUTER SIMULATION OF LARGE-SCALE SOCIAL SYSTEMS

Guy H. Orcutt

University of Wisconsin

## Policy Role of Simulation

The government uses many instruments that are believed to influence the behavior of the economy. The precise use of these instruments comprises the policy of the government. The task facing the policy-maker is to specify how these instruments are to be used.

Simulation of the economy will not tell a policy-maker which of several possible courses of development is preferable. Nor will simulation of the economy, by itself, provide instruments capable of modifying its behavior. The major contribution to be expected from successful simulation of the economy is to provide linkage between functioning of the economy and use of available policy instruments. The ability to simulate the economy successfully would enable the policy-maker to investigate the probable consequences of alternative policies without actually experimenting with them. Successful simulation could provide an essential requirement of useful policy formation but would not reduce the need for human decision making.

Improved forecasting ability is an additional benefit that might accompany successful simulation of the economy. The extent to which unconditional prediction of the future is possible is not known, but the increased understanding essential to successful simulation would contribute to forecasting efforts. Since the decision process takes time, and since policy instruments work with a lag, it is clear that improved forecasting would be useful to the policy-maker.

## Models

Simulation of a social system involves two major steps. First, a model of the system is devised. Second, the model is solved by running it. Both of these steps have presented major difficulties, but given the computer revolution of the last decade, the second step has become quite manageable. However, we shall continue to stumble over the first step. This paper is concerned with why, more than

25 years after Tinbergen's path-breaking effort, this should still be so.  In addition, we will consider what can be done to rectify this unsatisfactory situation.

A model of the system embodies a set of equations.  Given an initial state of the system and values of input variables of the model, it serves to predict a subsequent state of the system.  By repeated use it serves to predict time paths of each output variable of the model.  Solutions obtained in this way are specific rather than general, but inductive methods may be used to generalize from an adequate number and selection of specific solutions.

Data are essential for model building, and it is a central thesis of this paper that data deficiencies are the primary reason for lack of clear success.  Data are also essential for model running, but since the needs in this area are fairly obvious and likely to be well met, we will limit ourselves to the data needs involved in model building and testing.

Let $Y_{1t}, \ldots, Y_{mt}$ be m distinct criterion variables of interest to policy-makers as measures of the state of the economy at time t.  These variables would normally include one or more measures of national income, unemployment, prices, and balance of payments.

Let $Z_1, \ldots, Z_n$ be n distinct policy, or control, variables.  These are variables selected or developed to describe actual or hypothetical adjustments or uses of policy instruments.  They are used to describe such things as tax laws, spending policies, open market operation, and federal debt management.

The essential characteristic for models of the United States economy, if they are to make an important contribution to policy formation, is that they adequately represent the way in which the time paths of the Y's depend upon the time paths of the Z's.

## Essentiality of Related Time Series

The model-builder must seek a set of equations that adequately represents the dependence of the Y, or criterion variables, on the Z, or policy, variables.  The fundamental problem that must be solved is the discovery of stable relationships between the activity of behavioral components and the specification of federal government policy.  This problem is clearly an inductive one, and our present lack of success stems from the fact that the discovery of such stable behavioral relationships has not been demonstrated to any even remotely satisfactory extent.  If stable relations of the desired form have been hit upon, we are unable at present to distinguish them from a great multitude of other relationships with conflicting implications.

Predictions about the consequences of actions represent particular applications of relationships that can only be estimated and tested on the basis of accumulated data.  A necessary condition for satisfactory estimation and testing of a relationship is the availability of time series for both the output and input variables.  They must relate to the same component or components, and each variable must relate to an appropriate time span.  Unco-ordinated measurements are likely to be of little or no value for estimation of relationships.

Responses of behavioral components are typically distributed over time and lag the situation that gives rise to them. The form and average lag of responses are typically part of what must be estimated. Cross-sectional data may be useful but are unsuitable for estimation of lagged responses. The observed responses may relate to earlier unmeasured stimuli, while the observed stimuli may relate to future unmeasured responses. Recall data may help a little, but errors are likely to be larger for longer than for shorter recalls, and systematic biases are likely to be substantial. Cross-sectional data may be useful for establishing appropriate initial conditions and may provide a variety of possibilities for testing hypotheses. Nevertheless, related time series are essential if the dynamic behavior of the economy is to be studied.

## Losses Resulting from Aggregation Prior to Estimation

In general, aggregation of data prior to estimation will lead to some loss in efficiency of estimation of both regression coefficients and the variances of their estimates. This follows from the fact that aggregated data can always be derived from disaggregated data, but in general the reverse is not true. Information is lost in aggregation; the only question is whether the loss is significant. Of course, if inefficient estimators are used with disaggregated data, while efficient estimators are used with aggregated data, then it is easy to devise situations that seem to show that aggregation prior to estimation is actually helpful. There is more than one way of throwing away evidence, and it is possible to do so at the estimation stage as well as prior to it.

In a recent article, J. S. Cramer considers some of the effects of prior grouping of data on Engel curve analysis. [1] His objectives differed from ours, as he was mainly concerned with the effects of grouping cross-sectional data obtained from budget studies. Nevertheless, his analysis applies equally well to a situation that might arise in the analysis of time-series data. The only difference is that while efficient grouping may be possible for specific uses of cross-section data, it is not attempted and does not appear feasible in the case of time-series data.

Cramer considers the ordinary regression model for a sample of $N$ observations $(x_{ij}, y_{ij})$, which is divided into $t$ groups of $n_i$ observations each. The $x_{ij}$ are fixed and given, and the $y_{ij}$ are repeated samples defined by

$$y_{ij} = \alpha + \beta x_{ij} + U_{ij},$$

where $\alpha$ and $\beta$ are unknown constants. He assumes that the $U_{ij}$ are independent random disturbances, drawn from a single normal population with zero mean and constant variance $\sigma_U^2$. They are independent of the $x_{ij}$. No assumption is made about the nature of the $t$ groups, and for our use his normality assumption is unnecessary.

We will assume that there are $n$ spending units, and that the $y$ and $x$ variables are measured for each of the $n$ spending units for each of $t$ time periods. Each of Cramer's $n_i$ is thus set equal to n, and the total number of observational points, N, is equal to nxt. We thus are considering time-series data on each of two variables for each of a panel of n spending units.

One possibility is to estimate the regression parameters from the original time-series data on the panel of spending units. A second possibility is first to aggregate or average over the n spending units to obtain a single pair of time series for the entire group. Then the aggregated data may be used to estimate the regression parameters. Such aggregation is analogous to what we do in obtaining aggregated time-series data. The question is how much, if anything, might be lost by this aggregation prior to estimation.

As Cramer shows, the effect of prior grouping in the above case is to increase the variance of the regression estimate of $\beta$ by a factor

$$\left[ \sum_{ij} (x_{ij} - \bar{\bar{x}})^2 \right] \Big/ \left[ \sum_{i} n (\bar{x}_i - \bar{\bar{x}})^2 \right].$$

The reduction in efficiency will be given by the inverse of this fraction. In our interpretation the i is the time subscript, and the j is the spending-unit subscript. The i runs from 1 through t, and j runs from 1 through n; x is the grand mean of the x's, and $\bar{x}_i$ is the mean of the x's for the time period, i.

If the $x_{ij}$ within each time period are identical, then it can be seen that the above ratio will be equal to one, and no loss of efficiency in the estimation of $\beta$ will occur. This is, of course, the justification for saving computing expense by prior grouping of cross-sectional data on the basis of those variables used as explanatory variables.

If the $x_{ij}$ within each time period are not identical, then it can be shown that some loss in efficiency of estimating $\beta$ will take place. If the grouping of the $x_{ij}$ within time periods is equivalent to that obtained by a random grouping of the entire nxt observations into t groups, then the loss of efficiency will be of the order of (t-1)/(N-1). When it is remembered that N is equal to the number of spending units, n, times the number of time periods, t, it may be seen that in this case prior grouping of data would reduce the efficiency to approximately 1/n of what it would be without grouping. Since n is the number of spending units over which aggregation takes place, it is clear that prior aggregation would, in this case at least, result in throwing away almost all of the available information. Cramer's results also show that in this case the precision of the estimate of $\sigma_U^2$, and hence of the variance of the regression coefficient, is reduced by a factor (t-2)/(N-2).

In practice the x's grouped in arriving at aggregate time series are likely to be positively correlated, and the ensuing loss of information would therefore be less than in the above example. Nevertheless, considering the large amount of obvious variation present in cross-sectional data, it is difficult to see much basis for complacency about current practices. We may not be losing 99.999 per cent or more of the available evidence, but I think it would be extremely difficult to show that we are not inadvertently discarding 99 per cent of it.

### Necessity of Time Series on Microcomponents

It is my belief that insofar as availability of data permits, a proper study of socio-economic systems should have its foundations in research on the microcomponents from which such systems are formed.  I believe this is so despite the fact that many uses of models of such systems revolve around predictions of macrobehavior. The previous section indicates one basis for preferring data on microcomponents. This section presents additional reasons for seeking time series on microcomponents.

<u>Hypothesis formation</u>:  The essence of any model is the hypotheses embedded in its relationships and structure.  The social scientist can invest hypotheses relating to components of any desired level of aggregation, just as the physicist may promulgate hypotheses about the behavior of gases as well as about the behavior of molecules or components of molecules.  However, the social scientist has a peculiar advantage in producing hypotheses about the behavior of individuals, families, and firms that he does not have at other levels of aggregation.  He is an individual, and he lives at a microlevel.  Introspection and personal observation cannot be relied upon to be unbiased and free of gross distortion.  Nevertheless, fruitful hypotheses about human behavior are rare enough that social scientists should fully exploit whatever advantages may accrue from their being the most important type of component in the systems they wish to simulate.  This does not mean completely avoiding hypotheses about macrobehavior, but it does mean being willing to work with models based upon, or derived in large part from, hypotheses about the behavior of microcomponents.

<u>Specification of Causality</u>:  We want models of social systems that will enable policy-makers to predict consequences of alternative actions.  Furthermore, we want models that say more than that certain things have been associated in the past or even that, in the absence of control efforts, they will be associated in the future. We want models that will predict how the future will be different if particular actions are taken in preference to others.  Successful induction from past experience about even the immediate impact of actions is difficult enough in any case, but it seems most attainable in situations in which we can clearly identify the action, observe many repetitions of the action in varying circumstances, and observe developments in terms of many selected variables at closely spaced points in time, both preceding and following it.  All of the above requirements can frequently be met in studying the behavior of microcomponents.  They are almost never met at highly aggregative levels.

<u>Estimation and Testing</u>:  Social scientists do not yet possess a body of theory sufficiently developed and tested to permit the confident specification of variables to be included, of forms of equations to be used, and of appropriate lags for each variable prior to the estimation of parameters entering into equations.  Existing theory offers some guidance, but it is the most fanciful kind of wishful thinking to believe that it offers much guidance in the above respects.  It is obvious, therefore, that any effective testing and estimation requires very large numbers of observations.  This would be true even if the observations to be used were generated by experiments arranged according to the best available knowledge about experimental design.

Highly aggregative time series simply do not begin to contain enough degrees of freedom to permit extensive testing and estimation. This would be the case even if the observations in such series resulted from well-planned experiments. The fact that the available aggregative series are autocorrelated, multicollinear, frequently poor measures of what we want to measure, often not helpful in measuring short-run developments, and embedded in an operating system involving many relatively rapid feedbacks, only compounds the already apparent drawbacks of estimation and testing based only on highly aggregative time series.

Since much of the hoped-for payoff is at the highly aggregative level, it is of course reasonable to exploit fully the testing and estimation possibilities that exist at this level. However, anyone who recommends primary reliance upon estimation and testing based solely on the use of time series aggregated all the way up to a single set of series for the national economy is surely one of the world's greatest optimists. Estimation and testing problems still abound, even if observations on microunits are used, but at least one can have an enormous body of unplanned experiments to work with. These unplanned experiments may be observed in great detail at very frequent intervals, and they do involve wide ranges of variation in the variables. At the microlevel, there are frequent cases in which variables we would have liked to vary do in fact vary and in which other variables we would have liked to hold constant do remain constant.

In existing macroanalytic models, certain gains may be achieved by the introduction of additional product classifications or by use of finer industry classifications. Nevertheless, although additional data may be brought to bear with each such move in the direction of disaggregation, it also is true that new parameters are added at about the same rate as new data. The attempt is not to obtain replication of somewhat similar components but rather to obtain homogeneity within classifications. Thus each new component introduced requires a new and different set of equations to describe its behavior and its response to various kinds of treatment.

Microanalytic models were devised to improve estimation and testing possibilities. One central reason why they could be expected to do this is that although enormous numbers of components are introduced, these components are thought of as being replications of one or another of a very small number of types. A single household model is supposed to apply to each household. The parameters of a submodel of such a component type are supposed to be estimated on the basis of time-series observations on thousands or tens of thousands of households. The number of observational points brought to bear in estimating or testing a given relationship model may thus be thousands or even tens of thousands of times as numerous as the parameters to be estimated.

It is not my intention to suggest that the only thing that matters is the ratio of observational points to parameters that must be estimated. It is of critical importance to be working with the right variables and for the same time periods and components. It seems evident that it is almost, if not absolutely, essential to work with time-series data. Of course, one wants data that include a wide range of variation of variables used as inputs into any equation to be estimated. Multicollinearity is harmful. Autocorrelated errors are a handicap. Rapid feedbacks present substantial problems. Errors of observation are difficult to avoid and difficult to deal with. Nevertheless, almost all of the above problems are more manageable if the ratio of observational points to parameters to be estimated is high. Many of the above difficulties must be completely ignored if this ratio is low. No testing is possible if it is equal to one, and estimation becomes impossible as this ratio drops below one. Even in the ideal situation in which well-designed experiments can be carried out, it seems clear that no experimentalist would ever be satisfied to estimate and test a particular relationship with a ratio of observational points to parameters of the order of 10 or less. Yet we have been trying to do just this in the case of relations used in macromodels of the economy — and in the face of a very impressive array of deficiencies with respect to the data brought to bear.

### The Significance of Time Series on Matched Groups

Because the present supply of time series about microcomponents is grossly inadequate and likely to remain so, other possibilities of increasing the effective data base should be of great interest. One such possibility, which appears to be of major significance, is the systematic development of time-series data for parallel and approximately matched groups of behavioral components.

The typical situation currently faced in efforts to model the United States economy is that there exists at best only one set of time series for testing and estimating each relationship. By securing parallel sets of time series of the same variables for ten or a hundred subgroups of the population, the number of observational points available for estimation would be increased by a factor of 10 or 100. If the groups were selected so as to be approximately matched, the same equations should apply to each of the groups, and no increase need take place in the number of parameters to be estimated.

The multiplication of observations with little or no increase in parameters permits large gains in testing power and corresponding reductions in standard errors of estimated coefficients. Furthermore, an additional opportunity would then present itself.

With a single set of time series relating to what might be thought of as a single experimental subject, the only kind of controls possible is of the before-after variety. It is thus always extremely difficult to know whether any observed behavior is a response to a potential stimulus of interest or to one or more of the large number of other aggregate time series highly correlated with the explanatory variable of interest. By using parallel sets of observations on approximately matched groups, we can relate differential behavior to differential stimuli and so achieve more effective controls. In the first case, average responses are related to average treatments, and most of the available evidence is not brought to bear. In the second case, all other subgroups may be thought of as potential control groups for each subgroup. This would permit the effective suppression, or balancing out, of major feedbacks. This in turn might well permit appropriate and effective use of simple techniques for estimation and testing, along with far fewer assumptions about parts of the economy not under immediate investigation.

Since the population of households, for example, could be divided into approximately matched groups in many ways, the question arises as to which groups should be used. However, it is easily seen that a single optimal grouping is not to be expected.

Therefore, insofar as is feasible, we should provide for use of more than one basis of grouping.

The general objective in selecting groups should be to achieve groups that are as internally heterogeneous as possible with respect to variables the researcher wants to balance out, and as internally homogeneous as possible with respect to variables the researcher wishes to consider as potential explanatory variables.

Thus in studying expenditure behavior of consumers, the researcher might well want to suppress or balance out variables that vary a great deal over the life cycle of individual consumers or over the cross section of consumers. He might wish to do this because these variables largely cancel out when it comes to time variations of aggregate income. In this case the selected groups should be approximately matched with respect to distributions of such factors as age, sex, race, and education. To achieve this the consumers within each group need to be heterogeneous with respect to these variables.

For the purpose of developing dynamic models of the economy, the researcher studying consumer behavior might wish not only to suppress variables of the above type, but to focus attention on variations of income of the type that do aggregate to the major movements of national income. To facilitate this process, it is clear that we must have as much independent variation as possible among the groups with respect to variables measuring these kinds of income change. To achieve this the consumers within each group should be as homogeneous as possible with respect to the variations of such variables.

A prime and obvious attraction of the use of data aggregated or averaged over a group of microbehavioral components is that disclosure problems are greatly reduced or even eliminated. If the groups are small, appropriately selected, and numerous, it is possible that the loss of information inherent in aggregation can be kept small. A significant effort in this direction is now being made by Edgar Feige, of the University of Wisconsin, with the co-operation and support of the Board of Governors of the Federal Reserve System. In this approach each set of time series would relate to three or four banks.

A second very important attraction of seeking time series that measure average or aggregate stimuli and behavior of groups is that, if the groups are large, it permits deriving sets of time series from a succession of unlinked cross-sectional samples. At present, Arnold Zellner and I are trying to demonstrate the feasibility and promise of this approach by use of the successive cross-sectional surveys of finances conducted by the Survey Research Center of the University of Michigan for the Federal Reserve Board. The basic idea of this approach is simply that, since each nationwide cross-section sample actually draws a sample from many subgroups of interest, it is possible to estimate the mean value of each measured variable for each subgroup. This having been accomplished in successive surveys since the late 1940's, the estimated means can be linked into time-series estimates of the true time series of means for each subgroup used. This can be done even though the successive samples are unlinked, and consequently time series for individual microcomponents could not be derived. Since the sampling variance of sample means depends primarily on sample size, it is important to have sizable subsamples from within each subgroup of the population.  <u>The large total sample size of the Current Population Surveys of the Bureau of the Census makes it an ideal candidate for this kind of use.</u>

A third important advantage of seeking time series that measure average stimuli and behavior of groups is that an extensive set of time series related to the same groups can be built up by merging data from different microcomponents.  It is only necessary that each source secure the minimal amount of information needed to classify the selected microcomponents into the same set of selected groups.  This variant of the general approach also requires the use of sizable samples if direct matching is impossible.

## Summary Statement

By now the importance of model development and simulation studies is fairly widely appreciated.  Thus a substantial amount of money is invested in model building and simulation for the purposes of (1) development of weapon systems and military strategy;  (2) planning and control of production processes;  (3) preparation for space exploration;  (4) design of traffic-control and flood-control systems;  and (5) development of corporate policy.

Although the potential value of model development and simulation studies to economic and social policy formation is extremely large, efforts to simulate our economy have been on a small scale.  The importance of such efforts is beginning to be recognized by political leaders, but this recognition has yet to be translated into an appropriate measure of support.  Support and co-operation are required in several areas but are most urgent in data collection and provision for their use.

Relationships, or chains of relationships, that adequately represent the dependence of criterion variables on policy, or control variables, must be discovered, esti-mated, and tested.  But estimation and testing of behavioral relationships requires the availability of time-series data for the output variables and the input variables of each relationship considered.  Appropriate sets of time-series data are essen-tial; isolated cross-sectional surveys or isolated time series cannot provide the major part of the data base needed.

If it were available, the best data base would include an extensive supply of appro-priately selected time series for each member of large panels of households, firms, and other basic behavioral components of our economy.  Ideally, such time series would contain frequent measurement over long periods of time.  Unfortunately, model-builders are not about to be presented with an ideal data base.  Nevertheless, some individuals, such as Roger Miller and his associates, on the current Wisconsin Assets and Incomes Study, have shown how much even a relatively small group can accomplish if it has the co-operation of the government, necessary resources, long-range vision, and a lot of staying power.

The U.S. Bureau of the Census has taken a valuable and historic step in preparing and distributing the 1-1,000 sample from the 1960 Population Census.  Hopefully, additional bodies of data about microcomponents will be made available in this way.  However, it must be recognized that although a major step, it still falls far short of what is needed.  This sample yields a cross-sectional view of households; thus many variables record responses to earlier and unobserved situations, while many other variables measure stimuli to later and thus unobserved responses.  Furthermore, since locational information was omitted in order to prevent disclosure, it is difficult to supplement this body of data with needed current and lagged data about communities, labor markets, and states.

Time-series data are needed, but the publicly available supply of time-series data about microcomponents is likely to remain extremely limited, partly because of disclosure problems and partly because of the difficulty of collecting such data. Since the U.S. Government does collect, but does not release, a great deal of information from and about microcomponents, two possibilities, which deserve to be vigorously promoted, have been recognized for overcoming this problem.  One is that the government greatly strengthen and extend its own model-building activities. The existence of a more vigorous effort within the government would permit effective use of some bodies of data which are now largely wasted.  The existence of an in-house effort might also be expected to offer guidance to data-collection activities. In addition, it might provide a motivating force for carrying out linkage or merger of data bodies that are now separate and therefore of little research value.

A second possibility for greatly increasing the research value of data now collected is the establishment by the U.S. Government of a major data library — computation center designed to facilitate both government and nongovernment research. Such a center could store data and facilitate their rapid retrieval and use without disclosing confidential information about individual components.  If adequately organized, staffed, and financed, it could be of enormous social benefit by facilitating the expanded research use of currently available data.  It could greatly increase the value of existing data by providing for essential linkage and merger of data collected by both government and nongovernment collecting agencies, and could prevent the tragic loss of irreplaceable data, which now frequently occurs.

During the next 10 years, we can expect to make progress in the collection of time-series data about microcomponents.  Nevertheless, in view of some well-known and formidable problems, we are unlikely to secure an adequate supply of such data. In view of this belief, Section 6 of this paper presented a case for systematic development of time-series data for groups of microcomponents.  It stressed the importance of obtaining sets of time series for approximately matched groups.  It pointed out that the use of data about groups, rather than microcomponents, avoids the major disclosure problems.  It also offered the possibility of deriving sets of time series from a succession of unlinked cross-sectional samples, and it facilitated merger of data from surveys of different microcomponents taken at about the same point in time.  Sets of time series on matched groups probably cannot provide as good a data base as would adequate sets of time series on large numbers of individual microcomponents.  However, they would enable us to increase the effectiveness of our present data base by several orders of magnitude; moreover, they are obtainable.  Used with reasonably available data about microcomponents, they would permit highly useful modeling and simulation of the United States economy.

### Reference

1.    Cramer, J. S., "Efficient Grouping, Regression and Correlation in Engel Curve Analysis," Journal of the American Statistical Association, 59, 233 — 250 (1964).

## DISCUSSION

Carl Kaysen
Harvard University

In commenting on what Dr. Taeuber and Professor Orcutt have had to say, I will be brief. Professor Orcutt, for very good reasons, has requested more and more data; we need it in less aggregated form; we need it more frequently. I think the basis for making this request is a sound one. There is no question that systematic bodies of less aggregated data would advance the analysis of a great many kinds of economic behavior difficult to deal with on the basis of highly aggregated measurements alone.

From his quite different perspective at the Census Bureau, Dr. Taeuber has pointed out some of the significant legal and institutional restraints on making more data available, but has told us only a part of what the Census Bureau has done to make these constraints as minimal as possible. I might add, as a personal note, that I have had some experience with the Census in this regard, and I think that Dr. Taeuber has conveyed too modestly a sense of how helpful the Census people can be and how eager they are to make the data they collect usable. It would be easy for me in following these two speakers to take a reasonable position in the middle, but I do not want to do that; rather I want to take an extreme position and offer a quite different approach.

Professor Orcutt suggests getting more data by using, as one alternative, sample studies of numerous small groups rather than aggregate series for national or state totals; the data bank as another alternative; and the notion of more in-house model building as a third alternative. I would like to suggest a fourth alternative and argue its merits a bit: the fourth alternative is a great deal more disclosure. I fully appreciate the reasons why the Census Bureau cannot and should not take the lead in that direction. I do not think it should push for disclosure, nor do I think it should be asked by consumers to transgress the legislative rules and customs under which it operates. But I would argue that the professional users should make a case for changing the rules.

I want to distinguish here between the household sector and the firm sector. On the household side, I think a great deal of what Professor Orcutt asked for can be accomplished without raising serious problems of disclosure. The only obstacle, if it is an obstacle, is money.  It is perfectly feasible to produce data of various sorts on groups of consumers without raising the issue of disclosure so long as the number of members of the group is sufficiently large, even though narrowly pin-pointed as to such variables as age, occupational status, current employment status, residential status, city size, and geographic area.  If means and variances could be published for cells defined by such variables, all of Orcutt's aims would be sub-stantially accomplished.

Of course, there is the problem of measurement, namely, that some kinds of items, when measured from survey data, are still not very good qualitatively as compared with the same kinds of items when measured from national income data.  This is a very important limitation in the household sector.  But if we turn to the firm sector, the problems are much greater.  Here we have experience with time series on individual cells, based on conventional census data published by industry and size group, internal revenue data by industry and size group, and, more recently, some new census material by industry and age group in the company statistics program. Our experience with these is bad for reasons that reflect neither anyone's ill will nor failure to address the problems properly, but merely the nature of the data. Classifications tend to change or become obsolete, and it is inevitable that data-producing agencies interested in issuing current reports that make sense place less weight on consistency over time than on current definitions.  Anyone who has tried to use industry data with any fineness of classification over a period of time knows that the content of the industry has really changed quite a bit, and the aggregated data make it difficult to get inside the industry and reconstruct industries consistent over time.

In some parts of the census, especially in the Census of Manufacturers (the oldest, the best established, the most reliable, and the most stable body of economic data), some of these problems have been dealt with.  But they have not been solved, for by their nature they are insoluble.  With respect to the Internal Revenue Service data, which are by-products of tax collection, the problem is much worse.  Classi-fications by industry, and location of particular firms in industries, reflect the interaction of changes in the tax laws with changes in the decision of firms as to how they want to behave.  My own experience with data of this kind suggests that we can deal with the problem only if we can get data separately for individual firms.  It is worth noting that a very substantial part of the data that the Census collects is also now available in a variety of other forms without the restriction of confidentiality. Perhaps a quarter of the information contained in the Census of Manufacturers' reports for large firms is publicly available from a combination of individual finan-cial reports and the publications of investors' services, provided the investigator knows what to look for — a very important qualification.  The ordinary investigator frequently cannot make use of these data because it is too fragmentary and he does not know how to put the pieces together.

I would suggest that the business community ought to take the lead in making more data of this kind publicly available.  Firms can be protected against providing in-formation useful to competitors if there is an appropriate time lag involved in publication.  The disadvantages resulting from a two- or three-year lag in the pub-lication of information for individual firms would not be as disturbing to the analyst as the difficulties he now encounters in dealing with aggregate data.  Yet the firms' concerns about making data available to competitors might be sharply reduced if a suitable time lag were built into the publication process. I think it worthy of note that business firms in the regulated sectors have grown accustomed to publication of data in individual firms so detailed, so specific, and so extensive that it often overwhelms analysis. So while I think that on the household side the suggestions advanced by Professor Orcutt ought to be pursued, on the firm side we perhaps might look at a different goal.

We are not here discussing a scientific problem of what is the right kind of information; we are discussing a tactical problem of how to go about getting more information. Agreeing that we would like more information of all kinds, what efforts are more likely to yield fruitful results? That is why I distinguished between what might be done on the household side from what can be done on the firm side. Moreover, it is also true that in the household sector, within the cells defined, the data are probably reasonably distributed — perhaps not normally, but at any rate, reasonably symmetrically. This is rarely true, however, of any cell defined for firm data, and therefore the same device will not yield results as manageable when applied to large business units. For all these reasons, my own feeling is that the tactic for economists and other social scientists for getting more data from the business sector is to approach head-on the question of what disclosure restrictions are really necessary, what interests they serve, and what the countervailing interests are in trying to eliminate, or reduce sharply, these restrictions. As consumers of data and as advisors to governmental units who are users of data, I believe we must take the lead, with the hope that if we succeed, the Census will be glad to follow.

### Postscript

Two and a half years later my proposition for the best tactics for interested social scientists to pursue in getting more information seems to me to be still correct. The issues that have been raised by the proposal for a National Data Center[1] make clear both the possibilities for getting more data and the problems that such proposals create. The demand for privacy on information about individuals has entirely different justifications than the rules for nondisclosure of information on business enterprises. It seems to me clear that, unless that distinction is drawn, justified concern about the former may make more difficult an appropriate use of data on the business enterprise.

### Reference

1.   Bureau of the Budget, Report of the Task Force on Storage of and Access to Government Statistical Data, U. S. Government Printing Office, Washington, D. C., October 1966.

## DISCUSSION

**Edgar S. Dunn, Jr.**
**Resources for the Future, Inc.**

These two papers, and indeed the entire conference to date, are symptomatic of an amazingly significant phenomenon. I refer to the radical change that has taken place on both the supply and the demand sides of the information process. In these papers we have representatives of both sides of that process. I think that the explicit and implicit testimony of this conference has been that these revolutionary changes have increased the relative gap between the demand for and the supply of information. I would like to examine with you the extent to which this is true and my view of some of the forces at work. In the process I will make a few comments about each paper.

I will not take up the time of this group in discussing dimensions of this radical change in supply and demand. Certainly you are all intimately familiar with the changes on the supply side that have been brought about by the advent of the computer, and you are also thoroughly familiar with the methodological advances in research that have placed new strains upon the quality, scope, and availability of data. You are also aware of the increase in the complexity of the public and private decision process in recent years that has also increased the burden of our information requirements.

For the moment let me beg the question whether this relative information supply gap is increasing or not by asserting that it is. This will allow me to begin with some of my views about the reasons for this unsatisfactory performance. I shall return to the other question later.

One of the reasons why the relative information gap is increasing is a fairly substantial lag in the adjustment to the change of circumstances on the part of both users and producers of information. If I were asked what I consider to be the single most important consequence of the recent revolution in the information process, I would say it is that the producer and the user of data are intimately linked in ways not heretofore experienced. It has been something of a shotgun wedding, forced by circumstances. Neither party has been altogether willing, and on occasion each has been inclined to blame the other for his condition.

One result of this lag in adjustment is a production bias on the part of the producers of statistics that is not altogether appropriate for the new circumstances. There are several perfectly natural reasons for this.  First, until the advent of the computer the only efficient information-retrieval device for those agencies engaged in generating data for publication distribution was the traditional data monograph.  As a consequence, practically all of the agencies of the Federal Statistical System, for example, are organized as data publishers.  They prospect for the data, give it some initial benefaction of the tipple-head, and then publish it in a conventional format.  The consequence of this has been that most requests for data never impacted on the agencies themselves but were handled by the documentary centers.  Indeed, none of these agencies has any kind of refined idea about the nature or frequency of use of these data.  The outside pressures to which they have had to respond have more often been associated with respondents than with users.  The organizations have not typically developed the kind of reference or user services that are commonly associated with documentary files in more direct contact with users.  The advent of the computer is rapidly creating a situation in which these agencies need to function relatively more as libraries and relatively less as data publishers, and this is placing a strain on some of the older institutional arrangements oriented to a different time.  Secondly, since these agencies have not typically had many close ties with users inside or outside government, few of their people are trained or experienced in subject-matter research fields or even more pedestrian forms of data utilization in association with the public or private decision process.

At the same time, there is a users' bias that is equally as damaging as, if not more damaging than, the production bias just discussed.  This has several dimensions. On the whole, social scientists have had an appalling lack of interest in the problems of producing information.  In general, the attitude has been that this is dirty work to be left to specialists in data production.  I think this is basically the penalty of our discipline's developing outside of the experimental tradition.  Most physical scientists have a long tradition of responsibility for the generation of their own data as well as for its quality and relevance.  Most social scientists, however, have simply been content to work on what was available.  Moreover, in our graduate  schools we have given comparatively little training in the development and handling of information in research.  There are many bright young graduates who are quite facile in model building and in the use of sophisticated research tools, but who are excessively naive and inept when it comes to coping with the problems of an information base.

One of the things I am saying is that one of the vertical sectors of the information process is either missing or badly undeveloped in most institutional settings, whether it be government, business, or an academic research community.  The information process, like most production processes, has a number of vertical stages.  There is a basic resource stage, represented by the basic or primary information agencies.  There is an intermediate processing stage, often organized in completely different institutional form.  For example, such agencies as the Office of Business Economics are engaged in taking data from a variety of primary sources and constructing a set of intermediate data.  This intermediate processing, which produces national accounts or complicated index numbers and other such forms, adds value to primary data by giving it a form that increases its utility and relevance.  All of these primary and intermediate information products have an ultimate usage in either the business or the public decision process or in research. Yet most of the existing institutions involved in research or decision making have never developed adequate personnel or institutional arrangements for efficiently bringing together the producers of data and the decision maker or research worker. Mr. Orcutt calls attention to this fact in his paper when he recommends that the government greatly strengthen and extend its own in-house model-building activities.  This is a recognition on his part that a more direct involvement in the activities that link the data source and the user may be an important step in overcoming the production biases that exist.  It may be of some interest for this group to know that some progress is being made along these lines.  The Office of Business Economics has recently taken over the Klein model in one of its units in order to gain greater familiarity with this kind of exercise.  It is also attempting to establish an econometric division that will be in a position to carry on more of this type of research.  I myself am more concerned at the moment by something other than the deficiency in model-building capacity.  In most government agencies and departments there is an almost unbelievable absence of subject-matter specialists who are qualified to serve as efficient liaisons between those engaged in producing primary and intermediate data and those engaged in the responsible exercise of the decision process.  If this gap could be plugged, even at levels that this group would be inclined to consider pedestrian, the decision-makers would learn to appreciate the value of information in a new way, and in a way that I am afraid is essential if we are to gain the necessary support for substantive changes in the federal system.

These lags of which I speak are perfectly natural, of course, and they will work themselves out over time.  This evolution will proceed much more rapidly, however, if both groups recognize these lags and face them more explicitly.

I have no doubt that this young couple will learn to live together more gracefully as time goes on.  I am really more concerned about some of the obstacles to a happy and successful marriage they are likely to encounter.  I think the most important and the most persistent sources of the increase in the relative information gap are a result of discontinuities growing out of scale factors and external factors. This leads me to observe that my friends from the Bureau of the Census, who are with us today, and other program managers in the federal statistical system have often been charged with errors of omission for which they cannot fairly be held accountable.  Many ways in which they would like to accommodate the users are blocked by circumstances beyond their immediate control.

The foregoing observation takes me back to the question of the reality of this growing information gap.  One can assert with some logic that there cannot be a gap between the effective demand of and supply for any commodity, including information. It can be claimed, with some justice, that the information-producers are doing a good job of meeting the demand that is made effective in the market place.  In this context one might admit that there are felt needs that are not being adequately met in an absolute sense and still contend that anyone in the position to make his needs effective is being accommodated.

The trouble with this argument is that there are a number of serious discontinuities in both the demand and supply functions that make the traditional concept of

these functions more or less irrelevant and raise a serious question about the le-
gitimacy of the concept of effective demand.

Let us illustrate some of the sources of these discontinuities.  Consider first some
problems of simple scale.  If we wish to extend the scope of the information file to
plug some of the more serious gaps and provide information for certain forms of
research and decision making that are not at present adequately being served,  in
most cases we will need to institute new programs.  Almost without exception these
gaps represent areas where incremental costs will be high.  The data prospectors
have mined the most accessible seams first.  We run into similar problems if we
try to improve the efficiency of access to existing files.  Any change in system
design that might be directed at improving information retrieval in this system will
require for its efficient application a substantial change in the level of file maintenance.  In most of the statistical agencies the basic files are not maintained in a
sufficiently clean condition to serve a sophisticated general-purpose retrieval system.  One informed observer has told me that it would probably take an increase in
support levels equal to at least 5 per cent of current program budgets simply to
bring file maintenance to a level essential to support any basic changes in the retrieval system.  In short, any changes that will make a substantial contribution
toward closing the information gap will require order-of-magnitude changes in the
levels of support.

In addition to these scale factors, a number of serious external factors operate as
constraints.  There are more of these constraints than I can hope to discuss with
you today, but let me mention one or two.  Some of them arise out of the system
design requirements we must impose if we are to serve some of the most important uses that we can anticipate in the future.  In time, the various subsets of the
federal statistical system will need to be brought up to a higher order of integration so that components from one may be more easily associated with components
from another.  Formidable institutional and classification problems will have to be
resolved before a great deal of progress can be made along this line.  It is tempt-
ing to suggest that some kind of central data center be established in the federal
government to bring together all these sources of data in an integrated fashion for
the benefit of users.  This constitutes one of Mr. Orcutt's suggestions.  I would
like to say that, for my own part, I am quite bearish about this notion in the short
and intermediate period.  It seems to me that this is something that develops at a
much later stage in the evolutionary process if it is going to succeed.  An absolute
essential precondition to the success of such a venture would be fairly substantial
changes in the level and character of file management and program organization in
each of the agencies responsible for initiating a subset of the total system.  It
seems to me that we need to begin first to fulfill these preconditions in each of the
program agencies.  Furthermore, there have already been some experiments outside the federal government with data banks of one sort or another.  These have not
had a distinguished record to date.  One of the reasons for this, I am convinced,
is that many of these efforts have simply pulled together already available data
without any serious thought about the principal uses that were trying to be served.
The design of a centralized or integrated system, it seems to me, must be based
on a great deal more knowledge and understanding of user requirements than the
system has acquired to date.  I am not even sure that we have yet acquired sufficient understanding of what this future system looks like to be sure that a high degree of centralization is essential.

Other serious external constraints arise out of legal restrictions imposed on the federal agencies, such as the rules against disclosure. These restrictions enormously complicate the elements of system design that are essential in order to try to serve legitimate interests of users. These restrictions also introduce some formidable scale factors by substantially increasing costs. I must say that in this connection I am inclined to side with Mr. Kaysen and would have made some of the same points had he not. I think the time must come when we will have to deal with some of these disclosure problems in a much more straightforward fashion. I think that this may become possible because of some of the reasons that Mr. Kaysen mentioned, and I also agree that one cannot expect the agencies themselves to take any initiative in this field. One of the reasons why I think some change in this area must eventually be faced is that I am convinced that disclosure rules are frequently operating in a fashion that is contrary to the basic intent that motivated them. I can cite a number of instances in which large business firms and institutions with access to adequate intellectual and financial resources routinely have access to information that is barred by reason of disclosure simply because it can be assembled from a variety of sources if one knows how and can meet the expense. This is having the effect in many areas of increasing the advantage of some firms and institutions at the expense of others less able to fulfill this requirement.

There are other external constraints in the form of political, budgetary, and institutional anomalies of one kind and another. I will not even commence to recite the details of the problems that exist in these areas.

In short, I am saying that there are some very substantial threshold problems that will have to be dealt with before we can successfully address ourselves to the serious information gap that is inhibiting both the research and the decision process today. I am also saying that these threshold problems are very difficult to cope with at the level of agency management. I am worried about this state of affairs. There is an almost overwhelming temptation in this situation to rely exclusively on an evolutionary incremental adjustment to deal with this problem. I am seriously convinced that the incremental adjustments that are easily available to the producers and users of information are simply not adequate to bridge these discontinuities. I am also concerned that incrementalism in this situation might yield over time quite a different and less satisfactory solution from the one we would reach if we were able to deal directly with some of these scale problems.

I do not mean to imply that there are not a number of incremental efforts that might well be useful. Indeed, it is reasonable to believe that as the easier sorts of accommodation are exploited, we will move to a position from which it will be easier to deal with some of these basic discontinuities.

For example, let me mention some of the kinds of things that I think we should be undertaking more and more on the production side. First, I think a great deal can be done to supplement the programs of the existing production agencies with more explicit reference or user service functions. For example, one way of helping to solve the disclosure problem might be for these agencies to put themselves in a position to perform some basic operations on the data at the users' request. In such circumstances, inputs can be used free of disclosure, and output disclosures can then be analyzed. If the desired output is in the form of correlation coefficient or factor loadings, a great deal more information can be derived from a given set of data. These kinds of things, however, imply that producers and users will work together much more closely than they have in the past. Small beginnings of these sorts will also improve the understanding and cooperation between both users and producers of data in many ways.

Second, I think the time has come when some experimentation in the statistical agencies might point the way to some effective forms of resource reallocation. For example, some experimentation with factor analysis might allow us to reevaluate some of the variables with the objective of reducing possible redundancies and thus permitting other variables not adequately treated by the present system to be more fully explored and documented. I also wonder if the use of factor and discriminant analysis might not be applied to identifying aggregations or groupings of data, by sector and region, of considerable utility, which might lead to a reduction in the bulk of the publications expressed in the currently traditional formats. One does not know, of course, until one tries, how productive efforts of this sort might prove to be, but some experimentation with better tools for program management is warranted.

I think there are many changes to which we should address ourselves on the user side also. I think we need to modify the form of training in a number of our graduate centers to turn out future research workers with a much greater understanding of and capacity for dealing with problems of information production. I am convinced that there are many ways that ingenuity can be exercised to help shortcircuit some of the limitations currently imposed on the system. In this paper Mr. Orcutt provides an outstanding example of the kind of thing I mean when he proposes the use of matched groups of time series as a way to maximize the relevance of information for a certain kind of experimental purpose. More of this kind of concern needs to be exhibited and more of this kind of work needs to go on.

In these few remarks I have been drawing up an indictment of the information process for its current inadequacies. I have pointed out that these are partly a result of an understandable lag and of special circumstances that will require institutional, budgetary, and political innovations of a fairly substantial order. At this point I would like to point out that to the extent that I have made a complaint, the user and the producer represented in the two papers that stimulated this comment are far less legitimate objects of that complaint than most. Guy Orcutt has shown an interest and concern for information problems that is rare among social scientists. He is one of the genuinely outstanding leaders among the user groups, and his influence can be expected to make a substantial contribution to the modifications that must come in the community of users. Indeed, he is one of the marriage counselors who may save this union. Mr. Taeuber represents an agency that I can testify is one of the most outstandingly managed organizations in Washington. Its people have always attempted to do their best in meeting the needs of the information-user. I would say that the biases of which I have spoken are much less pronounced in the case of the Bureau of the Census than in most statistical agencies. Furthermore, the Bureau is in the process of thinking seriously about some of these problems and trying to evolve plans for dealing with those than can be addressed within the limits of its management constraints.

In closing, let me make this observation.  Because the producers and users have rapidly been brought into more intimate contact after being accustomed to a more dissociated existence, the recent dialogue between them has been dominated by the tendency for one group to say to the other, "You don't understand and appreciate my needs," and for the other to reply, "You don't understand and appreciate my constraints."  I would hope that we can devote sufficient honesty and effort to the task so that this dialogue can soon generate a more adequate understanding by both parties of these needs and constraints, and that we can soon arrive at the point where we can join forces more effectively in devising ways of reducing the information gap by bridging some of the formidable discontinuities that stand in the way.

# THE SOCIAL THEORIST: ON—LINE THEORY CONSTRUCTION AND CONCEPT VALIDATION*

James M. Beshers

Massachusetts Institute of Technology and

Joint Center for Urban Studies of M.I.T. and Harvard University

For the American Sociological Association, August 31, 1967

Computer systems are now being brought to bear upon three aspects of social theory: (1) the construction of formal models and the deduction of their implications in the form of an implied time series; (2) the manipulation of social data in the light of model construction and in the light of classification schemes that can be empirically validated; and (3) the construction of indices to social data archives and to literature on social theory. In my work these are conceived as related aspects of social theory; thus the systems being developed are integrated in the sense of being compatible computer systems, they are integrated in the sense that the tasks or activities of the user are compatible in any sequence that the user chooses to carry them out, and they are integrated in the sense that the user is able to conceptualize them as related issues. [1]

Here I would like to describe my work on two related projects utilizing the remote console and large disk computer configurations at M.I.T. (Project MAC and the M.I.T. Computation Center). The construction of formal models has been carried out on my project on Computer Models of Internal Migration (NSF Grant GS-1043) — I am principal investigator and also have done much of the programming myself. The computer systems for managing social data archives and for manipulating social data have been designed, programmed, and developed by Stuart McIntosh and

*Research for this project was sponsored in part by the National Science Foundation under grants GS-727 and GS-1043, and in part by Project MAC, an M.I.T. research program sponsored by the Advanced Research Projects Agency, Department of Defense, under Office of Naval Research Contract Number Nonr-4102(01). Reproduction in whole or in part is permitted for any purpose of the United States Government.

David Griffel (the ADMINS system) under NSF Grant GS-727 — Ithiel de Sola Pool
is the principal investigator and I am a co-investigator.    (NSF GS-1043 is administered through the Joint Center for Urban Studies of M. I. T. and Harvard; NSF
GS-727 is administered through the Center for International Studies at M. I. T. ).
My role on the ADMINS project is that of a user during the development phase,
seeking to establish ways in which social science users might choose to utilize the
system.

I hope to communicate to you some of the character of these computer systems
(they work) and some of the implications that emerge from my experience in using
them.    First I want to indicate some premises and over-all perspectives, then I
want to go into some detail.

These computer systems are conceived as tool kits under the control of a human
decision-maker (say a senior scholar).    The scholar is assumed to have some
particular purpose in mind (not a general purpose).    The system is available to
him as a tool in building models and in manipulating data bases, or in other tasks.
With the system one does things, audits their consequences, changes his mind and
does it some other way, audits those consequences, and so on until he is satisfied
that he got what he wanted (even though the purpose was very likely modified during
the process).    These decisions and audits are carried out by typing commands to a
large central computer facility from a remote console (resembling an oversized
electric typewriter).    Thus in an afternoon's work one can construct and reconstruct quite a number of models, or construct and reconstruct his social data base
in a variety of ways (including reclassification, the construction of new variables
or indices, building a complex file structure from several data source files, and
changing the complex file structure), or he can do both as related tasks in the
solution of his problem.

Note that we do not assume that social science is a general system, nor do we
assume that the computer is a superior robot performing the functions of a Delphic
oracle for mere social scientists.    The systems analysis is largely oriented to
abstracting ways in which people actually go about their work, as well as ways in
which they might prefer to go about their work if technology and associated costs
made it possible.    Thus these systems are being developed in response to user
experience.

A crucial problem in the use and development of these systems is the kind of
strategies that users will employ in tackling their particular problem.    With rapid
response, flexible audits, and the responsibility for deciding what to do next, the
social scientist finds himself in an entirely new work situation.    He runs a great
risk of trying to do too much at one crack, and then drowning under the detailed
system response.    He must take care to begin with small steps and with surgical
precision, rather than asking the computer to tell him everything about everything
(and obtaining an impenetrable mass of computer printout in return).    He must
also assume the responsibility for many decisions that he formerly delegated to
assistants with lofty and vague declarations.

My experience suggests that both model building and data handling are best done
in the light of conscious comparisons of alternatives, where the alternatives can be

stated relatively simply and clearly, perhaps deliberately caricatured. In this way the decision criteria can be reasonably explicit, thus allowing others to evaluate your judgments should they choose to replicate your research. These comparisons are made so as to focus attention on certain issues while deliberately suppressing others, just as a professional photographer deliberately blurs much of his image so as to focus attention. It now appears that skill in sequentially focussing on different aspects of the problem is a crucial element in the use of these computer systems. In particular the selective use of audits or of display is essential; in effect one develops habits of displaying fairly crude or aggregated outcomes, then seeking further detail in light of warning signals (this means that intermediate output and various diagnostic information is often sent to the disk, and not displayed unless or until the user orders its display — then displayed in the form that he orders it).

Now let me describe the model building in some detail. Here the guiding concepts are interpretation and verification. Let us consider interpretation first, considering tasks within the model-building programs alone. Present practice in simulation involves the construction of enormous models (from any point of view) with large numbers of parameters; frequently it is extremely difficult to manipulate these models intelligently, even though implied time series can be calculated. The output in the form of implied time series is voluminous; further, the number of combinations of conditions of the parameters is essentially infinite; thus sensitivity tests (study of variations in output in response to different parameter values) are very difficult to carry out.

In order to remove ambiguities I take the extreme position that the content of any model must be expressible in subject-matter language and in explicit mathematical form as well as in a reasonably simple computer program. This means that any computer output may be attributed to an initial situation that can be described from all three points of view (by the user).

Now let me discuss my present programs. The mathematical description may use set notation, graph notation, and matrix notation; the mathematical models constructed are discrete nonstationary Markov processes, so probability notation can also be used to describe them. A class of models can be described by (1) the nodes on a directed graph (the states of the system); (2) the elements that flow over the graph (conceived as a network); (3) a discrete time interval in which elements may flow between pairs of nodes; (4) the initial weights or constraints on weights on the links of the graph (including no arrow for absence of link); (5) an updating transformation that calculates new weights in each time period. This means drawing a diagram with points (nodes) indicated and labeled, with arrows among the points (not necessarily all pairs of points), with numbers associated with each arrow; and with an explicit rule that defines the calculation of probabilities from weights, and the calculation of new probabilities.

Within a class of models different cases can be obtained by varying the initial distributions of elements over nodes, by varying the initial weights on the links, and by varying the parameters of the updating transformation. (In some models there are alternative ways of transforming the weights on the links to conditional probabilities, but most often a matrix is constructed with the rows representing every

node as origin and the columns representing every node as destination — the entries
in the matrix are the weights on the links, and these weights are transformed to
probabilities by row normalization, namely, dividing each row by the row sum).

In matrix notation two equations define the process. [2]  Let us say that there are  n
nodes on the graph, or states of the system, that there is an initial distribution
of elements over each node defined by the vector m(0), that there is an initial
stochastic matrix P(0), and that there is an updating transformation G.  We will
need one equation to specify the calculation of m(1), and another equation to specify
the calculation of P(1).  Then the general form of these two equations can be specified for an arbitrary time interval, say from t to t+1.  Equation 1 is a conventional
linear transformation.

$$m(t + 1) = m(t) P(t). \tag{1}$$

$$P(t + 1) = G(P(t), \ m(t), \ m(t + 1)). \tag{2}$$

One can see that Equation 2 defines a first-order nonstationary Markov process.
Aside from that, however, one's choice of G is quite open.  It should be clear that
the choice of G is the essential theoretical task in defining a class of models.  From
the point of view of pure mathematics, the relevant task is to classify all possible
functions according to their implications for resulting processes.  (Many choices of
G will not go to equilibrium, exponentially or otherwise, except under special conditions — the lagged characteristics of these models allow them much richer variety than the conventional simultaneous equations that other models use. )

Let us get some subject-matter feeling for these equations, then let me show you
how the equations can be constructed in the computer programs.  Most social
science problems are defined over either or both of two graphs, which we may call
the micrograph and macrograph.  Let us restrict our attention to these problems
in which it seems useful to conceive of flows of things with respect to persons (a
micrograph) or of flows of persons with respect to characteristics of persons (a
macrograph).  Examples of the former might be flows of money, or of commodities,
of information, or of emotion among a set of persons; examples of the latter are
migration and social mobility, i. e., flows of persons with respect to areas or to
social status.  In the former case a node is a person; in the latter case a node is a
set of persons.  In general, the former graph can be transformed into the latter
graph by aggregation (by unions of nodes) — thus giving rise to the micro-macro
terminology.  An example of such aggregation occurs in economics; the micrograph represents flows of money among persons, the macrograph represents flows
of persons among income categories (thus defining the characteristics of persons
as a net result of the money flows).  Economists usually state their psychological
assumptions over a micrograph (a utility function) and state their social system
assumptions over a macrograph (a market or an input-output matrix).

Ordinarily, I use these models to represent macrographs of the person-flow kind
mentioned above, and I shall use this special case for detailed illustration, but
one should note that I or any other user could define the nodes and flows very differently if it suited the problem at hand.  In the case that persons are the elements
that flow among the nodes, and the nodes are sets of persons classified by some

complex of characteristics, it becomes clear that birth processes and death processes should be defined, and that age of persons must therefore be defined. Age
may be viewed as a subclassification of the nodes that is automatically provided
by the model (presently age interval and time interval must correspond, i. e. , if
you choose 10-year age intervals you get 10-year time periods and vice versa).

How do we handle birth processes, death processes, and age? The correct procedure can be taken from Whelpton's concepts of cohort fertility. We may view
the function G as augmented by the birth probabilities and the death probabilities.
More important, we keep track of every birth cohort (set of persons born in the
same time period) as they age. This is done by assigning to each cohort at birth
a transition matrix P defined over the nodes of the graph (except for age) and then
updating each such transition matrix separately. Thus each age group, at any time
period, has its own transition matrix, and this transition matrix may be calculated
as a function of the transition matrix associated previously with the same cohort,
that is, with the set of people one age group younger at one previous time period.
In effect, we partition up the function G into separate functions for each age group;
these separate functions may be identical or they may be different.

The result of introducing age cohorts into the function G is that we may interpret
the updating transformation as learning. With some reflection you will see that
mathematical learning theory can be introduced here en masse. Can we give even
better behavioral interpretations to these models? In effect, we would like to view
learning as a consequence of experience.

Let us interpret the transition probabilities as aggregate outcomes of individual
decision processes. To each set of persons at each node let us impute an average
utility function (preference function defined over the set of n nodes as alternatives)
and an average likelihood function (a subjective estimate of the probability that a
certain alternative, i. e. , node, can actually be chosen by that person). At each
node we calculate the average choice over all nodes (including staying at the present node) in the next time period, then we calculate the transition probabilities
from the average choices.

The calculations of utility, likelihood, and choice are currently done in the following way. To each birth cohort is assigned a matrix U and a matrix L (both n x n),
where the rows represent the nodes at which persons presently are, and the columns represent the nodes as alternatives for choice. Consider a particular row,
a set of persons classified by certain characteristics. Then a number is assigned
in the U matrix that represents the average relative preference for each alternative held by this set of persons, and a number is assigned in the L matrix that
represents the average relative likelihood over each alternative held by this set
of persons. We may now calculate a row of a new matrix, say C, by using scalar
multiplication of the elements in the corresponding row and column,

$$(c_{ij}) = (u_{ij}) \cdot (1_{ij}).$$

We then normalize the matrix C by its row sums and use it as a transition matrix.
This means that we have split the P matrix into two matrices; now we may partition
the updating transformation G accordingly and use separate functions for

calculating the U matrix and the L matrix for each age cohort. Often one wishes to have the U matrix constant over age, or changing slowly, so as to represent deep-seated values or attitudes of preference, while the L matrix is very sensitive to the current situation, or to changes in the situation, to represent learning from experience.

To write a function G that depends on the current situation, you make the function largely respond to the entries in the vector m(t + 1), the simultaneous distribution vector; to make G respond more slowly, emphasize the entries in the vector m(t), the distribution vector lagged one time period; to make G respond to changes, use ratios or differences of the elements of the two successive distribution vectors; to make G relatively stable, emphasize the entries in the previous matrices (either U or L). See Equation 2.

It should be clear that these models represent social structure as constraints on decision processes. [3] The nodes of the underlying graph merely have to be defined by the relevant social characteristics, say race, or occupation, or both. Then differential effects for these nodes can be expressed as constraints in the U matrix, the L matrix, and the updating transformations. Further, the behavior of some persons can be made dependent upon the behavior of other persons by judiciously selecting elements from the distribution vector specifying in the function G.

There is, however, a type of constraint not easily expressed by the methods above. These are the constraints due to saturation of a node, or overcrowding of the population of a node; they resemble the constraints in queuing problems. A simple example occurs in migration; everyone may prefer to live in Southern California, or some particular area, but there are structural constraints stemming from the local economy and the total economy that one would like to express in the problem. These constraints would naturally be expressed as constraints on the distribution vector; perhaps some asymptotic values would be compared with a calculated distribution. Note that such constraint effects should show up in the likelihoods, reflecting a process of learning by experience (sour grapes).

These saturation effects, it turns out, are very effectively handled by a market mechanism. One assumes that overcrowding drives up prices, and that rising prices drive down likelihoods. Thus overcrowding should be expressed as a relation between supply and demand.

For specificity consider migration among metropolitan areas as a function of labor markets, the supply and demand for labor. Assume that some numbers representing demand for labor can be provided for the whole system, and perhaps also disaggregated over some subsets of nodes. (Demand may be exogenous or endogenous or mixed, depending on your choice.) Supply of labor is defined by sums over elements of the distribution vector, perhaps using age to obtain partial sums.

Now suppose you have 12 nodes representing a cross-classification of three areas by two skill levels by two races. (This is a problem that I have worked out.) Suppose demand for labor can be specified as a number for each of the three areas, and can even be disaggregated by skill level, so six demand numbers are available for comparison with a labor supply that is further disaggregated by race and age.

It seems likely that the employers would be biased both by race and by age, and that this bias would reveal itself as a last hired — first fired phenomenon; when supply exceeds demand the first-fired effect should be revealed, when demand exceeds supply the last-hired effect should be revealed. This kind of effect can be represented by a utility function average of the employer within each of the 6 nodes for which we already have demand numbers. At present this utility function is a constant, assumed not to be influenced by anything. (If the utility function were variable, it might represent power.)

From our previous discussion of likelihoods and learning by experience, we would expect that the employers' bias would show up in the employees' likelihoods, namely by lowered likelihoods, and this is what happened in a test of the model. To recapitulate, in a market problem there are bidders and bid-receivers. The bid-receivers may be aggregated into a single bid-receiver, or they may be viewed as several bid-receivers, where one would create bid-receivers that had different demand characteristics or different biases toward persons in the labor market. Persons in the labor market also have utilities and likelihoods that will constrain their decision processes.

I have also worked on a model of migration within a metropolitan area in which the housing market is viewed as the constraint, and in which the migration probabilities of the whites greatly depend upon the actual migration of the Negroes. The dependence is of a "tipping-point" variety; white migration may accelerate abruptly, as in panic. Here, I use a central area and two rings for area nodes.

Perhaps these illustrations suggest to you the kinds of model building that one could try today. There are various ways that power may be introduced into these models, as constraints on the conflict processes already described, for example.[4] My impression is that many of the problems in mathematical game theory of the n-person game variety can be solved within the context of these models.

There are two important issues in model building that I have not resolved in general form in the present system. One of these is the case of several markets defined over several different kinds of elements with partial mutual influence — for example, take houses as elements that are born, age, and die, as well as households as elements that move from house to house and also are born, age, and die. The difficulty is to define partial influence. The other is the problem of negative flows; such concepts as Freud's ambivalence, especially in relations within a family, or the self-hatred concept as applied to racial or ethnic groups seem to require much more subtle work than is shown above.[5] A related problem is the relation between punishment and the absence of reward.

Some words are now in order as to how the user actually works with such model-building techniques while sitting at a console. The structure of the program is a main program that handles input issues, storage issues, output issues, and otherwise calls six subprograms. The user would be well advised not to monkey with the main program. The six subprograms, however, contain the various aspects of the function G. They consist largely of conditionals and of mathematical equations; the user can simply delete these and substitute his own, recompile (a couple of minutes at the console), and then run the new version. The six subprograms handle births, deaths, the utility likelihood option, a "learning" aspect of the updating transformation, and a supply-and-demand aspect of the updating transformation (this requires two subroutines). There is a modest library of examples of subprograms to suggest alternative ways of doing things to the user. (The whole program is quite simple and reasonably quick; there is no reason to exceed a minute on any particular run. )

The user decides the number of states that he wants and the time interval, and types these in when the program requests it of him; in addition, the user may select options as to how he wants to define the initial distribution and the initial transition probabilities, including input options.  The output gives for each time period the total population in the system and the total population at each node while running; if these seem interesting the user may push the quit button, and then print a disk file containing the full age distribution and the associated transition matrices (or likelihood matrices) for everyone at that time period.  At the end of a run the program reassembles the population by date of birth rather than by current date and prints out those totals (summed over age, but for every node and every birth date).

Now let us turn our attention to verification.  We extend the interpretation of the model to empirical issues.  For many people this would mean selecting a single model, or a single class of models with the same generalized parameters, and then estimating the parameters of the model from a single data set — often in effect as a least-squares curve fitting, since the parameters and the criteria of goodness of fit come from the same data set.  Here we take a different view.

Verification is most meaningful if it takes place in the context of the comparison of several alternative reasonable models.  Reasonable is defined by the prior knowledge of the scholar and by his purpose in a particular problem.  The archive system should provide him with search procedures for the prior theory and research of other investigators, as well as for the various data sets that might prove useful.

Suppose the alternative models have been constructed and that various hypothetical time series have been calculated from them.  Should we now select that model which best "fits" some particular historical data set, or on the average best "fits" several historical data sets?  The answer is no.  We would like to have a theoretical time series of distribution vectors that resembles some empirical time series of the same quantities, but we are more concerned that the "system response" of our models make sense than we are that the "fit" of these two time series is especially close.  As the updating transformation is the crucial issue in model construction, the system response is the crucial issue in verification.  Thus the relevant historical data are those selected to reveal system response, e. g. , social change.

Note that, in contrast to much current work, we do not seek to infer the causality or the process from a cross section of data.  Instead, we state a model with an updating transformation selected to represent the causality, then deduce the implied time series, namely, a sequence of cross sections.  The whole implied sequence of cross sections can then be compared with empirical data; in particular, different implied sequences can be generated under different assumptions, namely, the reasonable alternative models mentioned above.

The alternative models, of course, are not developed in one fell swoop, and the comparisons with empirical data are not withheld until the models have been refined and polished.  Depending upon an investigator's purpose, he may choose to spend years on the model building (as a sequential process of trying them out and reconstructing them), or he may choose to stay quite close to certain sets of data that fascinate him or otherwise seem relevant.  Whatever style of work is chosen, great simplifications in procedure can come from a flexible on-line data-handling system.  It becomes convenient and quick to construct alternative variables from raw data, and to examine the consequence of such choices or measurements. There is ordinarily some ambiguity in the interpretation of theoretical concepts in empirical terms; in effect, one is experimenting with alternative operational definitions.  If these experiments are carried out foolishly, then tautological conclusions may be reached, but we may hope that these instances will be both rare and transparent.

Let us now turn directly to the use of the ADMINS system for social science data handling.  Suppose there are two styles of work, one in which the investigator is very familiar with the subject matter, the models, and the empirical data with which he is working, and one in which these issues are only dimly perceived — the investigator hopes to work his way through pragmatically.  Currently, I am using the ADMINS system in each style.  The former style is appropriate to migration data, which I am currently attempting to recapture from a large household survey on transportation in the Boston region; the latter style is appropriate to a modest restudy of the Office of Education study, Equality of Education Opportunity, often called the Coleman Report. [6]  The analysis of the migration data has much to do with the interfaces between the models programs and the data-handling programs. There are five interfaces either recently programmed or not yet debugged, so there is relatively little experience to report that is not already implicit in what I have said.

Let us therefore concentrate our attention on the Coleman Report, and on the issues raised in this kind of social survey analysis.  The fundamental issue is, how should one use classification procedures to make valid comparisons of social phenomena? What tools are available in ADMINS for attacking such subtle and intricate problems?

The ADMINS tools are especially powerful in three kinds of application:  (1) problems of "messy" data; (2) the construction and reconstruction of new variables; (3) the construction and reconstruction of complex file structures.  In all of these applications the console serves as an audit and as a control device; the disk allows complex data structures and file structures to be used (in contrast to the rigid linear or serial single files that are so often seen in tape-oriented computer applications).

The first application, that of messy data, is a great boon, but it is not especially well illustrated in the Coleman Report data, and it is not a novel problem for most of you.  Suffice it to say that the user takes a copy of the original data, audits it, and decides for himself what is an error and what to do about it; thus the user may transform variables, may ignore "errors," or may conduct elaborate detective work in order to resolve ambiguities — such as doubting the codebook itself, or suspecting interviewer bias.

The second application, the construction of variables, is commonly done with methods from psychology, or with methods of ad hoc inspection of frequency distributions and other characteristics of the data.  With ADMINS the methods of ad hoc inspection become far more powerful; they are flexible, convenient, and quick, and it is quite easy to implement decisions in transformations.  For both audit and transformations the Boolean, or set, operators are available as primitives; it is easy to ignore fields in the original formats and create new concepts that cut across the data base in complicated ways; it is easy to assign names to your constructions and to change these names; and a complete record of your work is automatically maintained, so you may always ask the system about your prior decisions, constructions, names, and so on. Thus ADMINS opens up new and rich possibilities that most social scientists are not prepared to take advantage of; there is a surfeit of possibilities. A paradox emerges here: on the one hand, an investigator is encouraged to develop his own personal style that suits his immediate purposes, but this very freedom will extort costs when he seeks to make his conclusions public to his colleagues. The result is that one is pressed to make one's purpose explicit and clear, so the basis for decisions is clear to oneself as well as to others. How one proceeds to make his purpose clear is quite open; obviously, the models approach discussed before is one way, but many others are available. At this time it appears that the rationale for the comparison of social entities is the crucial issue; frequently this may lead to some crude sketch of imputed causality.

In the third application, file structure, the problems mentioned above become more acute, yet more tools for extricating oneself also become available. The issues in file-structure problems may not be familiar to you. The solutions to these problems often turn on the use of highly flexible naming conventions — these would be very difficult to describe to you. Some inkling of the issues is conveyed if we consider two features of the file structure, multisource files and multilevel files.

A multisource file is one that originates from several data source files. These source files may be described by the same codebook, or they may be described by different codebooks. In the Coleman data, for example, one might choose to regard each twelfth grade as a separate source file, although all twelfth grades are described by the same codebook, while teachers, principals, and superintendents may also be viewed as separate source files with differing codebooks. These source files may be brought in with separate names according to some naming conventions (that you have to make up yourself), those described by identical codebooks can subsequently be merged if one chooses, those described by different codebooks can be related in other interesting ways. In particular, a subfile instruction allows one to create new files, while a map instruction allows one to send information from one file to another (say by matching on I.D. numbers of persons or of schools).

From the user's point of view, the multisource file capacity allows him to discriminate many social systems that he wishes to compare. In my Coleman work, for example, I have started with a single twelfth grade, and I am attempting to construct self-image and psychological climate variables that are relative to the students in this one twelfth grade. When I am satisfied that I have milked this system, then I shall try another twelfth grade; perhaps up to 6 to 10 twelfth grades will be examined as separate subsystems in a detailed microanalysis, with a basis for comparison hopefully emerging (I plan to stay in the Northeast metropolitan schools initially). At some point I will want to bring in the teacher, principal, and superintendent data for these schools, or perhaps information from lower grades. These will all involve multisource file problems.

A multilevel file is one that contains information at two or more levels of aggregation. Thus the student records are available by grade, but the teacher records are only available by school (unless one wants to use grade usually taught as a basis for creating subfiles of teacher records). In general, some sort of hierarchical structure will describe file structures at more than one level. The user frequently likes to aggregate over the microdata, without losing the microdata and without prejudice to a subsequent decision to aggregate differently.

Now let us look at ADMINS as a tool for archive management. Much of what has been said above can be repeated, with the restriction that the input data are different. Here, however, we have higher-level organization problems; in effect, we must supply some structure for relating concepts. The approach to be taken remains the same. One must take a particular problem with a particular purpose, then use ADMINS as a tool kit. Since ADMINS was designed to have the capability of a management information system and of a generalized archive, the available tools will turn out to be applicable.

My own first experiment along these lines will be an urban information system. I hope to develop it as a by-product of my migration research. Work is progressing well, but there is little to report. Obviously the census data and the conventions of concept formation used by the census play a significant role in providing structure for many other concepts.

Subsequent experiments might be along the lines of the Sociological Abstracts Index, or more along the lines of Berelson's Human Behavior; it is too early to tell what direction might be most rewarding. In any case I am hopeful that the work on model construction on which I reported in the first part of this paper will turn out to be useful in specifying conceptual structure. Additional problems in pure mathematics will arise in this work, especially in classification systems. [7] These will concern higher-order relations that may be expressible as strings of Boolean operators (or as graphs or as matrices). The essential problem is to devise a procedure by which one determines if two classification systems are identical, and if not, how they differ. [8]

Let me bring the discussion to a close. It is clear that much remains to be learned about the use of these computer systems. In particular the next step for me is to improve the interface between the models programs and the ADMINS programs, and to gain experience in the use of these programs together.

To recapitulate, the main conclusion to date is that intelligent specification of purpose, in particular an ability to focus sharply, is essential to the use of a sequential decision procedure — such as is provided by these on-line computer systems. The purpose must be specified to define sequential strategies and to determine the nature of the display hierarchy for auditing procedures; this is true even though we expect the purpose to be modified during the course of the work, perhaps modified substantially, for each revised purpose also must be specified. Lesser conclusions are that the model construction will be dominated by comparing and classifying the updating transformations, while the data manipulation will be dominated by the use of complex file structures to implement the comparative analysis of social systems.

## References

1.  For an earlier discussion of such systems, see Beshers, James M., Ed.,
    Computer Methods in the Analysis of Large-Scale Social Systems, Joint
    Center for Urban Studies, M.I.T. and Harvard University, Cambridge, Mass.,
    1965.

2.  An early discussion of these methods is given by Beshers, James M., and
    Stanley Reiter in "Social Status and Social Change," Behavioral Science, 8,
    1 —13 (Jan. 1963).

3.  This point of view is elaborated by Beshers, James M., in Urban Social
    Structure, The Free Press of Glencoe, New York, 1962; and in Population
    Processes in Social Systems, The Free Press of Glencoe, New York, 1967.

4.  See Urban Social Structure, op cit., chaps. 7, 8, and Appendix; and
    Beshers, James M., "Urban Social Structure as a Single Hierarchy,"
    Social Forces (Mar. 1963).

5.  The difficulties here are similar to those encountered in the Herder theory of
    balance; however, here we chose to treat the problem from a dynamic point
    of view in contrast to the existing mathematical literature.  From private
    conversation I judge that Charles Hubbell has the most interesting viewpoint,
    but I do not believe his work is published.

6.  Coleman, James S., et al., Equality of Educational Opportunity, National
    Center for Educational Statistics, U. S. Government Printing Office,
    Washington, D. C., 1966.

7.  For a similar viewpoint, see Yamamoto, William S., and William F. Raub,
    "Models of the Regulation of External Respiration in Mammals," Computers
    and Biomedical Research, 1 (Mar. 1967).

8.  One attack on these Boolean string problems is that of David Rosenblatt.
    See, for example, "Aggregation in Matrix Models of Resource Flows," I,
    Boolean Relation Matrix Methods, The American Statistician (June 1967).

# INDEX

This book is one of a series published under the auspices of the Joint Center for Urban Studies, a cooperative venture of the Massachusetts Institute of Technology and Harvard University. The Joint Center was founded in 1959 to organize and encourage research on urban and regional problems. Participants have included scholars from the fields of anthropology, architecture, business, city planning, economics, education, engineering, history, law, philosophy, political science, and sociology.

The findings and conclusions of this book are, as with all Joint Center publications, solely the responsibility of the author.

Other books published in the Joint Center series include:

## HARVARD UNIVERSITY PRESS

*The Intellectual Versus the City: From Thomas Jefferson to Frank Lloyd Wright,* Morton and Lucia White, 1962.

*Streetcar Suburbs,* Sam B. Warner, Jr., 1962.

*City Politics,* Edward C. Banfield and James Q. Wilson, 1963.

*Law and Land: Anglo-American Planning Practice,* Charles Haar, 1964.

*Location and Land Use,* William Alonso, 1964.

*Poverty and Progress,* Stephan Thernstrom, 1964.

*Boston: The Job Ahead,* Martin Meyerson and Edward C. Banfield, 1966.

*The Myth and Reality of Our Urban Problems,* Raymond Vernon, 1966.

*Muslim Cities in the Later Middle Ages,* Ira Marvin Lapidus, 1967.

*The Fragmented Metropolis: Los Angeles, 1850–1930,* Robert M. Fogelson, 1967.

*Law and Equal Opportunity: A Study of the Massachusetts Commission Against Discrimination,* Leon H. Mayhew, 1968.

*Varieties of Police Behavior: The Management of Law and Order in Eight Communities,* James Q. Wilson, 1968.

*The Metropolitan Enigma: Inquiries into the Nature and Dimensions of America's "Urban Crisis,"* James Q. Wilson, 1968.

**THE M.I.T. PRESS**

*The Image of the City,* Kevin Lynch, 1960.

*Housing and Economic Progress: A Study of the Housing Experiences of Boston's Middle-Income Families,* Lloyd Rodwin, 1961.

*The Historian and the City,* John E. Burchard and Oscar Handlin, editors, 1963

*Beyond the Melting Pot: The Negroes, Puerto Ricans, Jews, Italians, and Irish of New York City,* Nathan Glazer and Daniel P. Moynihan, 1963.

*The Future of Old Neighborhoods: Rebuilding for a Changing Population,* Bernard J. Frieden, 1964.

*Man's Struggle for Shelter in an Urbanizing World,* Charles Abrams, 1964.

*The Federal Bulldozer: A Critical Analysis of Urban Renewal, 1949–1962,* Martin Anderson, 1964.

*The View from the Road,* Donald Appleyard, Kevin Lynch, and John R. Meyer, 1964.

*The Public Library and the City,* Ralph W. Conant, editor, 1965.

*Urban Renewal: The Record and the Controversy,* James Q. Wilson, editor, 1966.

*Regional Development Policy: A Case Study of Venezuela,* John Friedmann, 1966.

*Transport Technology for Developing Regions: A Study of Road Transportation in Venezuela,* Richard M. Soberman, 1966.

*Computers Methods in the Analysis of Large-Scale Social Systems,* James M. Beshers, editor, 1968.